D0178478

ML

Taking Research to Market

How to Build and Invest in Successful University Spinouts

ANDERSONIAN LIBRARY
★
WITHDRAWN
FROM
LIBRARY
STOCK
★
UNIVERSITY OF STRATH

**Books are to be returned on or before
the last date below.**

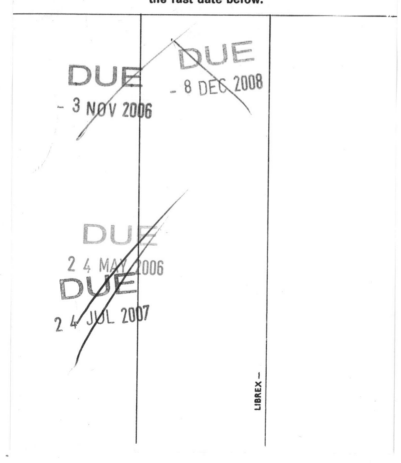

DUE
- 3 NOV 2006

DUE
- 8 DEC 2008

DUE
2 4 MAY 2006

DUE
2 4 JUL 2007

LIBREX —

Taking Research to Market

How to Build and Invest in Successful University Spinouts

Edited by

Dr Kenny Tang, Ajay Vohora and Roger Freeman

Published by
Euromoney Institutional Investor Plc
Nestor House, Playhouse Yard
London EC4V 5EX
United Kingdom

Tel: +44 (0) 20 7779 8999 or USA +1 800 437 9997
Fax: +44 (0) 20 7779 8300
www.euromoneybooks.com
E-mail:hotline@euromoneyplc.com

Copyright © 2004 Euromoney Institutional Investor Plc

ISBN 1 84374 132 6

This publication is not included in the CLA Licence and must not be copied without the permission of the publisher.

All rights reserved. No part of this publication may be reproduced or used in any form (graphic, electronic or mechanical, including photocopying, recording, taping or information storage and retrieval systems) without permission by the publisher.

This publication is designed to provide accurate and authoritative information with regard to the subject matter covered. In the preparation of this book, every effort has been made to offer the most current, correct, and clearly expressed information possible. The materials presented in this publication are for informational purposes only. They reflect the subjective views of authors and contributors and do not necessarily represent current or past practices or beliefs of any organization. In this publication, none of the contributors, their past or present employers, the editor, or the publisher is engaged in rendering accounting, business, financial, investment, legal, tax, or other professional advice or services whatsoever and is not liable for any losses, financial or otherwise, associated with adopting any ideas, approaches, or frameworks contained in this book. If investment advice or other expert assistance is required, the individualized services of a competent professional should be sought.

Typeset by Julie Foster
Printed by Hobbs the Printers

UNIVERSITY OF STRATHCLYDE
28 SEP 2005
UNIVERSITY LIBRARY

D
658.404
TAK.

Contents

CONTENTS

Author biographies

Editors' biographies

Dr Kenny Tang, CFA, is founder and CEO of Oxbridge Capital and has postgraduate degrees from Oxford and Cambridge University. He worked in corporate finance and business strategy with the Union Bank of Switzerland in London and has strategy consultancy experience with KPMG Consultants and Stern Stewart, pioneers of the use of economic value added (EVA) in shareholder value creation. In June 1999, he set up his first start-up company, Oxbridge Investments Asia to take UK electronics companies to the major technology centres of South-east Asia to access major technology partners for original equipment manufacturers licensing deals and to access venture capital. This provided the platform to set up Oxbridge Capital – an investment and advisory house chaired by Sir Paul Judge, benefactor of the Judge Institute of Management Studies at Cambridge University – which specialises in commercialising early stage technology and accelerating technology transfer and technopreneurship linkages between Europe and Asia Pacific.

Kenny earned his Bachelor's degree in Actuarial Mathematics from City University in London and his Master's of Science degree from the University of Oxford. He earned his Doctorate in international strategies of European telecommunications firms at The Judge Institute of Management Studies, Cambridge University's business school.

Kenny is a member of the judging panel of the London Business School's Summer Entrepreneurship School and Business Plan competition as well as a judge at the Ideas Challenge competition of Tanaka Business School's Entrepreneurship Centre at Imperial College, London. He was invited to judge at the Global Start-up@Singapore competition in Singapore in October 2003 and at Singapore Management University's 2004 Lee Kuan Yew Business Plan competition.

Kenny is a member of the Board of Governors of Middlesex University, London.

He is a Chartered Financial Analyst (CFA) – the international qualification for asset management and investment banking – from the CFA Institute in the United States and also holds the Investment Management Certificate (IMC).

Ajay Vohora, based at Cambridge University, is a leading academic researcher, consultant and commentator in the areas of university technology transfer, spinout companies and venture capital. Ajay's primary research interests straddle the areas of strategy, entrepreneurship and finance, focussing on the economic and strategic implications of innovation change. His work has been published in a variety of journals including *Research Policy*, *Journal of Business Venturing* and *Journal of Technology Transfer*. The European Commission, Bank of England, HM Treasury and Department of Trade and Industry have all drawn on insights from Ajay's research while reviewing and developing policies on science, technology and innovation.

Previously, Ajay worked for IBM in the United Kingdom and Microsoft in the United States. In 2000, Ajay joined an exceptional team of entrepreneurs and scientists to successfully launch and develop a spinout in the field of optical sensors.

Ajay was awarded a BSc (First Class Honours) in Computer Science from the University of Leeds and an MA in Corporate Strategy and Governance from the University of Nottingham and holds an Executive Diploma from MIT.

Roger Freeman is a consultant to PricewaterhouseCoopers and chairman of their Corporate Finance Advisory Board. He was previously a partner. He is chairman of Thales UK plc and a director of Thales SA. Thales is Europe's largest defence electronics company.

Roger is chairman of a Cambridge University spinout, Metalysis Ltd. Between 1981 and 1997, he was an MP and government Minister in the Departments of Defence, Health, Transport and a Cabinet Minister.

Roger is a Life Peer and now a full time businessman. He is a chartered accountant and a former partner of Lehman Brothers, the US investment bank. He was the editor of 'UK Rail Privatisation 1992–1997', published 2000.

Contributors' biographies

Ben Anderson co-founded Renoir Christian & Timbers in 2001 and is the UK firm's managing partner. Renoir Christian & Timbers is an executive search firm focused on technology and telecommunications companies in the United States, Europe and Asia. Prior to Renoir, Ben was executive director of Robert Walters plc and a member of the main board team that built the company to US$350 million revenue, took it through initial public offering and finally to a publicly quoted company in 1996. Ben was educated at Auckland University in New Zealand and lives near London with his wife and two children.

Richard Anton is director of Amadeus Capital Partners. He has 10 years' experience of backing early stage technology businesses. A graduate of Cambridge and INSEAD, Richard began his career with Bowater plc before deciding to move to the technology sector. Before joining Amadeus, Richard was director of finance and development at Autonomy Corporation, helping to develop Autonomy's strategy and team in the run up to its 1998 initial public offering. At Amadeus, Richard has led investment in six companies, including university spinouts, and currently represents Amadeus's funds on the boards of Valista, a business producing electronic and mobile payment platform software, and Clearswift, a leading email and web content filtering software business.

Keith Arundale leads the European venture capital programme for the Global Technology Industry Group (GTIG) of PricewaterhouseCoopers LLP. He is the author of PwC's 'Money for Growth' European technology industry private equity investments report and surveys for EVCA and BVCA on private equity activity. He also wrote the BVCA's 'Guide to Private Equity'. Keith is also responsible for the development of marketing strategy for GTIG in Europe and its business development programmes, including those for fast-growth, venture-backed technology companies that are part of PwC's Vision to Reality programme. Keith holds BSc and MSc degrees in Physics and Applied Optics from Imperial College, London. He is a chartered accountant and a chartered marketer.

Dr Claire Baxter has been the director of the Business Liaison Office at the University of Sydney since 1995. The office is the commercial arm of the university, responsible for collaborative and contract research, consultancy, intellectual property management and commercialisation, including facilitation of development of startup companies. After a research career in the United States and Australia, Claire became managing director of Dioclone Australia in 1983. She holds a BSc (Hons) and a PhD from the University of Sydney and a Master of Professional Accounting from the University of Southern Queensland. Among other appointments, Claire is a vice chair of Knowledge Commercialisation Australasia. She will take up the position of executive director of business development at Charles Darwin University in September 2004.

Ravi Belani focuses on software and services investments at Draper Fisher Jurvetson, a global seed and early stage venture capital firm with approximately US$3 billion in capital commitments managed across its offices around the world. Prior to Draper Fisher Jurvetson, Ravi worked in enterprise software product management at Zaplet and, formerly, at Extensity. He began his professional training at McKinsey and Company, working with high technology and biotechnology corporations on a variety of strategy development, marketing and operational issues. Ravi is a Phi Beta Kappa and Tau Beta Pi graduate of Stanford University, holding a BS with distinction and an MS in Industrial Engineering and Engineering Management.

Dr D. Jane Bower, professor of entrepreneurship at Glasgow Caledonian University, worked for sixteen years in biomedical research at Edinburgh and Stanford Universities and the MRC Human Genetics Unit. Jane then became involved with the academic spinout process, both directly as a founder and also through advisory and training roles. In 1998 she planned and raised funds for the Nova Fund, an oil and gas technology venture fund. She has designed and directed a number of entrepreneurship training programmes, including the business training programme of the highly successful Royal Society of Edinburgh Enterprise Fellowship Programme for academic technology entrepreneurs.

Dr David J. Brophy is a member of the Finance Faculty of the University of Michigan Business School and director of the Center for Venture Capital and Private Equity Finance. He is founding director of the Michigan Growth Capital Symposium, through which he has assisted some 800 companies in raising venture capital. David is a leading researcher and lecturer on venture capital and has served on the editorial board of several leading journals of entrepreneurship and venture capital. He is also a founding member of BioStar Fund and Plymouth Ventures and is adviser to Compass Technology Partners and Crystal Point Partners. He serves on the board of Nighthawk Radiology, the Munder Funds and Nantucket Capital.

Richard E. Campbell is a partner in the Intellectual Property Group of Procopio, Cory, Hargreaves & Savitch LLP in San Diego, California. He concentrates on the creation and execution of intellectual property strategies in the electronics, telecommunications and software fields, focusing on patent related matters, technology licensing, developing intellectual property strategies and related trademark and trade secret matters. Richard received his BS in Applied Sciences in Engineering with a concentration in electrical engineering and computer science from Rutgers University in 1985, and graduated in 1989 from Marshall-Wythe School of Law at the College of William and Mary. Richard is a member of the San Diego County Bar Association, the American Electronics Association and the University of California, San Diego CONNECT Forum.

Sarah Cooper graduated with a BA (Hons) in Geography from the University of Nottingham in 1985. She joined Heriot-Watt University, Edinburgh, in April 1986 and spent six years as a research associate before moving into lecturing in management at the university. In 1997 she was awarded her PhD from Heriot-Watt University for work on the location of high technology small firms. Sarah joined the Hunter Centre for Entrepreneurship at the University of Strathclyde in January 2002 as senior lecturer in entrepreneurship. Currently she is undertaking collaborative research on learning and knowledge transfer in regional technology clusters. Her research has been conducted in a number of contrasting regional environments within the United Kingdom and North America.

Charles Cotton is a director of Library House, chairman of Level 5 Networks and a business angel. Previously, he was executive chairman of GlobespanVirata Inc. He was CEO of Virata Corp. prior to its merger with GlobeSpan. Charles took Virata public on NASDAQ in 1999, executed five acquisitions and established a venture fund. Previously, he was CEO of Shandwick Europe, president of Thermal Scientific Inc, and sales and marketing director at Sinclair Research Ltd. Before that he held senior operations, finance, marketing and product planning positions at British Leyland and Ford. He is a Physics graduate of Oxford University.

Dr Kate L. Farmer has significant experience of technology transfer, having spent the last four years as a business development executive for the University of Nottingham in the United Kingdom. During this time she has specialised in the commercialisation of biomedical and pharmaceutical applications. Kate is also a Sainsbury Life Science Management Fellow and has recently completed an MBA at Nottingham University Business School. Her scientific background prior to this includes industrial post-doctoral projects, a PhD in Molecular Microbiology and a BSc in Biomedical Sciences.

Paul Field is responsible for the delivery of business acceleration programmes to startup biotechnology companies in the ATP innovations precinct at the Australian Technology Park in Sydney. He brings to these companies a background in technology marketing, biotechnology commercialisation, start-up company formation and seed funding. He is a non-executive director of three life science companies. Paul came to ATP Innovations from the University of Technology, Sydney (UTS) where he was technology commercialisation manager for seven years. He was involved in numerous technology licensing deals and the formation of three spinouts from UTS. Paul's professional memberships and associations include the Australian Institute of Company Directors (GAICD) and the technology commercialisation peak body group Knowledge Commercialisation Australasia (KCA), for which he serves as vice chair.

Dr Michael H. Gera is a partner with Pond Venture Partners – a London and Silicon Valley Venture Capital firm investing in the information and communication technology sector. He joined Pond from Merrill Lynch's Investment Banking Division. Prior to Merrill, Mike was based in Berlin, Germany, with ESF, focusing on software engineering design and distributed systems. Mike holds an MBA from INSEAD, and a Bachelor's degree and PhD in Computer Science, both from Imperial College London.

Thomas Gibson, president of The Gibson Network in Cleveland, Ohio, has handled public relations activities for Morgenthaler Ventures and many of its portfolio companies since 1983. In that capacity, he has worked closely with engineers and other technologists to connect them with both technical and general business media. He has written many articles under client bylines for a variety of national and international publications including *Semiconductor International*, *Lightwave*, *America's Network*, *C/NET*, *Technology Review* and *Barron's*. Prior to his work with Morgenthaler, he was Frankfurt Bureau Manager for *Business Week* magazine.

Brian Graves is head of the physical sciences and engineering technology team at Imperial College Innovations. Brian is widely experienced in business development and marketing in the engineering industry. Previously, Brian worked for John Crane Ltd, part of the TI Group plc (now Smiths Group plc), most recently in business strategy and analysis. Before that he was based in Chicago, responsible for business analysis and competitive intelligence. The earlier part of his career, based in the United Kingdom, focussed on new product development, marketing communications and pricing strategy for European and international markets. Brian is a graduate of Durham University with a BSc in Engineering Science and Management.

Dr Hermann Hauser has, for over 25 years, been instrumental in starting and funding numerous early stage technology companies, including Acorn Computers, which was subsequently rolled into ARM, and GlobespanVirata. In 1986, he joined Olivetti where, as vice president of research, he established Olivetti's global network of research laboratories. In 1997, he co-founded Amadeus Capital Partners, which has since invested in over 45 companies in the United Kingdom and continental Europe, including Cambridge Silicon Radio, floated on the London Stock Exchange in 2004. In 2003, in recognition of his service to the UK enterprise sector, Hermann was awarded an honorary CBE.

Peter Hiscocks is director at Cambridge Enterprise at the University of Cambridge. Cambridge Enterprise supports the academics within the University of Cambridge in the effective commercialisation of their inventions and business concepts. Peter has taught Innovation Management at the University of Cambridge since 1994 and also teaches at LBS. He has spoken at a number of conferences on entrepreneurship and innovation, including the European Economic Forum (part of the World Economic Forum) and the Institute of Financial Engineers. He has also published a number of articles on innovation management and core competencies and is the inventor on six pending patents. He is a director of Progressive Asset Management Ltd, Cambridgeshire Business Services and Toric Ltd.

Dr Kim Puloma Kamdar joined MPM Capital, a healthcare-focused venture capital firm, in 2003 as a Kauffman Fellow. Kim began her career at Ciba/Novartis, where she built and led a research team that utilised the biology, genetics and genomics of model organisms to uncover small molecules that modulated signaling pathway networks. Kim is a founder of Aryzun Pharmaceuticals, a biotechnology company utilising protein–protein interaction mapping for small molecule discovery with an initial focus on anti-infectives and oncology. Kim holds a BA from Northwestern University and a PhD from Emory University, and is the author of 10 papers and the inventor on seven issued or pending US patents.

Sebastian Kayll is a founding member of Renoir Christian & Timbers and is responsible for business development for the group. His current responsibilities include working closely with the venture capital community on existing and proposed investments, as well as all branding and marketing for Renoir Christian & Timbers. Sebastian also works in the board practice, working with private technology companies to strengthen and restructure their boards. Prior to March 2001, Sebastian spent five years running the IT sales and marketing team of a major global recruitment organisation. This team delivered pan-European and global resourcing solutions to major IT vendors, including IBM, Sun Microsystems and EMC. Sebastian lives in the Thames Valley with his wife, Amanda, and sons, William and Henry.

Giffin Lorimer is a director of G4h, a leading sales and marketing execution agency that turns concepts, products and services into viable market propositions with sustainable revenue streams. Giffin has held international leadership roles in a wide range of blue-chip firms that span the technology sector, including IBM, GE and Cable & Wireless. During a 24-year career, he has spent three years with IBM USA as a pioneer of Object Technology, invented and developed several multimillion dollar products and services, and co-founded a life-sciences software firm. Giffin is an accomplished conference speaker and has written eight IBM technology 'redbooks' and numerous press articles. He has an Honours degree in Business Studies and the CIM post-graduate Diploma in Marketing.

Matthew McCooe manages Columbia University Science and Technology Venture's (STV's) portfolio of new ventures. STV has over 45 portfolio companies and is currently structuring deals with another 15 startup companies. Prior to joining STV, Matt successfully led several large, rapid growth operations. He has also launched three companies from the business plan stage. The revenues generated by these businesses today range from US$30–750 million. Currrently, Matt serves on four startup company boards. Matt earned his MBA at Columbia Business School, where he concentrated in Management and Finance. Previously, he worked at TCW as a venture capitalist in emerging markets.

Dr Stéphane Méry has been fund manager of the Bloomsbury Bioseed Fund since November 2000. Previously, he worked as a management consultant at the American consulting firm ZS Associates, specialising on sales and marketing issues within the pharmaceutical industry. He was then involved in the startup of a strategic consulting company specialising in research and development and marketing strategy for the biotechnology and healthcare industry, Double Helix Development. Stéphane is a doctor in veterinary medicine, a trained veterinary pathologist specialising in Nasal Toxicology at the Chemical Industry Institute of Toxicology in North Carolina and holds an MBA from INSEAD.

Hazel Moore has spent the majority of her career identifying attractive investment opportunities and marketing them to institutional investors, initially in the listed stockmarkets and more latterly within the venture capital arena. In 1999, she co-founded FirstStage Capital, a corporate finance adviser specialising in providing fund raising, mergers and acquisitions and strategic advice to venture-backed technology companies. Prior to this she was a Director of W.I.Carr, a leading Hong Kong-based stockbroker. Hazel is a Chartered Financial Analyst and has an MA in Natural Sciences from Cambridge University.

Wassim R. Mourtada is the founder and managing director of CrystalPoint Partners, a venture capital firm focused exclusively on founding and funding spinouts from research institutions. He is a founder and director of Ligazyme and Myrmidon Biomaterials, both of which are spinouts from research institutions. He is also a director of Genetics Squared, which is in the field of personalised medicine. He was formerly Associate Director of the University of Michigan's Center for Venture Capital and Private Equity Finance, where his primary research focus was studying issues faced in the commercialisation of research institution-originated intellectual property as well as the evolving structure of the private equity industry. Wassim has earned two degrees from the University of Michigan in Economics and Engineering.

Kjell Nace is director of research and founding member of Library House. Prior to Library House, Kjell gained wide experience in strategy consulting in Europe and the United States and has worked on cases in strategy, mergers and acquisitions, as well as projects in venture capital and private equity in a variety of industries. Following his career in consulting, he worked as a senior manager in the Enterprise Group for Dell Computer Corporation with responsibility for planning, finance and operations. He has a BSc from the Wharton School, an MSc from London School of Economics and an MBA from the University of Cambridge.

John O'Donohue is managing director of Motorola Ventures in EMEA. His role is to identify, execute and manage strategic, minority equity investments in Europe that are strategic to Motorola's core and emerging businesses. The focus areas are wireless, broadband, telecom software and the digital consumer. Prior to Ventures, John spent four years in Chicago, where he led Strategy & Business Development for the wireless infrastructure sector and also corporate strategy initiatives. John has specialised in the creation of strategies that disrupt markets and create new business opportunities. He focused on changing the infrastructure portfolio to create a platform for renewed innovation and growth. John received an Engineering degree from University College Dublin and an MBA with distinction from Imperial College London.

Renee Rottner is a doctoral student in Organization and Strategy at University of California, Irvine. Her research interests include the organisational and strategic issues in technology innovation and the commercialisation of scientific and engineering research. Formerly, Renee was the executive director of Caltech's Entrepreneurial Fellowship Program. She has co-founded three technology companies, which include a spinout from Caltech to develop web-based tools for education and science, an incubator for technology transfer from a nonprofit research and development lab, and an electro-optics manufacturer formed within the incubator. Renee holds an MS degree in Management Science and Engineering from Stanford University.

Ellie Runcie leads the Design Council's campaign in technology, which encourages the strategic use of design by early stage emerging technology startups. She is responsible for ensuring that design is successfully adopted by the technology and investment communities, resulting in a greater number of successful products and services.

Dave Sands is the founder director of START, Shell Global Solutions International BV, a management consultancy made up of talented people from all walks of life, ranging from energy, venture capitalism, communication and commerce. START is supported by 'unconditional thinking', modular tools, techniques and processes. There are more than 100 elements that are combined to offer a unique approach to problem solving – not a standardised or inflexible way of working. As part of its portfolio, START has a special interest in innovation and in designing businesses, preferably sustainable ones. START is created in Dave's own image – eccentric, eclectic, diverse, creative and full of the unusual.

Susan Searle is managing director of Imperial College Innovations and is responsible for a range of activities including business development, technology transfer, new ventures and portfolio management. She is a leading technology transfer practitioner and highly experienced in intellectual property strategy, company formation, business funding and company directorship. Since joining Imperial Innovations, Susan has been instrumental in creating over 30 spinout companies and many licence agreements. Susan has been a director of 10 spinout companies, including Turbo Genset when it was floated in 2000. She is currently Imperial College's appointed director for the London Technology Network, a collaborative venture with LBS, UCL and Kings College. Susan has a degree in Chemistry from Oxford University.

Bob Smailes is managing director of Edinburgh Research and Innovation Ltd and director of research services at the University of Edinburgh. His role is to market the university's resources, including people, equipment and intellectual property; to generate research funds from publicly, commercially and charitably funded bodies; and manage all aspects of technology transfer. Over the past five years, more than 50 spinout and startup companies have been created from the university, which has one of the highest royalty income from licenses within the United Kingdom. Bob graduated in Chemistry from the University of Salford in 1973 and gained his PhD in Physical Chemistry from the university in 1976. He obtained an MBA with distinction from the University of Dundee in 1993.

Colin Spiller is a partner at G4h, a sales and marketing execution agency that has developed a proprietary sales process for turning products and services into viable market propositions with revenue streams. Colin is a general business consultant and manager with extensive sales, marketing, client relationship management and market launch experience in the software marketplace, particularly in Europe. Recently, Colin has been heavily involved with a value investor in high growth technology businesses; primarily this has involved coaching, training and developing staff, particularly in the companies they invest in, while promoting the name of the venture capitalist in their target markets. He holds an honours degree in Mechanical Engineering and completed the Charted Institute of Bankers Exams in record time to become an ACIB.

Iain Wilcock is the director responsible for Quester's healthcare investment activity and university relationships. Quester is a leading UK venture capital firm with over £250 million under management. The firm also manages specialist funds for nine of the United Kingdom's leading universities, including the University of Oxford. Over the last eight years, Iain has successfully developed Quester's involvement in the healthcare and medical sectors, having supervised investments in over 15 private companies, some of which are now publicly quoted businesses. He is a non-executive director of several private biotechnology companies, including Avidex Ltd, Oxxon Therapeutics Inc. and Xention Discovery Ltd. He is a biochemistry graduate of Oxford University and has a tax qualification.

Dr Phillip Wing is a partner of Technology Venture Partners (TVP), a specialist Australian-based information technology and telecommunications venture capital firm, and is an active non-executive director on TVP's portfolio companies. Prior to joining TVP, Phillip was a senior executive in IBM's global and Asia Pacific management team. He held Asian responsibility for a major industry business unit and was also general manager of the IBM consulting business that grew from six to 150 consultants during his leadership. Phillip has worked extensively in the United States and Asia, has a Bachelor and Masters of Economics and has completed a PhD in Management (business transformation). Phillip is a specialist angel and institutional investor in early stage technologies, including spinouts from university research efforts.

Chris Winter, a partner at New Venture Partners, is responsible for the venture discovery process at British Telecom's research and development facility, analysing and reviewing new technologies and intellectual property for their potential commercialisation. Chris is chairman of Microwave Photonics, an NVP Brightstar portfolio company. Chris graduated from Oxford University in Biochemistry, gained a doctorate in Solid State Physics and was awarded an 1851 research fellowship. He is currently a Visiting Professor at the Systems Engineering Department of Brunel University. He has published extensive research papers and patents, is author of two books on the future of IT systems and has frequently presented on radio and television.

Foreword

Lord Sainsbury of Turville
UK Minister for Science and Innovation

With a growing range of technological opportunities and more intense global competition, exchanging knowledge and working in partnership are becoming increasingly important for successful innovation. Universities have a key role to play in this. The excellent quality of UK university research means we are well placed to benefit from this trend.

Spinout companies provide one route for universities to commercialise and develop knowledge for the benefit of the wider economy, and there has been an exciting increase over the last few years in the number of companies launched – a sign of a major cultural change in our universities in their approach to knowledge transfer. There is more, however, for us to do to ensure that the most promising ideas are selected and developed. This book provides a useful contribution to best practice guidance in launching, nurturing and successfully growing spinouts.

Foreword

Kenneth P. Morse
Senior Lecturer and Managing Director, MIT Entrepreneurship Center

When it comes to building very successful world-class technology companies everyone has a role to play. High-tech entrepreneurship is a vital component to the sustainable development and prosperity of every country. Improved productivity and competitiveness depend on it. The continuous creation of new technology-based companies enables great leaps forward.

To stand a chance of creating successful high-technology companies, universities first need to try to lose their possible sense of aloofness. An ivory tower mentality is not conducive to great research, great teaching or creating great companies. Creating genius inventions is not enough: new scientific discoveries need to be reduced to practice, and effectively commercialised and evangelised until they become a global standard.

Investors need to bring more than money to spinouts. They need to behave as serious, value-added partners committed to helping entrepreneurs build great companies. Superficial speculators who lack hands-on operational experience do not create great companies.

Through its policies and institutions, government has a key role to play in creating the conditions necessary to enable entrepreneurship to flourish. Government can help ensure that society understands that failure is acceptable and a necessary part of learning. There is no such thing as 'winners and losers', only 'winners and learners'. A cultural mindset that cannot embrace failure as a positive learning experience cannot expect to achieve great things. Societies that embrace diversity stand a better chance of realising the benefits of innovation.

Leaders should demand a culture of transparency and openness in order to build trust, credibility, and a sense of community with effective communication and collaboration. Opacity leads to information asymmetry, bad decisions and poor performance. Unnecessary regulation is the enemy of innovation.

Above all, passionate people are the most important part of the entrepreneurial process: everyone has a role to play if our society is to achieve our ambitions to build very successful world-class technology companies with fulfilling, high value jobs.

This book brings all these elements together. It illustrates that entrepreneurship is neither easy nor straight forward, but the rewards along the journey more than compensate for the effort and commitment. That is why we do it!

Foreword

Mizuhiko Hashimoto
General Manager, International Investment Group, NIF Ventures Co., Ltd

Until recently, relatively few professional investors considered investing in university spin-outs as a part of their institutional portfolios. The growing understanding of these university spinouts – their characteristics, sources of value creation, returns and risks – has resulted in an increased focus and attention among the venture capital community. This first ever book in the field of university spinouts is an innovative and timely addition to the field's future development. It will help to promote an in-depth and insightful understanding of university spinout finance among the investment community, not only in Europe and the United States, but in the emerging markets of Asia too.

NIF Ventures is the only active Japanese venture capital firm to invest in European technology and as we seek ICT and biotechnology investments, products and services that address large emerging markets we are delighted to recommend this book to our Japanese and Asian entrepreneurs, our Asian counterparts in venture capital and to Asian universities' technology transfer offices. I wish this book was around when NIF Ventures started investing in university spinouts!

Universities in Asia, with the increasing emphasis on innovation and entrepreneurship, could find their universities a rich source of productive capacity for spinout company formation. Asian institutions, universities and entrepreneurs will benefit greatly from this book and its excellent chapters written by leading global experts in the field of early stage university spinouts. Asia has the opportunity to replicate and indeed surpass the successes of Europe and the United States in the exciting hyper-growth engine room of university entrepreneurship and innovation in the next decades.

What a great line-up of insightful chapters by leading global experts in the field, sharing knowledge of best practice in launching, nuturing and successfully growing spinouts. NIF Ventures recommends this book for our global network of strategic partners and our portfolio of venture-backed companies everywhere in the world.

We believe that *Taking Research to Market: How to Build and Invest in Successful University Spinouts* will not only be instructive to read, but be an essential part of your educational process and library.

Editors' preface

University spinouts exploit novel scientific discoveries across a range of scientific research fields, including computer science, engineering, physics, life sciences, medicine and chemistry. These companies typically depend on the creation of intellectual property (IP) as the core ingredient to developing innovations that lead to new product and service applications in a variety of market sectors, including telecommunications, healthcare, energy, aerospace and electronic devices. If successful, spinout companies can produce significant economic and societal benefits as well as create wealth for investors and inventors. Despite the obvious potential benefits of these vehicles, very little has been written on the process of creating, developing and financing spinout companies from universities, government laboratories and research institutes.

From our own experiences there has been some exceptional value created from university spinouts – particularly in the United States, the United Kingdom, continental Europe, Canada and elsewhere. Universities in these countries have spawned companies that exploit 'disruptive technologies' with the potential to change marketplaces and create new opportunities for firms to compete with each other. Furthermore, as the science, engineering and technology base continues to advance at a rapid pace in developing countries such as China, India, Malaysia (eg, BioValley) and Singapore (eg, Biopolis), we will see universities, government laboratories and research institutes emerge as rich sources of intellectual capital for potential spinout company formation.

There are already a number of successful venture capitalists (VCs), universities and research institutes that have developed a track record in spinning out companies. However, it should also be acknowledged that behind every success story lies several failures. The landscape for spinouts, in common with new high-technology startups, is littered with failures and the walking wounded. In fact, the list of post mortem causes is long. Furthermore, there exists a multitude of investors, entrepreneurs and universities seeking to learn how to emulate the success stories of those that have managed to achieve their ambitions. We explore all three aspects throughout this book and present case studies illustrating the lessons that have been learned along the way, be it through success, failure or through simply trying.

The triggers for this book: highlighting the 'knowledge gaps'

The editors have been involved in creating, developing and raising finance for university spinout companies. This familiarity whilst working with and in spinout companies has provided a rich source of first-hand knowledge of the pitfalls and challenges that all stakeholders face. In particular, the experiences of the lead editor of this book and his former professor – Ian Page – from Oxford University Computing Laboratory during a speculative roadshow to Singapore led to an unexpected but rewarding entrepreneurial journey. In the course of four packed days, they met four VCs, three universities, two government agencies and four potential technology partners. To their surprise, the response from Asia was overwhelming! The realisation of the commercial potential of commercialising university IP and its attractiveness to Asia provided the first trigger for the inception of this book.

Smart entrepreneurs and academics have not been the only ones to recognise that there are potential gains to be made from commercialising university research. In fact, the second trigger that led to the inception of this book was a noticeable and significant increase in government interventions in recent years through funding and support programmes. For example, in the United Kingdom, Lord Sainsbury of Turville, the Minister for Science, Innovation and Technology has been a passionate advocate of university spinouts as a mechanism for capturing social and economic returns from government sponsored research. It is gratifying to note that policy makers worldwide, seeking to develop greater innovation capacity in their economies, have followed and matched Lord Sainsbury's enthusiasm.

In many cases, public policy initiatives have lead to a wave of university spinouts being created. It is of great concern to us that too many of these companies have been created without the benefit of specialist expertise, know-how and guidance to enable them to achieve their potential for creating fulfilling jobs and wealth.

Addressing the 'knowledge gaps'

It is generally accepted that outside the United States, the venture capital industry is relatively young and is still in the process of developing into an established asset class. It is our belief that eventually investing in university spinouts will become a sub-asset class of its own. It is our contention that the key challenges of building successful university spinouts do not simply revolve around what is commonly perceived to be a 'financing gap'. It would be more accurate to say that 'knowledge gaps' occur across the entire university spinout creation and development process where the experience and know-how either does not exist or is prevented from working effectively. Those who have the right knowledge to create, build and present credible spinouts that are investable and financeable generally do not find capital to be a significant hurdle.

This book is a handbook for university spinouts and their entrepreneurs and investors. The intention is to help emerging entrepreneurs avoid the common mistakes that may end up costing them time and money, and limit their chances of success. It shows them what to do before they embark on a university spinout, how to think through the various possibilities, how to set their spinout on the right foundations, and how to enhance their chances of winning both early customers and venture capital and actually achieve their entrepreneurial dreams.

We recognise that knowledge gaps also exist between academia, industry and finance. Academic scientists speak the language of research and discovery, industrialists are focused on the realities of the marketplace and creating value for shareholders, while financiers speak about managing the risks and generating returns on their investments. We hope this book provides 'unipreneurs', technology transfer offices (TTOs), universities, business angels and venture capital investors with a common understanding and appreciation of each other's expectations, objectives and potential to contribute to the entire spinout creation and development process.

Acknowledgements

Our thanks to Lord Sainsbury of Turville, Professor Kenneth P. Morse and Mr Mizuhiko Hashimoto for contributing forewords to this book. Thanks also to external reviewers, including Dr Hermann Hauser and Sir Robin Saxby, as well as informal reviewers, including Richard Jennings and Miranda Weston at Cambridge University, and Rob Arnold at PricewaterhouseCoopers. There are fewer factual errors and fewer erroneous insights thanks to your unstinting efforts.

Our grateful thanks must go to all the chapter and case study contributors – they are the real stars of the book. It is their devotion to further the cause of their industries and professions and to disseminate best practices that have brought them together to share their thoughts, experiences and practices in this book. We thank them for their commitment – especially against the constant promptings of the editors – whilst continuing with their normal daily schedules. Thanks for your time, energy and commitment in completing your excellent contributions! Together we have set a high standard for future editions of this book.

Thanks must also go to Dr Elizabeth Gray, managing editor at Euromoney Books, for her support and encouragement to push this book all the way to the printing press. Her colleagues, Johanna Geary and Kim Gross, provided invaluable editing and production support. Prunella Purdy and Emma Brookman of PricewaterhouseCoopers also provided much valuable support.

Kenny Tang would also like to thank everyone connected with Oxbridge Capital, especially Sir Paul Judge (chairman), Gordon Young, Nigel Rich, Peter Pearson, Sir Geoffrey Pattie and Yap Hon Seeng for their continuing support in the venture. Special thanks from Kenny to his wife, Lorraine, for her consistent support and encouragement to take on this project; to his son, Joseph, for being such an energetic bundle of joy; as well as to the latest addition, Hannah, whose gestation closely paralleled the development of this book!

Dr Kenny Tang, CFA, Oxbridge Capital
Ajay Vohora, University of Cambridge
Roger Freeman, PricewaterhouseCoopers

London, United Kingdom
Summer 2004

Part I

Introduction

Chapter 1

University spinouts: what are they and how do they work?

Dr Kenny Tang, CFA
Oxbridge Capital, London

Ajay Vohora
University of Cambridge, Cambridge

Roger Freeman
PricewaterhouseCoopers, London

University spinouts are an economically powerful form of high-technology venture. Some of these spinouts have developed into public companies that have generated significant amounts of wealth. In some industries, such as software, telecommunications and biotechnology, spinouts have emerged from university research laboratories to deliver substantial benefits to society.

What are university spinouts?

In this book, the definition of a university spinout is: 'a startup company whose formation was dependent on the intellectual property (IP) rights of the university and in which the university holds an equity stake'.

University spinouts can be regarded as a sub-set of innovation-based companies. These firms have several key characteristics, that affect their financing.

- Their value is linked primarily to the longer-term growth potential, derived from scientific knowledge and IP.
- In their early stages, they may lack tangible assets.
- Their products initially have little or no track record and are largely untested in markets.

Not all spinouts are alike or have the same potential to generate wealth. There is a distinction between creating spinout companies to develop technology outside the lab, and creating spinouts that seek to become substantial ventures and attract equity investment from private investors.

Furthermore, there are important differences between spinouts from universities and new technology-based firms, and these differences must be taken into account when seeking to raise finance. The university environment raises a number of potential issues that may promote or inhibit the creation and development of spinouts.

Why are university spinouts attractive?

The phenomenon of spinout companies has prompted increased interest in these 'engines for economic growth' from many university administrators, policymakers, entrepreneurs and investors. As a result of this attention, a greater allocation of university, public and private funding has been invested into these new ventures and startup programmes. Many universities have established and developed technology transfer offices (TTOs) that seek protection for new IP.

According to research published in the United States and Canada,[1] and the United Kingdom,[2] the volume of patenting and licensing activity of university inventions and the employment levels of university licensing offices have grown dramatically over the last 10 years. Furthermore, many institutions have established incubators, venture capital funds, business plan competitions and support systems to enable more academic entrepreneurs to create new spinouts as a route to commercialising university IP. For example, a survey by the Association of University Technology Managers (AUTM) found that US institutions generated 402 spinouts from a research base of £19 billion (US$34.8 billion), contrasting with 213 from £3 billion (US$5.5 billion) found in the United Kingdom HE-BI survey during the reporting period. US institutions formed one spinout for every £47.6 million (US$87.3 million) of research expenditure compared with around £15 million (US$27.5 million) per spinout in the United Kingdom.[3]

Policymakers, seeing the positive effect of these new ventures on regional economic development, have encouraged these efforts. As well as being required to perform research and teaching, universities are now being deemed to have a mission to promote the local economy. However, in practice, achieving these results has been far from straightforward. Key challenges are yet to be addressed concerning how these new ventures can be created, developed and financed in order to maximise private returns and social benefits.

Knowledge gap

To fully realise the potential benefits and satisfy market demands requires significant human and financial resources beyond those usually found in research institutions. In particular, with regard to financing spinout companies, there is currently insufficient mutual understanding among key stakeholders: academic faculty members, university management, TTOs, entrepreneurs, investors and policymakers. As a consequence, financiers report finding it tough to select spinout companies to meet their specific investment requirements. At the same time, because of relative inexperience, a lack of resources and capabilities, and as a result of their cultural environment, research institutions and would-be academic entrepreneurs find interacting with investors problematic. This often results in a lack of funding or insufficient funding, constraining the ability of these spinouts to develop into resilient firms that are able to produce potential benefits.

This book aims to adopt and provide a common language between spinouts (and their management) and their business angel and venture capital investors as well as those acting as a conduit – the TTOs. This book therefore addresses the knowledge gap that exists between the stakeholders.

The purpose of this book

This book aims to improve the ability of investors, entrepreneurs, academic inventors and universities to realise potential benefits from the commercialisation of IP through spinout companies. The geographical scope is Asia, Europe and the United States.

Specifically, this book has three core goals.

- First, it seeks to plug the knowledge gap that exists between key stakeholders involved in creating, developing and financing spinout companies. The following chapters will enhance the ability of these stakeholders to avoid unnecessary mistakes, and to create more resilient spinout companies that have the potential to generate sustainable private and social returns.
- Secondly, the book will inform, educate and manage the expectations of investors, universities and would-be academic entrepreneurs. This will enable these parties to operate more effectively, based on a better understanding of each others' requirements.
- Thirdly, the book aims to facilitate greater interaction and develop closer involvement between private equity investors and research institutions engaged in the commercialisation of IP.

Why such a book and why should it be read?

Whether the reader is an academic entrepreneur seeking to create a spinout company and raise equity finance, a technology transfer professional involved in spinning out companies, a private equity investor intending to work with universities, or an investor interested in spinouts as a potential investment, this book will be required reading. The book aims to become the essential guide for anyone involved in the commercial exploitation of IP through spinout company formation, by helping to uncover potential problems and show what to look out for. In short, this is intended as a handbook for both entrepreneurs and investors to bridge the knowledge gap.

With contributions from experts experienced in university spinouts and leading investors in this growing asset class, this book provides detailed insight into this expanding area of finance.

This book targets five distinct audiences. First, it is intended for university researchers who have created IP and wish to learn more about how to exploit it commercially. Using this book, academic scientists will be able to obtain a good basic understanding of all aspects of a university technology transfer or spinout programme – from conception to research to spinout to financing to exit. Beyond that, the book aims to encourage these entrepreneurs to approach the spinout company creation and development process with the confidence that comes from knowing a large part of what to expect.

A frequent complaint is that while spinouts have been relatively successful in their initial spinout formation and customer reference stage (the 'zero-to-million dollar' stage), they are less successful in kicking off from such a platform to become 'billion-dollar' companies (the so-called '800-pound gorillas' of their industry). Part IV of the book provides some guidance on this issue, discussing sales and selling, post-investment relations and strategic partnerships.

The second target audience consists of professionals from incubators or TTOs of universities and research institutes with experience in one aspect or stage of the spinout programme, but who would like to learn more about other aspects or stages. The book provides a convenient opportunity for professionals to learn about new areas of the spinout process.

The third target audience is individual business angel investors (namely family and friends, high net worth individuals, serial entrepreneurs and experienced corporate executives) who can use the book to cost-effectively learn what they need to do to add value to university spinouts during the early stages of development. It is well established in the United States that early-stage technology ventures depend critically on angel investors.

The fourth and most critical target audience is venture capital investors. It is well known that early stage venture capitalists provide more than just funding – they provide advice and guidance on strategic matters, access to resources and introductions to corporate partners. The book will be relevant to investors seeking to develop relationships with universities and investing in university spinouts for the first time.

Finally, the book provides policymakers in national and regional governments with a practical insight into creating and developing university spinouts. Recent government policies require universities to play a vital role in fostering and increasing industrial competitiveness, and working with other economic actors to create private and social economic returns. However, policymakers require a better understanding of what is achievable from spinouts and how well-designed policy can be implemented to ensure that various institutions and stakeholders can operate more effectively. The book seeks to increase an awareness amongst policymakers that creating, developing and financing spinout companies is a highly complex and intensive endeavour. The book will emphasise that realising success is based on a multitude of factors and that national and regional governments have a role to play in facilitating this process through policy.

The structure of the book

This book is divided into four parts. Part I, 'Introduction', encompasses the first three chapters. Chapter 2 focuses specifically on the interactions between stakeholders and players in university spinout activity. Chapter 3 examines why universities are engaged in the commercialisation of their research base. It discusses external factors, such as government and the sponsor's requirements, as well as how to resolve internal drivers for exploiting the research base for (a) economic development, (b) societal benefit and (c) financial gain.

Part II, 'Preparing for spinout', incorporates the next five chapters. It discusses the key techniques in achieving proof-of-concept and managing university seed funds from a university standpoint (Chapter 4), and the key steps in the process by which university technologies are created from scholarly research, and then move from seed to venture capital financing, from a venture capitalist's perspective (Chapter 5). Chapter 6 analyses the process from discovery to market opportunity from the viewpoint of a leading corporate consultancy company, focusing on the transformation of the invention into a product or service and the development of a market. Chapter 7 traces the creation and disclosure of technological inventions, and the patenting of the technologies. Finally, a university TTO, a venture capitalist and a recruitment selection firm discuss the selection, recruitment and development of the evolving management team (Chapter 8).

Part III, 'Financing the spinout', includes Chapters 9 to 14. It focuses on the acquisition of financial capital and discusses the steps to making the spinout investable and investor-friendly. It starts by analysing how to develop winning business plans (Chapter 9). It then discusses the role of business angels in the funding and financing process (Chapter 10), the process of identifying, presenting to and selecting the right investors (Chapter 11), and the process of due diligence conducted by the investors (Chapter 12). Finally, it analyses the structuring of the transaction, focusing on the key elements of financing, including discussion of the term sheet and key technical terms (Chapters 13 and 14). Readers who are not familiar with the venture capital industry or how venture capital funds operate should read Chapter 13 for a brief overview.

Exhibit 1.1

Relevance of chapters

Spinouts	For those with intentions to spinout	Chapters 2–8 most relevant
	For those yet to receive funding	Chapters 4–8 most relevant
	For those entering the funding process	Chapters 9–14 most relevant
	For those who have received funding	Chapters 9–19
	For hyper-growth spinouts	Chapters 15–20
TTOs		Chapters 2–14 most relevant
Angels	For those have not invested before	Chapters 2–14 most relevant
	For existing investors and directors	Chapters 4–19
VCs	For those new to spinout investing	Chapters 2–14 most relevant
	For existing investors	Chapters 4–19

Source: Authors' own.

Exhibit 1.2

Timeline: from birth to exit

Duration	*0–12 months*	*0–12 months*	*0–12 months*	*18–24 months*	*12–24 months*	*0–12 months*	
Stage	Founding stage	Spinout stage	Seed stage	A round	B round	C round	Exit
Activities	Research, identification	IP protection	Initial customer visits, VC visits	Customer visits, VC visits	Sales and selling focus	Sales and selling focus	
Outcome		Academic prototype, proof of concept	Commercial prototype, customer traction	Sample customers	Customer orders	Sales ramp	
Key players	Academics + TTOs	Academics + TTOs	Investors + Academics + TTOs	Investors + Academics + Spinout managers	Investors + Spinout managers	Investors + Spinout managers	
Chapters: preparation	2–8	4–8	4–8	4–8			
Chapters: financing			9–14	9–14	9–14	9–14	
Chapters: operating				15–19	15–19	15–19	

Source: Authors' own.

Finally, Part IV, 'Running the spinout', consists of six chapters devoted to discussing the implications for the management team of running a spinout company. This is the stage at which successful spinout companies with some initial sales and customer traction can proceed in hyper-growth mode in the quest to be billion-dollar companies. The first two of these chapters discuss the role of strategic design in the operation of a spinout (Chapter 15) and the role of selling (Chapter 16). The subsequent two chapters from leading venture capital investors discuss building and managing productive relationships with the spinout's investors (Chapter 17), and the value of venture capital and what to expect from a venture capitalist (Chapter 18). Chapter 19 discusses the key role of major corporates and their strategic alliances and partnerships with young early stage spinout companies. Chapter 20 focuses on the active management of spinout companies from a TTO.

How to use this book

Exhibits 1.1 and 1.2 provide an outline on how to use this book. Exhibit 1.1 indicates the chapters most relevant to specific industry players, while Exhibit 1.2 indicates the chapters relevant to the stage of the spinout.

---

[1] Association of University Technology Managers Licensing Survey, *FY2002: A Survey of Technology Licensing (and Related) Performance for US and Canadian Academic and Non-profit Institutions, and Patent management and investment firms*.

[2] Higher education-business interaction survey 2001–02, The Higher Education Funding Council for England (HEFCE), 2004.

[3] Higher education-business interaction survey 2001–02, The Higher Education Funding Council for England (HEFCE), 2004.

Chapter 2

Components of a university spinout: aligning goals, drivers and expectations

Dr D. Jane Bower
Glasgow Caledonian University, Glasgow

Dr Kate L. Farmer
University of Nottingham, Nottingham

Introduction

This chapter considers the parties to spinout formation: the researcher, the university, the university's technology transfer function, and the investor(s). Each stakeholder has different goals, drivers and expectations from a spinout company. The chapter describes how careful planning and preparation, proactively managing potential conflicts of interests, and teamwork can provide the elements of success.

The term 'spinout' gives the impression of an effortless and speedy exit. This is deceptive. The process of spinning a company out of a university can be challenging and dogged by obstacles. Inevitably, there will be a number of stakeholders involved whose expectations and requirements are rarely aligned.

- The academics who seek to found a new spinout may not be the only researchers with a legitimate interest in the intellectual property (IP).
- The institution will usually have an ownership interest in the IP.
- The institution has an interest in the spinout process itself, and how it fits with its mission and agenda.
- Engaging in commercialisation activities raises conflicts of interests.
- Investors' return on investment (ROI) requirements may not fit with those of the other parties.

The success of most spinouts requires that all these parties sign up to achieve the same endgame and then play their own parts effectively up until that objective is reached.

The researcher

A great number of universities and research institutes are incorporating entrepreneurship training in their staff development programmes. However, these courses are usually optional. In any case, until scientists have expressed the desire to start a business based on their own technology, it is unlikely that they will have devoted much time or thought to the matters raised in entrepreneurship classes. Academic scientists have very heavy demands on their time and must prioritise their efforts. Until they have an active interest in starting a company they rarely give much thought to the skills and knowledge base required for technology entrepreneurship.

University versus corporate spinouts

Academic researchers who aspire to spinning out a company based on the technology they have developed in the university have all the problems that a spinout from a commercial business has to grapple with, and a few more besides. Founders of spinouts from large firms are likely to have:

- greater prior knowledge of market needs and how to serve markets in the industry they have been working in;
- existing contacts to draw upon that will provide the new venture with legitimacy; and
- greater commercial awareness and familiarity with much of the territory on which they must operate.

Academic founders of university spinouts, on the other hand, may:

- enter the business environment with a less developed commercial skill-set and knowledge base;
- belong to a culture of adding to the sum of human knowledge and be used to free dissemination of this knowledge to the world;
- be unfamiliar with the concepts of commercial markets and financial ROI;
- be less at ease with the constraints of commercial confidentiality and secrecy;
- be unfamiliar with the industry they are entering, and its language and customs; and
- unknowingly under-sell their skills, knowledge and expertise.

The university

The institution that employs the inventing scientists will usually have an important contribution to make when a nascent technology is commercialised through a spinout.

Smoothing the way towards commercialisation

The university or research institute in which the invention was created may have ownership rights to the IP. Since the early 1980s in the United States, and increasingly so in other countries, the IP generated in government-funded research has belonged to the institution. Whether the IP belongs to the inventor or the institution, several complex ownership issues arise.

- A number of scientists' work may have contributed to the IP.
- The work may have been carried out at more than one institution.
- There may have been prior agreements that assigned IP to sponsors.
- Students may have some ownership rights in IP if they have contributed to the research programme.

Apart from IP, there may be other matters that involve the university. For example, the founders may need to use university laboratory space and facilities for some time before it is desirable or possible to exist as a separate entity. These factors will at some point involve the cooperation of the university if founders of spinouts are to have a chance of moving their venture out of the laboratory.

Too many cooks?

Senior management of the university and its governing body often take a very close interest in spinouts. This often leads to protracted delays in decision-making as a series of academic committees ponder the question of how to extract as much public profile, equity and financial returns from the venture as possible. The extent to which this problem arises varies between universities. It has attracted adverse commentary from frustrated investors.

Universities and equity stakes

Very few people would claim that universities are good at running high-growth companies. The expectations of a university may be out of line with what is achievable. For example, even when there is no market interest in the technology, there has been a tendency for universities to value a spinout on the basis that it is worth the sum of all the money that was spent on the research in the past, plus an unrealistic expectation of what will be generated in the future through revenues or sale of the company.

Remember, 50 per cent of nothing is nothing whereas 5 per cent of a very large amount of money is quite a lot of money.

Universities insisting on large equity stakes and large up-front fees from royalty agreements will find it difficult to incentivise the other partners to create value. If financial investors are not attracted by the terms of the deal, the spinout may not happen, or may fail to develop quickly.

As a spinout company develops, there may be continuing tensions for as long as the university and the spinout are closely interrelated. If the university holds a large equity stake, and/or a board position, it is able, and indeed compelled, to put the interests of the university above those of the company when a conflict of interest arises. This is unlikely to be always in the interests of other shareholders.

The technology transfer office (TTO)

Although TTOs may have considerable delegated authority, factors peculiar to academic spinouts restrict their operational capacity. The TTO usually reports to the senior management group of the university. Line management authority over star academic scientists who are generating the IP may not be very effective, without total support from faculty departments. As a result, some TTOs are left exposed by not having sufficient decision-making rights and may lack ownership of the technology transfer process.

Conflicting interests can make it difficult for the TTO to maintain a friendly and cooperative relationship with the academics.

- Academics may be under pressure from their faculty departments to publish promptly. If there is any question of commercial potential, the TTO will want them to maintain confidentiality while this is assessed and a decision to patent is made.

- The prestige of leading academic scientists gives them influence that may limit the TTO's effectiveness. For example, pressure on the TTO to enable an academic to publish earlier may prevent a proper assessment of the potential commercial opportunities for applications of the technology.
- Academic scientists may ignore requests for confidentiality while patentability is considered, which can result in loss of IP rights or ambiguity over whether disclosure has, or has not, taken place. As a result, members of the research team may be prevented from spinning out a new venture.

TTOs can labour under a burden of conflicting expectations from stakeholders within their universities. A lack of clarity over the policies and guidelines and failure of university management to enforce these policies at every faculty department can make launching a university spinout a difficult task.

The investor

All categories of investors vary considerably in their experience and expertise in dealing with academic spinouts. They also differ in their ability to bring complementary business and industrial skills and contacts to support the spinout.

On the one hand there are a number of small public funds linked to the universities and some public/private funds that are focused on achieving proof of concept. They have usually been set up to bridge a perceived funding gap and can be instruments of regional economic development policy.

On the other hand, there are investors who are looking for a substantial financial return and will only invest in ventures with high growth potential. This latter group may in some cases be able to draw down some public matching funds, but only where it does not compromise the financial objectives. This category includes business angels and venture capitalists (VCs).

Bringing the components together

Soft start versus hard start

University spinout companies come in different shapes and sizes. Two characteristic routes to spinning out research are the 'soft start' and the 'hard start' (see Exhibit 2.1).

Exhibit 2.1

Soft start versus hard start

The soft start	*The hard start*
The academic(s) develops the business and explores the market opportunity by offering consulting services. This generates cash, client contact and some business skills. If the prospects are promising s/he may eventually commit to developing the business full time.	The academic(s) leaves the university and commits full-time to the company. Venture capital supports the development from an early stage.

Source: Dr D. Jane Bower.

The soft start allows an academic to get a venture started and to develop the business organically for a period of time before deciding whether or not to seek funding from private investors. In some cases, soft start spinouts start out by using their know how to sell specialist consulting services to generate revenues.

Hard start spinouts often require substantial funding over long periods of time from venture capitalists and/or corporate partners to develop their proof of concept into marketable products or processes. If successful in attracting funding, hard start spinouts can embark immediately on a rapid development trajectory to seize a window of opportunity in the marketplace.

Whichever route is taken, it is important the stakeholders realise the level of commitment, flexibility and patience expected of them if they are to achieve a successful outcome.

Aligning interests and securing equity investment

Investors interested in providing funding to university spinouts must be prepared to negotiate with the university as well as the academic founders. There are several issues to deal with.

- *Equity ownership* – all parties must agree on who gets what.
- *IP ownership* – will the company own it and, if not, what are the terms of any licences?
- *Use of university facilities* – does the spinout have a continuing need to use the equipment or services of the university?
- *The management team* – do the founders have the right skills for the stage of the venture and are the team members in the right roles?
- *Time* – will potential investors walk away from prospective deals because the institution cannot make a decision within commercial timescales?

Exhibit 2.2 describes an investor's worst-case scenario. The factors described would lead to rejection of a spinout investment proposal. Exhibit 2.3 presents what investors are looking to achieve in terms of alignment of interests.

Universities, academic inventors, entrepreneurs and investors all have different agendas. The risks involved in creating a spinout company can be minimised if:

- constraints and objectives of each are made clear from the outset; and
- all parties are well-informed about the likely costs and risks associated with each stage of the venture, and who will have to deal with them.

Terms of any agreement must be such that the interests of all parties are aligned in order to underpin the success of the venture.

Managing conflicts of interest

Whenever universities encourage faculty and staff to transfer IP to the private sector, conflicts of interest may result because of the following issues:

- altered professional judgment by academics to further personal gain;
- control over research findings and withholding publications or data;
- source of research funds to the faculty's lab;
- use of university facilities by a spinout; and
- bias or lack of objectivity by academic entrepreneurs to favour their commercial interests.

Exhibit 2.2

Factors likely to lead to rejection of investment proposal by an investor

Stakeholder	Goals, drivers and expectations
Investor (existing), eg, business angel or university seed fund	Expects very high returns based on the technology, expects little dilution, and has a poor appreciation of the cost and difficulty of building a business.
University	Seeks to capture money from short-term licensing IP, wants to retain ownership of the IP if the company fails, wants company to continue research at the university at high per hour rates.
Inventor	Wants to run the business, dismisses importance of other requirements for commercialisation, thinks investors are providing him or her with more research funds, thinks future research will continue at university pace or believes the job is done and does not want to engage with the company.
CEO	Non-commercial terms of retention.
Other	Insufficiently secured IP, 'academic' business plan.

Source: Mike Quinn, Chairman, Innovation Capital.

Exhibit 2.3

Factors most likely to lead to funding being offered by an investor

Stakeholder	Goals, drivers and expectations
Investor (existing), eg, business angel or university seed fund	Few shareholders, sensible and pragmatic decision-makers, realistic understanding of their ability to contribute to the next stage, sensible valuation, clean and simple corporate structure.
University	Realistic decision times, good balance of technical and commercial experience, flexibility in deal structure, will back the deal with its own money.
Inventor	Clearly understands how he or she would like to be involved in the future, shows understanding of where the research fits into the building of a company, exhibits enthusiasm for a future role.
CEO	Tight with money, likes to supplement a tiny team with highly experienced functional experts on a consulting basis, wants to hire the best people in the world.

Source: Mike Quinn, Chairman, Innovation Capital.

It is important to understand that conflicts of interest are not inherently 'bad'. In fact, conflicts of interest are common, to be expected and often unavoidable. In this light, they can be looked upon as issues that need to be managed. This can be done successfully if a university:

- is clear about where it is going to draw the line;
- is prepared to monitor activity and enforce its policies; and

- has a conflicts of interest committee to ensure that problems can be reviewed and policies updated and revised accordingly.

When determining what inventors/faculty staff are allowed to do, universities should ask themselves:[1]

- Who can receive equity?
- Is there a limit to the amount of equity that can be held?
- Who can serve on the board of directors and/or scientific advisory board?
- Can an academic consult to the spinout?
- Can the academic receive research support from the company?
- Can the spinout use university equipment?
- Can students be employed by the spinout?

Successful spinouts are built on teamwork

Finally, it is essential to emphasise that teamwork creates value and success – lone wolves build perpetually small companies. For example, Massachusetts Institute for Technology (MIT) is aware that teamwork is essential for scientists and engineers to get spinouts off the ground – the figures speak for themselves:

- 80–95 per cent of 'purely technical' MIT spinout teams fail; while
- 80–95 per cent of MIT spinout teams that combine marketing, business and technical skills succeed.[1]

Like all winning teams, successful spinout teams tend to have the following characteristics:

- individuals who are committed to being team players;
- responsible division of the workload;
- deliverables are met on time;
- consensus is built around a shared vision;
- a diverse make-up to broaden the perspective; and
- work to achieve common goals is done collaboratively.

Like all dysfunctional teams, poor spinout teams tend to:

- have individuals that try to take over the group or 'free-ride';
- blame team members and other people when things do not turn out as expected;
- debate rather than decide;
- fail to organise effectively as a team; and
- procrastinate and whine.

The case of Voltage Security Inc., a spinout from Stanford University, illustrates how the components of a spinout discussed in this chapter can be brought together to enable a new venture to emerge. In particular, the commitment from scientists, a considerate approach by highly experienced venture capital firms and excellent teamwork transformed a scientific breakthrough into products that generated revenues. Furthermore, care was taken to ensure that a supportive culture was developed so that all partners had the opportunity to achieve their goals.

Case study

Voltage Security Inc. – building the elements of success

Tom Gibson, Morgenthaler Ventures, Menlo Park, California

The problems with Public Key Infrastructure (PKI) are well known. Developed in the 1970s as a way to ensure secure electronic communication, PKI requires a separate public and private key for each user that is independent of the organisation using it.

Thus, if Alice in purchasing wants to communicate with Bob in finance, Alice first needs to retrieve Bob's certificate, which has to be stored in a database. This certificate lookup process is prone to error. For example, Alice could be off-line and working on her laptop, or Bob's certificate could have expired. Moreover, if Alice leaves the organisation or loses her private key, this must be made known to all other users of the PKI system, including Bob. Indeed, with PKI, Bob must take conscious action to ensure that his e-mail knows that Alice's identity certificate has been revoked. This cumbersome process grows exponentially more difficult with the size of the organisation.

When, to make matters worse, members of separate PKI organisations use PKI to communicate, secure communication becomes so entangled in procedure it becomes all but impossible. Such difficulties, more than anything, have inhibited the widespread adoption of what should otherwise have become the gold standard for secure communication.

Adi Shamir, one of the inventors of PKI, suggested in a 1984 article that the management of PKI could be vastly simplified if each message could be directly encrypted with the recipient's identity. Such 'identity-based' encryption would, in turn, eliminate the need for an outside infrastructure. The burden of maintaining up-to-date, accurate user identities could then be carried by the underlying mathematics, thereby freeing the security system from most human error.

Shamir's proposed system, however, required mathematics so difficult it had not yet been invented. From that point on, in fact, the problem of developing a practical, identity-based encryption system joined the pantheon of nearly-impossible-to-solve challenges that always attract the efforts of the best, most ambitious minds in mathematics. For nearly two decades, all such efforts failed. Then, in 2001, Dan Boneh and Matt Franklin, professors at Stanford University and the University of California, Davis, respectively, happened to be mulling over the problem over coffee at the Café Borone in Menlo Park, California. There they came up with a solution. Eventually, the two published milestone articles on the subject. Finally, a practical, identity-based encryption system for secure communication seemed within reach.

The next challenge, however, looked equally daunting: to turn great mathematics into a great business.

The art of the non-plan plan

Boneh and Franklin's conceptual breakthrough provided fodder for countless graduate and undergraduate student projects. Three of Boneh's students emerged as particularly adept at translating the encryption mathematics into real-world applications. Matt Pauker and Rishi Kacker, two undergraduates, focused on secure e-mail and Guido Appenzeller, a graduate student, focused on secure Virtual Private Networks.

The three eventually incorporated their work into a business plan, which they entered in the Stanford BASES Entrepreneurs Challenge, the university's annual business plan competition. There they landed with a near thud.

'There was nothing notable in their original business plan,' recalls Ken Gullicksen, a Morgenthaler Ventures partner who was one of the first round judges. 'They sort of had some thoughts about how this technology is 'cool' and how it's kind of viral because it's easy to enrol into and pass on to others. Pretty soon, they said, the whole world will be sending secure e-mail. They didn't have any meat in their plan about taking their system to market.'

Moreover, they presented their original business plan at a time when investors' collective memory was still fresh from some two dozen secure e-mail companies that had all failed. 'When the other judges heard the term 'secure e-mail,' Gullicksen recalls, 'their eyes glazed over.' Gullicksen, however, had engaged the security problem earlier in his career at Nortel Networks. 'I was familiar with the history of PKI and its challenges,' he says. 'So the presentation was a real 'aha' for me. I could see that this was not an incremental innovation.' Gullicksen's backing proved sufficient to push the threesome's plan through to the next judging level.

Gullicksen advised the team: 'to be much clearer about their value proposition.' Instead of presenting the concept as 'secure e-mail,' Gullicksen suggested that they describe it as: 'a fundamental breakthrough in cryptography that used e-mail to demonstrate that breakthrough.' In addition, he says, the team rehearsed their new presentation to the point where they became more confident delivering it. Says Gullicksen: 'They said, "This is important and fundamental stuff and let us tell you why," instead of the typical academic thing of "Isn't this cool and you should be able to interpolate why."'

The change in emphasis took the team's plan all the way to first place in the final, international competition. Gullicksen stresses the importance of what the team consciously left out of their final presentation. 'In general, I would not suggest that people who come from a research environment spend long hours writing a formal business plan. Start with the vision and put it in the form of an elevator pitch. Why is the problem so damned important? Why is this solution so great? Why is it protectable? If they can do that effectively, they can get a world-class investor interested, they can get funded and they can get help completing their business plan.'

Assembling a cohesive team

The team began regular meetings with Gullicksen and Ann Winblad, a co-founding partner at Hummer, Winblad, who was a judge in a subsequent round of the business plan competition. Potential investors and founders then worked together in an iterative process both to develop a comprehensive business plan and build a management team.

But first, the founders had to decide whether they really wanted to build a venture capital-backed company and all that goes with it: majority ownership for venture capitalists, a new executive team of professional managers, rapid growth and the goal of an initial public offering (IPO) within five to seven years. 'There was a huge amount of discussion about how to build and finance the company,' recalls Gullicksen. 'The founders were wary of venture capitalists and, because they were at Stanford, there were any number of successful entrepreneurs they could ask for advice, which varied. They had to sort through the noise.'

The extreme youth of the founders necessitated a slow, deliberate process. Above all, the venture capitalists wanted to preserve the core team, which had already demonstrated so much talent and passion for the project.

After months of discussion, the founders ultimately opted for the high-growth, venture capital model. From the entrepreneurs' perspective, Appenzeller says the process 'was beneficial because it gave us time to talk about the nitty-gritty details of company building. How will the board of directors function? How do we bring in executives? Who are our first hires?'

The founders and venture capitalists focused on developing a culture that would simultaneously fit the founders' collective personality while making room for new management disciplines and partners.

States Gullicksen: 'Instead of cramming a candidate for a given management position down the founders' throats, the venture capitalists presented them with a range of people who were all qualified, but who still had different strengths and weaknesses. The key was that the founding team had to own the final decision on each position. Otherwise, we wouldn't have a company.'

Looking back, Appenzeller agrees. 'The number one lesson for me out of the whole experience,' he says, 'is how incredibly important it is to start out with the right people. Many people beginning a startup think opportunistically and try to pad the team with good-looking résumés. But they don't think about whether these are people they trust or who have a similar mindset. So much can go wrong at the early stages of a startup that you must have people around you whom you trust blindly – people who, if you're not in a meeting, will say the right thing with no politics.'

'This is a process that is very hard to speed up,' he says. 'With a startup, execution speed is everything, but this is one of the few places I would not compromise. Even if some market opportunity were running away from us, I would not be willing to incorporate with someone without sitting down and talking them through different scenarios. 'What is important to you in this company? What kind of projects do you want to undertake?' And so on.'

Each hire added a new dimension to the emerging business plan for the company, ultimately named Voltage Security. First came a vice president of engineering who instituted software and Application Programming Interface (API) development schedules. Second came the CEO, Sathvik Krishnamurthy, who had previous experience in the security market and who had a comparable technical background to the founders. Says Gullicksen, 'Someone who was less technical would not have synched up as well with the team.'

Then, with considerable input from the new CEO, the team added a marketing vice president. 'The founders liked the new marketing guy,' says Gullicksen, 'but they didn't really understand why we would hire him at all. Once on board, he came up with very crisp positioning for Voltage's first product line and developed a whole launch plan. The founders realised that marketing was a big, comprehensive activity that required its own expertise. Within a month after hiring, all the founders said, "Oh, now I understand why we have a marketing guy."'

Talking (and listening) to customers
In parallel to the team expansion, Winblad, in particular, introduced the founders to potential customers. Says Gullicksen: 'They learned how to interact with customers – not just making a good presentation, but correctly setting expectations so that they could deliver what they promised.

Several potential customers – a bank and a health insurer – agreed to serve as sites to help test Voltage's first product prototype. Says Gullicksen, 'We didn't get good, detailed feedback until we had something we could put in their hands. That's the only way to capture all the nuances of how a product has to function.'

'There's no magic in the process,' states Appenzeller. 'It's all about finding smart people who can talk to the customer and see how they use the prototype. Your customers will say, "This part of your product is not very useful, but this detail is very, very interesting." Then, as a team, you huddle and come back with the next iteration. By definition, the researcher is focused on the novel aspect of what he's developing, ignoring everything else. Marketing is the other extreme. Marketing guys don't care so much what's under the hood as long as they can solve the customer's problem and tell a compelling story. The big shortage in technology entrepreneurship today is finding people who can span this gap.'

Voltage emerges
With multiple product prototypes, a few functioning Beta sites, and a complete management team, Voltage finally presented itself to the wider world in July 2003. The advance

was big enough and initial customer enthusiasm was high enough that Voltage's emergence made the pages of the *New York Times* and the *Wall Street Journal*. The *Times* headline read: 'A Simpler, More Personal Key to Protect Online Message', and the *Journal*: 'Voltage Unveils Encryption Program: New Software Is Designed To Help Users Send Protected Messages, Boosting e-Mail Security'.

The media attention brought in hundreds of additional inquiries, including some from new groups of security customers – such as utilities – that Voltage management had not previously considered. By the spring of 2004, Voltage had introduced such products as secure e-mail, secure files and secure instant messaging and was beginning to see accelerating revenue growth.

Conclusion

Spinning a company out of a university is a complex undertaking. Every spinout is different and there is no optimal formula for success. There is a significant risk of failure even under the most favourable circumstances. However, anyone contemplating taking the plunge should understand that all the components have to be brought together if potential rewards are to materialise.

Practical suggestions for practitioners

- The university should have clear, written policies about technology transfer that are known to its academic staff and potential investors.
- Time is precious. Before starting to negotiate a spinout, set up an agreed timetable for the process and stick to it. This should include time required for any university committees or investor boards to approve.
- The TTO should identify any academics and/or students with an interest in the technology who may have IP rights, or who may need to have continuing access to the technology for their research.
- The university, the would-be entrepreneurs and potential investors should each make clear their own objectives and constraints at the outset.
- Identify the risks and rewards that are relevant to each party.
- All the parties have significant, differing sources of credibility and status. Highlight them and assess how any of them would be threatened.
- The university should specify what ongoing support it can provide and at what price – space, facilities, services, access to research and so on.
- Conflicts of interest should be expected, anticipated and managed with clear university policies that are enforced.
- Any would-be entrepreneur should be encouraged to seek independent legal advice.

---

[1] Kenneth P. Morse, senior lecturer and managing director, MIT Entrepreneurship Center.

Chapter 3

Academic enterprise and sustainable wealth-creation

Bob Smailes
Edinburgh Research and Innovation, University of Edinburgh, Edinburgh

Sarah Cooper
Hunter Centre for Entrepreneurship, University of Strathclyde, Glasgow

Introduction

This chapter discusses key internal and external drivers for the commercialisation of academic scientific research through the creation and development of spinout companies and outlines the impact of spinout company creation on university policies and procedures. The authors describe how, in order for financial gains, economic development and societal benefits to be realised, spinout companies require resilience to deliver new innovations, products and solutions to satisfy consumer wants and needs. Government, universities, entrepreneurs and investors should focus on achieving sustainable wealth-creation when starting new companies.

Universities worldwide are increasingly becoming engaged in the exploitation of their research base. Examples are frequently taken from the United States that show how the effective licensing of the output of research activities within universities has resulted in substantial economic benefit to key regions and significant financial returns to both institutions and individuals. Universities sometimes have been regarded as 'engines for economic regeneration', creating wealth through company formation, encouraging inward investment and strengthening the product lines of local companies through licensing. However, governments (local and national), universities, entrepreneurs and investors should take care when setting expectations of what can realistically be accomplished to ensure activities undertaken and outcomes produced lead to sustainable wealth-creation.

In order to assess what might be achieved from effective commercialisation of the research base of the university sector in a particular area, the reasons why universities engage in commercialisation must be considered as well as the external and internal pressures they face. These will vary from country to country as well as within regions and even between individual institutions. These key motivators influence the nature of the deals that are structured, the policies and procedures that an institution needs to have in place and the mode and operation of the technology transfer office (TTO). It also has to be realised that what can be expected to be achieved is related to the volume of the research base – a fact frequently overlooked when drawing comparisons between the United States and elsewhere.

Why are universities engaged in commercialisation?

The development of more commercially aware universities is a positive step. More attention is being paid to ensuring that technology that has been developed, and that has commercial potential, finds a route to market, via licensing to an existing company or a newly created spinout.

Universities are engaged in commercialisation of their research base for five principal reasons or drivers. Two are external and three internal. The external drivers are:

- *expectations of government* – including their agents, for example, regional economic development agencies; and
- *requirements by sponsors of the research* – including industry.

The internal drivers are:

- *economic development* – for example, the desire of the institution to affect the local, regional and national economy positively;
- *financial gain* – for example, wealth-creation for the institution, academic inventors and the investors concerned; and
- *societal benefit* – for example, by the delivery of a new cure or medical advance.

The internal drivers are the ones that the institution controls and therefore have the biggest impact on the way that it chooses to operate. However, they have to be considered in the context of the external environment.

External drivers

National and local government expectations

In attempting to identify ways to enhance levels of innovation and economic activity occurring at the local, regional and national level, governments are focusing increasing attention on the roles that universities play in contributing to the development of local, regional and national economies. The emergence of regional technology agglomerations, such as Route 128 and Silicon Valley in the United States and Cambridge in the United Kingdom, has been linked to the presence of specialist research laboratories and educational establishments that have acted as a focus for public and private sector investment. In turn, this has helped to stimulate the emergence of firms exploiting newly emerging technologies.

There has been a clear move by the governments of many developed nations to encourage universities to exploit their research base. This has been largely due to successes that have been achieved in the United States. After the introduction of the Bayh-Dole Act, US universities were allowed to exploit their intellectual property (IP) and retain the financial gains made.

Successive surveys by the Association of University Technology Managers (AUTM) have shown how many jobs and much wealth has been created by allowing universities to own and exploit IP arising from their research base. This was emphasised by the 1997 BankBoston study into the economic impact of just one US University – the Massachusetts Institute of Technology (MIT). It indicated that the companies formed by MIT graduates and faculty employ over 1.1 million people and have annual sales of US$232 billion. The performance of US universities in terms of exploitation efficiency widely has been regarded as significantly better than their contemporaries overseas.

Governments worldwide have sought to emulate this performance by introducing a range of initiatives and, in some cases, changes in the law to remove actual and perceived barriers. In Japan, recent changes have seen the universities being allowed to retain ownership of IP that previously had been automatically allocated to the government. In Germany, the 'professor's privilege' has been withdrawn. In Scandinavia, there has also been a review of the practice of academics owning their own IP. In Denmark and Norway, the law has been changed to confer ownership on the institutions, although Sweden has retained the current practice of academic ownership. In the United Kingdom, the previous monopoly on university inventions by the National Research and Development Corporation, now the British Technology Group (BTG), was removed in 1985. Now almost all universities have technology transfer offices (TTO).

A large number of government initiatives have been launched on the basis that significant economic benefit will flow from harnessing and commercialising the IP within the university sector. Yet two questions need to be asked: how realistic are these expectations and what level of resource input is required to generate different types of return? It may be the case that a relatively large amount of sponsored research is required on average to create a sustainable spinout company, that is, a company that has the resilience to develop to a point where new highly skilled jobs and wealth are created. It would be instructive for government and the various economic development agencies to review how realistic are their expectations of outputs and exploitation of their research base.

Sponsor requirements

The second type of external influence on universities seeking to commercialise their research base are the terms and conditions that the various sponsors attach to their funding.

Research funding for universities would widely come from three general sources. These are government-sponsored research bodies, charities and funding for contract research. In general, the first two fund basic research while the last is more directed toward the specific objectives of the sponsor. This last group is largely made up of government departments and industry. The mix between these three categories varies worldwide and within countries, and also between institutions.

In funding research, industry normally has clear objectives for the proposed programme. It will understandably require exploitation rights to any IP generated. The research may be based on background IP developed and owned by the university. Handled properly, it can be regarded as an effective form of technology transfer for the appropriate category of IP. Care has to be taken that background IP that has been paid for by the public sector is not lost through such deals, and that the universities' freedom to undertake future research with other sponsors is not restricted. With the exception of industrially funded research, the sponsor does not seek to own the IP, but does impose obligations on the institution to protect and effectively exploit it.

Internal drivers

Although individual institutions can choose to exploit their research base to achieve economic development, financial gains or optimise societal benefit, it is often more realistic to try to achieve a balance of the three. In any event, the institution needs to be clear as to the balance between the three drivers it is to adopt, as this will affect the policies and procedures governing the commercialisation process within the institution and the mode of operation of the TTO.

Economic development

All universities play a significant role in their local economy by attracting a large number of students to the area, some of whom become employed locally after completing their academic studies and training. Local companies can gain technical benefits from employing academics to undertake specific consultancy activities. The quality of the graduates taught and the research undertaken is a powerful incentive for companies to locate in the area. Over and above these measures, some universities elect to favour local/national firms for licences to use their technology.

Creating new spinout companies to commercialise university IP fits well with national and local government economic development initiatives. The university may also gain by receiving grants and awards in recognition for turning research into business opportunities. If circumstances are favourable, a positive impact on the region may also be seen through the creation of regional clusters, increased inward investment by larger companies and new highly-skilled jobs being created in technology-related sectors. It cannot be emphasised enough that these benefits are only achievable if the spinout companies created are of sufficient quality to survive in a commercially competitive marketplace.

Financial gain

Universities may consider that the new IP they are generating though research is a valuable resource. Given the financial pressures almost all universities face, they may favour exploiting IP commercially by the route that gives the maximum financial return. In some cases, this may be through licensing the technology to industry. However, there tends to be a great deal of uncertainty surrounding novel scientific inventions and disruptive technologies (for example, nanotechnology), making it difficult to find a licensee company or a development partner. Investment is required to achieve proof of concept and proof of market, which demonstrates the commercial potential for applications of the technology.

Licensing the technology to a spinout company with equity as part of the consideration provides one alternative route to attracting investment to develop this potential. These licence agreements may include equity shares in the spinout and, in certain cases, a combination of the following:

- substantially reduced up-front fees (if not waived in consideration of equity shares);
- a realistic percentage royalties on sales; and
- a reasonable percentage of sublicence income.

Universities, investors and entrepreneurs should all ensure that whatever deal is arranged, there is maximum opportunity for the spinout to become a success. Hard bargaining will not allow any of the stakeholders to increase their potential returns.

Licence agreements with equity consideration are another way to improve faculty retention by augmenting academic salaries and providing incentives to identify new ideas for research and development. Spinouts provide academic scientists and inventors who do not wish to leave their university posts with the opportunity to develop ongoing research, and commercialise new IP. In return, as well as a possible equity stake, this involvement enables academics to keep up with the latest developments in their field.

Societal benefit

Universities, particularly those with a medical school, are in a position to exploit the scientific discoveries for wider societal benefit. For example, patients suffering from illness may have no discretion over where a new therapeutic drug is made, only that it is available, affordable and it works. Societal benefits such as these are difficult to quantify but are vitally important nevertheless. Spinout companies are an effective vehicle for attracting the investment required to develop promising research into commercial products and solutions that can satisfy existing problems.

Can these three internal drivers co-exist?

It might be thought that the three internal drivers might always be acting against one another, but this is not necessarily the case (see Exhibit 3.1). It may be possible to find a local licensee to effectively bring the product to market and pay a fair return to the university in the event of success. Similarly, the optimal way forward may be to establish a local company.

The key point is that the exploitation route selected should be the one most likely to take the invention to the marketplace. Unless the product is made and sold there is no real economic impact, financial gain or societal benefit. Artificially distorting the process will not

---

Exhibit 3.1

Drivers 3D model

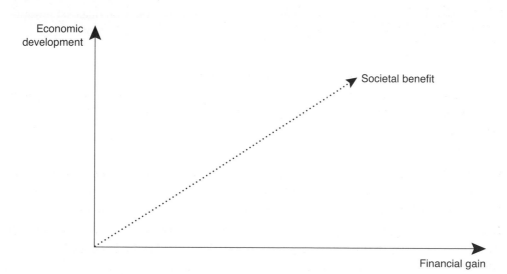

Source: Authors' own.

---

have a lasting benefit. Spinout companies formed for the wrong reasons will fail and the IP may be lost. Even those that survive may have to move out of the area as they mature if outside investors require it and market forces drive it in that direction.

The impact on university policies and procedures, and the role of the TTO

Those universities that place great emphasis on exploitation for financial gain will require policies and procedures that emphasise control. There can be no question over ownership of IP or who is responsible for the decisions regarding exploitation. They will need to have clear conflict of interest policies and act to enforce them. The potential for cash generation will allow the institution to provide incentive policies based largely on financial gain.

The impact of this approach on the way that the TTO operates is even more apparent when university management places specific financial targets on the TTO. This will in turn drive it to be very selective in its patenting process. Decisions on the exploitation process will be made on strictly business terms which will also affect the licence negotiations and post-award monitoring and even litigation. The TTO will require a significant investment both to cover patent costs and a substantial number of high-quality professional staff. Returns on this investment will be long-term and highly speculative. To date, only a handful of TTOs worldwide have produced significant financial returns from their spinout companies. Those that have tend to have achieved this through a small number of inventions, usually in the life science area. As such the university may elect to work with an external financial partner or even contract out the operation to a third party.

Where the university sees exploitation to be mainly for local economic benefit, the policies and procedures under which it operates will be slightly different. The university will need to be clear on IP ownership issues but may be more relaxed on conflict of interest issues if it is actively encouraging its academics to participate in local ventures whilst maintaining their university work. As financial returns may be less likely, the institution may have to adopt broader measures to give recognition to inventors rather than rely solely on financial rewards. These could be recognition in the promotion process for patenting, and public recognition awards for entrepreneurship.

For the TTO there will be a significant impact. They would anticipate a low to zero financial return and therefore the university is unlikely to invest significantly unless augmented by regional government grants. These types of grant may be conditional on supporting local firms. The nature of the deals will tend to be softer, possibly giving preferential terms to smaller firms and possibly looking to create new companies more often than the business case justifies.

Those universities putting wider societal benefit as the principal driver will tend to take a softer touch with their policy and procedures. The TTO will tend to give general assistance rather than take a specific lead and the institution will put relatively little resource into the office. Indeed, the university may partner to outsource or share some of the work with larger institutions that have well-developed and better-resourced technology transfer systems.

The following case study on Cambridge University outlines the steps the University has taken to foster entrepreneurship and the impact this has had on the local economy.

Case study

The Cambridge experience

Peter Hiscocks, University of Cambridge Entrepreneurship Centre, United Kingdom.

Cambridge is famous these days for its high-technology new business community, but this is a relatively new phenomenon. Thirty years ago Cambridge was a small market town in the east of England with a great University; now it arguably has the largest concentration of high-technology new businesses in Europe with about 1,600 high-technology firms in the Greater Cambridge area. These new businesses are grouped in a number of technology clusters in the Cambridge area. Most important are the information technology clusters of hardware and software, the biotech cluster and the telecommunications cluster. The result of the development of these high-technology clusters has been a considerable growth in the local economy. This has accelerated the Cambridge region from the bottom quartile of GDP per capita to number three in the United Kingdom behind the London Region and the South East.

The University has played an important role in this transformation, but it has not been the leader or the planner for this change. An analysis of the Cambridge high-technology business community shows that only about 10 per cent of these firms have spun out from the University, but the University has been critically important to many of the Cambridge companies in the provision of skills, knowledge, top-quality recruits, facilities and IP. The University has been an important but passive partner in the establishment of many of these new businesses.

The causes for the initiation of these clusters of new businesses in the late 1970s and early 1980s have been reviewed in a number of publications, most notably *The Cambridge Phenomenon* (Segal, Quince Wickstead (SQW), 1985) and *The Cambridge Phenomenon Revisited* (SQW, 2000). Some of the elements important to the establishment of these technology clusters are:

- people (or teams) that are passionate about the development and commercialisation of their ideas and inventions;
- leadership in encouraging enterprise and innovation in a number of sectors (technology, investors, business development, university and local government);
- building a culture of enterprise and entrepreneurship within the local community; and
- developing sources of early stage funding for new ventures.

Encouraging organisational and cultural change
The result of government funding was the establishment of several new organisations within the University of Cambridge to teach, support and encourage enterprise, entrepreneurship and the commercialisation of the University's knowledge assets:

- Cambridge Entrepreneurship Centre (CEC);

- Technology Transfer Office (TTO);
- University Challenge Fund (UCF); and
- Corporate Liaison Office (CLO).

One of the most important aims of these organisations has been to 'develop a culture of entrepreneurship within the University of Cambridge'. In practice this has meant making entrepreneurship a relevant career option within the University, and encouraging students and research staff to look for commercial opportunities that could arise from their research work – and then helping them make that commercialisation become a reality.

These new organisations within the University have produced a considerable increase in the 'commercialisation output' including a significant increase in new business ventures, licensing income, consultancy and collaboration with major corporates. More importantly, there is a growing culture within the University that recognises that enterprise, entrepreneurship and the commercialisation of ideas and inventions is a part of the way we work. It is the development of a 'culture of entrepreneurship' that is critical to achieving a lasting change in an organisation or a region.

Improving access to entrepreneurial finance

Another key element necessary for successful new businesses is money. Sources of investment for new high-technology ventures are a critical part of the mix that enables an area or a region to develop clusters of new ventures. In the 1970s and early 1980s there were very few sources of investment for starting high-technology companies and this was one of the barriers to growth at this time. However, some of the entrepreneurs at that time persisted and gained funding from a variety of sources, sometimes local banks in Cambridge, but more often by going to London to find specialist investment organisations such as investment banks or venture capital firms.

Venture capital is a key component in the growth of high-technology companies and high-technology clusters. Once it became obvious that there were good opportunities to develop high-technology firms in the Cambridge area, venture capital businesses began to move in. This also encouraged other types of investor such as seed funds and business angel networks. The result in Cambridge has been the development of a high-technology financing community that is unmatched in Europe. Cambridge now has more venture capital per head of population than any other part of Europe. In 2003, about 25 per cent of all venture capital funding carried out in the United Kingdom was in the Cambridge region.

Sustainable wealth-creation

Venture capital, seed funds and business angels want to invest in high-growth firms. One of the key sources for high growth is the development of products that are much better at meeting the needs of customers. The development of these better, newer products is usually achieved through using improved technology. In some cases, technological breakthroughs can lead to completely new types of product and can result in the development of new markets, such as personal digital assistants (PDAs), digital cameras or new drugs. These breakthrough technologies, in turn, rely on the deep technological knowledge base that comes from high level capability in basic research. For a long time, the University of Cambridge has had great scientific and technological capabilities. Now it has learned how to be entrepreneurial and has built an investment community to support, nurture and fund successful new high-technology businesses. We expect this virtuous circle to continue and to produce many more new successful firms.

Ensuring sustainable wealth-creation

When deciding to start a new spinout company, institutions should ensure that the exploitation route is correct and that the company is formed for the right commercial reasons.

In most cases, only if the creation of a new spinout company results in a new product being taken to the marketplace will there be substantial financial returns to equity shareholders, significant economic impact and true societal benefit. The following points are useful for universities, academic inventors, entrepreneurs and investors set on achieving all or any one of these three outcomes in a sustainable way.

Tips for investors and entrepreneurs

- Governments and their various sponsors are increasingly urging universities to exploit their research base effectively. Universities can adopt different stances depending on their own priorities among financial gain, economic benefit and broader societal benefit.
- Governments and their agencies need to be realistic in their expectations of what might be achieved. Universities, on their part, need to be clear as to why they are undertaking commercialisation and set clear objectives that all members of the institution understand and accept. There is a range of technology transfer models. However, few have made substantial returns to their institutions, most generating relatively small returns as a percentage of research turnover.
- The universities also need to maintain a sense of balance between the three internal drivers and not artificially adopt exploitation processes for short-term political gains. True impact can only be achieved if the correct exploitation process is adopted that maximises the chance of products coming to the marketplace.
- A university, having identified its position on the three drivers, should establish transparent policies and procedures to allow it to meet those objectives. University management should ensure that every department and faculty is in agreement with these policies to ensure that first, incentives and actions are perfectly aligned and second, potential conflicts of interest are recognised and avoided.
- A university's TTO will be critical in helping to meet the agreed objectives, which are likely to be based on a blend of drivers. Where the driver is primarily financial, the institution should be aware that in setting such an expectation on the TTO it should be looking

at long-term as opposed to short-term returns. Otherwise, this could result in the TTO negotiating terms and conditions on agreements that suit the survival of the TTO but not long-term sustainable wealth-creation for all stakeholders involved.

• Finally, every university is unique. Successful models rarely translate to elsewhere on the globe or even elsewhere in the same country. A lot depends upon the local environment as well as the aspirations of local governmental and institutional leaders.

Part II

Preparing for spinout

Chapter 4

Achieving proof of concept

Matthew McCooe, MBA
Columbia University Science and Technology Ventures, New York

Introduction

A number of scenarios can keep a promising invention from advancing towards becoming a successful commercial application. This chapter describes the importance of achieving proof of concept and the benefits to be gained. The authors provide hints and tips, guidance, and practical examples to illustrate how proof of concept can be achieved by academic entrepreneurs, as well as how universities can effectively manage and fund the process.

The disconnect between basic science and investor readiness

Unproven ideas often have little opportunity to advance beyond their theoretical stages and potential spinout companies lack the funds to develop the technologies. The following obstacles make it difficult for valuable research to move from the laboratory into the marketplace.

- Research universities by nature of their mandate (which is partially attributable to the mandate from funding agencies) are primarily focused on conducting basic research.
- Investors must try to contain their risk – particularly when technology is involved. One of the most vexing problems in technology transfer is sourcing the early stage investors and companies willing to risk their time and money taking ideas from the university's laboratory.
- Proof of concept activities are not traditionally considered work of an academic nature. There is little incentive to motivate researchers to achieve proof of concept, especially if the work involved is not publishable.

There is clearly a 'disconnect' between academia and marketplace – an 'innovation gap'. The difficulty of bridging this gap is driving the need for very early stage, or seed, funding that provides financial support to perform the experiments and trials, develop the compounds or write the software code.

Bridging the innovation gap

The resources required to launch a new venture are tremendous. Licence agreements must be negotiated with the technology transfer office (TTO), a committed team needs to be recruited, offices and laboratory space have to be set up – the list is endless. Furthermore, while the money and effort must be expended in advance, none of these activities guarantee that the scientific discoveries described in publications and patents will be reduced to practice and made to work (statistics prove that most new technologies fail). It is little wonder that most venture capital firms run for the hills when the TTO or faculty member calls to describe their truly groundbreaking invention.

Three golden words, 'proof of concept', can keep investors from running. Hard evidence demonstrating that the technology works may actually ease their concerns (especially if validated by a third party). If a credible person declares that the technology has proof of concept and addresses unmet needs in a huge market, the chances of getting investment improve dramatically. Tack on the name of a celebrity scientist's involvement and the good early stage investors should be willing to hear the rest of the story.

Proof of concept – what is it?

Proof of concept – and sometimes even proof of market (customers) – helps investors to focus on the reward and make the leap into the high stakes early stage investment arena. But what do 'proof of concept' and 'proof of market' actually mean for investors, universities and investors?

Proof of concept work can be defined as the reduction to practice of a hypothesis laid out in technical papers. Typically, this consists of feasibility studies that convert the theoretical to the practical. An example of such is given in the case study involving Columbia University below. Proof of concept projects usually occur after:

- advances have been made during curiosity-driven or strategic research;
- an invention report has been submitted to the licensing office and, most often, a patent application has been filed with the patent office;
- the inventor articulates why this invention matters to the addressable markets; and
- a plan is drafted outlining the resources and time needed to demonstrate feasibility.

In general, proof of concept projects precede:

- full-scale demonstration of the technology;
- product development, such as lead compound optimisation or commercial-grade software and manuals; and
- availability of commercial funds for development due to the high level of technical and market risk.

Case study
Establishing proof of concept at Columbia University

In 2003, Columbia University Science and Technology Ventures (S&TV) helped set up a small company to advance a Columbia scientist's proof of concept work. The company applied for and won a Small Business Technology Transfer Program grant (STTR). The STTR is a US Federal Government-sponsored programme that funds feasibility studies primarily in university research labs, awarding up to US$850,000 over two phases and three years.

Columbia holds the use patent application for a discovery relating to permanent and semi-permanent hair removal, made by one of the world's leading dermatology researchers, Dr Angela Christiano. While her original research was widely published and quite compelling, the animal models she created were made using ribozymes, a technology that has since fallen out of favour.

She decided she needed to repeat the experiments using small interfering RNA (siRNA), an important new technology that has captured the attention of the scientific and venture communities. The scientist needed funding for additional work demonstrating that siRNA would work as well at degrading the target messenger RNA (mRNA) in mice as the ribozymes did in the original experiments. Immediate results were generated (as was a new patent application), demonstrating that siRNA does inhibit the gene's expression far more easily and effectively than the ribozymes in mice.

The company began negotiating a term sheet within one month of their first presentation to the venture community, partly due to the proof of concept experiments completed in the laboratory.

Proof of market

Before deciding to invest in developing an early stage spinout, any financier will need to gain a better understanding of the market dynamics and market size for the eventual products. In the early conversations, investors for the most part will take the researcher's word when assured that the market is large. Goodwill notwithstanding, the dollars available to invest in proofs of principle are scarce, and choosing amongst different technologies is difficult and fraught with uncertainties.

Market information and risk are typically easier to analyse than new technology, and the data is more reliable. This explains why investors place a great deal of weight on market factors. Therefore, as highlighted in the case study below, it is crucial to demonstrate a sound understanding of the market dynamics and provide evidence showing the market for the product is real and growing. As a bare minimum, there should be evidence to back up the answers to the following questions:

- Is there a market?
- If so, how big is the relevant market(s)?
- What are the unmet needs that the invention intends to fulfil?
- Is there really room for improvement?
- What routes are there to enter the market(s)?
- Can the product easily gain access to any of these routes to market?
- What are the competitors doing in this field?
- Could someone else do the same thing or generate something equivalent?
- Realistically, based on answers to all the above questions, how big might the company actually become?

At Columbia University S&TV, experience shows that:

- The best academic entrepreneurs are able to answer market-related questions with authority, while still maintaining their air of impartiality and dignity.

35

- Sophisticated financiers understand the enormous value to be gained by investing in not just a brilliant academic, but one who can sell his or her work. If the scientist can convince all types of people that their science is truly breakthrough work in need of further investment dollars to move the concept to market, the investor has an incredibly valuable asset indeed.
- The researcher's (in)ability to sell often defines the dividing line between the successful spinouts and the ones that never get off the ground. It is not the best science that is funded, but rather the scientist best able to sell the ideas to the market that win the precious investment capital. This precept is anathema to most academics.

Case study
Establishing proof of market at Columbia University

One researcher at Columbia, Dr James Im, a major recipient of seed funding, overcame a significant scientific hurdle by creating high-quality crystalline silicon films on glass or plastic substrates. He is highly motivated to see his ground-breaking technology reach this multi-billion dollar market. Dr Im is gifted with a killer technology, a stellar academic reputation and enormous charm. Columbia University S&TV's significant investment in his laboratory was based on this potent combination.

S&TV filed more than 20 patents globally, and established a budget for the necessary trips to Asia. His technical vision and ability to communicate his ideas provide him with the personal contacts needed to see his work evaluated by the commercial world. The first commercial breakthrough achieved the establishment of an agreement with a Japanese manufacturing company that invested in building the thin film transistor for testing his technology (the company ultimately will make the machines for producing the commercial grade product). The scientist, along with the director of the TTO, then travelled the world to establish collaborations with the leading display manufacturers for implementation of the technology into their products.

The resulting films will, it is hoped, provide the base semi-conducting layer for the fabrication of thin film transistors for liquid crystal displays (LCDs) and Organic Light Emitting Diode Displays (OLEDs). S&TV was able to execute several licence and research agreements based on this technology at an early stage due to the massive market size, and their ability to communicate effectively the potential impact of this new technology to the industry.

A golden opportunity for inventors and investors

When Columbia University S&TV discusses creating a new spinout company with academic scientists, and the potential financial windfall that could come their way, one message is emphasised early and often: create as much value as possible in the beginning, before the investors come in.

Put simply, if the scientists hold 50 per cent of the company, and the investors give the company a US$4 million pre-money valuation (ie, the value of the company before money is invested), the scientists are receiving US$2 million of equity at an extremely low price (assuming all goes well). The early stage investor is hoping for a 10-times return on their investment. So, if the company is one of the investors' two in 10 that should achieve this type of return, the scientists' US\$2 million dollars' worth of equity could be realised at a valuation of US\$20 million dollars at an initial public offering (IPO) or trade sale. Conversely, if the venture firm perceives that this company has a higher risk of failure than similar companies receiving funding, the company will receive a lower pre-money valuation. If the investors give a pre-money valuation of US\$1 million, then the 50 per cent founders' equity is worth only US\$500,000 at the close of the first round and potentially US\$5 million dollars when the equity is sold (using the same assumptions as above).

The benefits of performing the proof of concept work are many, but the struggle to make a successful marriage of basic academic research and technologically relevant results can be trying. It is extremely difficult to juggle grant writing, publishing, teaching, managing a laboratory and attending conferences and to stay abreast of developments in the global technology market. The following are some of the major reasons why academics choose to take the extra step of proving their concept for a non-academic audience.

- Proof of concept helps to explain the idea and convince people it is real. It can turn sceptics into believers.
- Proof of concept enables inventors to raise more capital at seed stage from investors with deep pockets, experience and contacts in the given field. In turn, being able to raise a large initial round of funding means the spinout team can focus on developing the technology for market instead of immediately beginning to worry about raising more capital.
- Proof of concept enables investors a clear route to market and a prototype will help when it comes time to set the valuation and negotiate term sheets, garnering favourable terms from tier one investors.
- Proof of concept enables spinouts to hold onto their intellectual property (IP) until the concept has been proven (rather than licensing early), providing a more marketable asset to the company.
- The university shares in the success of funded ventures through negotiated equity, royalties, licence fees and reimbursed patent costs.

At Columbia University S&TV, experience shows that:

- Every extra effort put forth prior to the first professional round of funding clearly has an enormous leverage effect when the academic can finally sell the equity stake in the company. This may be the single greatest opportunity academic entrepreneurs have in their lifetimes to create significant wealth for themselves.
- It is in everyone's interests to limit the risk as much as possible at the start. In exchange for removing some of the technical risk, the investor will happily give the academic founders a more highly valued stake in the company – a win-win scenario.
- At no other point in the company's lifespan will the academic's individual efforts be so closely correlated to the success of the company.

What does it take to achieve proof of concept?

In practical terms, different techniques are required for proof of concept across academic disciplines. While each academic scientist should seek internal and external input on the specific types of experiments that the market would consider to be validating, the following give an idea of what to expect, as well as some of the lessons learned.

Biotechnology tools and medical devices

Biotechnology tools or enabling technologies (such as high throughput DNA sequencing, imaging, x-ray crystallography and reagent kits) need a prototype that works better, faster and/or is cheaper than what is currently on the market. The academic scientist should seek funding for the instruments that would allow a demonstration of the technology. The laboratory should produce data showing resounding advantages over what can be obtained using existing tools.

For example, in 2003, Columbia filed a patent application for a novel assay for screening drugs for the treatment of anxiety, Alzheimer's disease and depression. The research was performed in one of the leading neuroscience laboratories in the country. The discovery related to using neurogenesis as a marker for these poorly understood but widespread diseases, and was featured as a lead article in the journal *Science*.

Assays alone are not usually funded by the venture community, so a simple proof of concept experiment was designed to discover whether the assay worked with several candidate off-the-shelf drugs. Given the importance of the scientist's work and the potential for treating these indications, Columbia's TTO contributed a small amount of money to synthesise candidate compounds, house and treat the mice, and perform the real-time PCR experiments.

The reason for granting the seed money was that no one in the laboratory was inclined to do these routine experiments. The results from these experiments proved to be an important part of the licensing story, demonstrating to the venture community the efficacy of the assay in discovering new targets for CNS therapies. A spinout has since been formed, a chief scientific officer with 10 years of drug discovery experience in Big Pharma has come on board and term sheets from two venture capital firms are in hand.

Material science

Material science usually requires samples displaying the properties described in papers to attract industry's attention. Full-fledged commitment from the principal investigator to the commercial process is also essential.

For example, in 1998, the scientists in Columbia's concrete materials laboratory created beautiful concrete tiles using waste glass (recycled on campus from beer bottles). These tiles were sufficiently attractive to entice an outside angel investor with enough interest in the environment, as well as the aesthetics, to fund three years of fundamental research on the use of waste glass in concrete materials. Unfortunately, the spinout company funding the work went out of business after the three years of funding. There was no place to turn outside the University to keep the researchers working in the laboratory.

In early 2003, S&TV stepped in with a seed fund investment to keep the programme going. The rationale for the funding was that S&TV believed these environmentally important products would reach the market in the near term, based largely on conversations with the failed company's industrial partner. Thereafter, the research and development work was finalised in the laboratory, as well as in the industrial partner's plant. Columbia created formulae for a wide variety of the company's concrete products using waste glass, and then worked with the industrial plant to complete the transfer of the technology and the industrial testing. The products began selling within 18 months of S&TV's funding, and significant licensing income is expected to flow back to the University from this technology.

This important project would never have left the laboratory if the principal investigator had not been committed to reducing his work to practice and translating his ideas into a commercial product. He relentlessly pursued every party along the way to receive the necessary funding to turn his vision of 'greener' building materials into a reality.

Nanotechnology

Nanotechnology research is still in its infancy, and much of the work taking place continues at the fundamental level. Experiments are required to demonstrate these new technologies can work and are commercially relevant. Given the amount of attention nanotechnology is receiving, there are many resources available to help scientists with bright new ideas. There are many nanotechnology experts who, in the interest of moving the field forward, will advise on potential innovative applications of a technology and proof of concept experiments, as well as potential collaborators and investors.

For example, in 2002, a clinical pharmacologist at Columbia, along with a collaborator at the University of New Mexico, were the first to use artificial DNA molecules assembled into circuits to make complex decisions. The ultimate purpose is to create a new drug delivery device for delivering therapeutics on an as-needed basis. To prove that synthetic enzymes can be programmed, the scientist designed a game of tic-tac-toe[1] (also known as noughts and crosses). The work continues inside the university, where strides are being made to move the idea close enough to market to attract outside seed financing.

Computer science

University software code is often brilliant and inventive, but it also suffers from being sloppily written ('spaghetti code') that is encumbered by third-party software. Potential investors find it difficult to evaluate the computer scientist's academic work when it does not follow the same conventions as the commercial work to which they are accustomed. This is the case even though a spinout company, or corporate licensee, will end up rewriting most of the code so that it is modular and properly documented. The innovation gap lies in the investor's expectation that the academic's highly functional software will also have an easy to use interface, with patent and/or copyright-protected code. The academic must rewrite the code to make its development into commercial applications easy to visualise.

For example, while the work is not glamorous, nor necessarily publishable, if an academic researcher wants to start a company or license their work to a corporation, they must first do the forensic analysis of the code's origins, as well as be prepared to do significant additional programming. The patent attorney and the academic should confirm in advance of all this extra work that the software will not easily be reverse-engineered and duplicated.

For patents and copyrights protecting the code to be enforceable, it must be possible to determine if the code is being used without a licence. Otherwise it is difficult for an infringement suit to be brought forward (some code is buried so deep in a product or process that it is hard to know if it is being used).

In short, if significant funding for a spinout is hoped for, the academic's IP must look as professional, and be as strong, as that which comes out of a corporate laboratory. The benefits, ranging from funding for the laboratory, potential income and the thrill of working with an outstanding commercial partner will more than compensate for the extra hours and effort.

Life sciences

Molecular biologists developing targets for drug discovery must supply not just in-vitro data but, more importantly, have data on the genetically manipulated animal models and the mechanism of action for the system, up and down stream.

For example, a Columbia scientist conducted proof of concept experiments in his laboratory demonstrating that he could rapidly perform differential screening of genes involved in disease, and then create animal models showing that the genes and gene products, including one called MDA-7, were active in fighting cancer. The faculty member raised capital in 1999 for a spinout built around his functional genomics technologies, as well as the MDA-7 therapeutic. The company was sold to a publicly traded company within two years of its founding (with a nice return to the investors), the product has advanced into Phase 2 clinical trials for several cancer indications and patients' lives are being extended by the treatment.

Funding proof of concept

A small but growing number of universities are committing internal funding to proof of concept projects. The justification for this funding varies, but the most pragmatic explanation is that small grants seem to have a very high leveraging effect. The funds represent a powerful commitment by the university to exploit its research and to encourage innovation.

Research has shown that projects receiving seed funding at the University of Wisconsin (UW) brought in eight times more federal and private funding as a direct result of these grants. Furthermore, a high percentage of these projects were turned into products by industry once the proof of concept work was completed. The results at UW and elsewhere are similar to the experiences at Columbia, where the office grants awards from a modest proof of principle fund.

One notable project funded by Columbia University S&TV eventually brought in more than US$30 million in licence and equity income (and the patent has several more good years). The university would have received a much smaller piece of this income had it not taken the risk to cover some of the legal fees at the start, as well as to purchase its pro-rata share of this patent licensing joint venture with several industry partners. This sole investment would justify the continuing investment in the fund for many years to come and has built a case for continuing to run a university seed fund.

Turning ideas and inventions into commercial applications

Relatively small amounts of funding allow researchers to take risks and explore uncharted concepts. These types of project, usually funded with as little as US$90,000, are novel, technically feasible, and have a high chance of commercial success. Depending on the outcome of these exploratory projects, they also might position projects to receive further funding to take a concept to full development.

Large grants for as much as US$400,000 can remove obstacles and keep the innovation process on track and moving forward. Ultimately, the aim is to build a package that is 'venture capital ready': the investment should be used exclusively to address the potential major concerns of follow-on investors. In some cases where IP has been developed, an additional demonstration of success is required. Perhaps one or more potential target customers have been identified for the use of the technology, but the uncertainty associated with applying the technology commercially needs to be reduced.

A framework for funding proof of concept

Seed capital is risky by nature as there are a lot of unknowns involved with an early stage venture. Nevertheless, proof of concept projects must be assessed as true business opportunities.

The earlier proof of concept funds are applied, the better the outcome. At best, commercial value is recognised early on and resources can be quickly applied to capture this value. At worst, early proof of concept projects show that a technology is commercially unfeasible, preventing any further waste of resources and time.

From experience, well-managed university seed and proof of concept funds:

- aim to simplify the spinout of businesses out of academia;
- bring the investors' point of view and expertise to the beginning of the evaluation of a scientific project;
- make quick decisions to invest money into an idea if a project is attractive;
- provide future founders with access to mentors to help them increase their business literacy;
- provide rapid funding to accelerate the translation of a scientific idea into a commercial concept;
- have a tiered funding approach;
- allocate a large number of smaller grants to a preliminary 'pathfinder' evaluation process that is focused on exploring the opportunity and conducting early due diligence; and
- back the most promising projects with more substantial grants in order to address the potential major concerns of early stage investors; and
- are not run by university committees that add bureaucracy and delays to the process.

Case study

The realities of managing a university seed fund in the United Kingdom

Dr Stéphane Méry, Bloomsbury BioSeed Fund, London

Proof of concept and university seed funds come to life

Increasingly, there is more proof of concept funding and seed stage funding becoming available to universities, often supported by national or regional government. The objective of these funds is to add value to early stage technologies by helping to overcome obstacles in the innovation process between invention and commercialisation.

In 1999, the UK government launched such an investment scheme called the University Challenge Seed Funds (UCSFs). This involved creating 18 university seed funds to bridge the funding gap between academic research and external private equity funding.

The average size of these funds was £4 million (US$7.35 million). In most cases, several universities located in the same region shared access to a fund.

Each UCSF was free to design how the fund operated and to utilise the funds available as it saw fit. The only constraint was that no more than £250,000 (US$460,000) could be provided to any given project. As a result, the 18 seed funds implemented 18 different investment strategies. They differed by the way they were managed (by the TTO group versus independent fund manager), their remit (generalists versus specialists) and their investment strategy (funding punctual needs such as filing a patent or buying a piece of equipment versus investing only in viable companies).

The ups and downs of the Bloomsbury BioSeed Fund (BBSF)

BBSF is a life science UCSF managed by a dedicated team. The £4 million (US$7.35 million) fund is open to all inventive scientists related to University College London, Cancer Research UK, Institute for Cancer Research, The Royal Veterinary College and The School of Pharmacy.

We invest in any project related to life science, be it drug discovery, medical devices, diagnostics or research tools. Our investment strategy is one of a true pre-venture capital fund. The aim is to create a business that is venture capital ready. The investment is used exclusively to address the potential major concerns of follow-on investors. These may relate to the state of the technology, but will almost invariably involve developing the commercial strategy and/or management team.

By early June 2004 BBSF had invested in eight companies. Most of our startups have attracted co-investment from various sources ranging from established VCs to angel investors. In addition, our first two startups Xcellsyz and SpiroGen, raised £1.2 million (US$2.2 million) and £7 million (US$12.87 million) respectively in follow-on funding. These early successes look encouraging but the environment is not easy.

Seed funds usually trade on a very fine line between success and failure. Luck is certainly the most important factor in the fate of these funds. However, luck can be helped a little if one can find ways to overcome the specific weaknesses that are associated in Europe with investing in early stage companies. BBSF's has gained experience over the past three years with ways to deal with these weaknesses as discussed below.

Most seed funds in Europe are unable to provide enough seed level funding

Life sciences academic spinouts usually require between £750,000 (US$1.38 million) and £1 million (US$1.88 million) to achieve meaningful proof of concept for their technology and to retain enough cash to stay afloat whilst looking for follow-on funding. The £250,000 (US$460,000) limit imposed on the UCSF in the United Kingdom is clearly insufficient.

BBSF's attempt to address this problem was to seek co-investment from the start. As an example, Xcellsyz, the first spinout, raised £100,000 (US$188,000) from a seed investor in Barcelona (where one of the founders was located) and a further £150,000 (US$827,000) thanks to an agreement with GSK, NovoNordisk and Novartis to create a consortium to develop one of Xcellsyz's cell lines.

Unfortunately, there are limited sources of co-investment available in Europe. In the United Kingdom, there is only a handful of seed investors and their number is decreasing dramatically as several of them have ceased to exist in the recent past. One alternative, however, is to apply for commercial grants. As such it has become a policy at BBSF to make an application to the Wellcome Trust's commercial grant (UTA) a proviso to any investment.

Most spinouts cannot access good management
In general, the seed phase (for life science) is centred on the scientific proof of principle. Spinouts usually do not need – and cannot afford – full-time management. Yet, part-time management is critical to establish early commercial deals or to manage fund raising.

BBSF's experience with part-time managers has not been very good so far, mostly because there are only very few good experienced part-time managers available and also because part-time managers usually have other competing activities (such as consulting) that prevents them from providing the flexibility that spinouts require.

To remedy this, BBSF has recently hired an entrepreneur in residence. This very experienced individual with both scientific and commercial expertise is paid by the Fund and seconded to two or three startups. In addition, BBSF's fund manager has taken over the role of part-time CEO in one of the spinouts.

Valuations are extremely punitive for seed investors
In the current environment, valuation at the series A funding round is very low, especially if the seed investors do not have funds to participate in the next financing round. As a result, the seed funds hardly see any up-lift in valuation (and down rounds[2] are common).

So far, with its first two investments, BBSF has been fortunate enough to attract corporate investors, which are usually more flexible on valuation. As an example, Ipsen invested into SpiroGen at a good valuation in exchange for the right to license Spirogen's lead compound.

Lessons learned
The simple truth is that public-private schemes have been a mixed success in the United Kingdom. On the positive side, over 200 new spinout companies have been started with this scheme. This has fostered entrepreneurship in UK universities. However, many of these spinouts will be unlikely to receive follow-on funding, partly because they have been under-funded. Overall, the original objective set by the UK government, that UCSF should become self-sustaining, is likely to prove difficult.

Schemes such as USCFs could be successful if a few things were changed:

- Seed funds should be in position to invest in fewer companies but with more money.
- Seed funds should be prepared to take harsh decisions about their investee companies to only continue support to those companies where there is evidence to show that they are likely to succeed.
- Spinouts financed by seed funds should be allowed to access as many grants as possible. This is not possible at present because of the European Union rule that stipulates that a spinout is not amenable to government grants if a university owns more than 25 per cent of its equity. This is nearly always the case.

The funding process

Exhibit 4.1 outlines a proof of concept funding process. After the initial meeting with the inventor, if the fund manager believes that the project is a genuine business opportunity, the investment occurs in two phases – the pathfinder phase and the investment phase.

Pathfinder phase

At this point, the fund can make an immediate decision to invest money into the construction of a business plan and a critical due diligence assessment (the pathfinder phase). As an example, an experienced consultant may be paid by the fund to work with the inventor to develop a strategy. If no show-stoppers have been identified (a key criterion is whether the progress that will be achieved once the initial capital has been spent will be enough to attract large investors or commercial partners for the next round of funding), the pathfinder is then presented to the fund's investment board for consideration.

Investment phase

If approved, the fund manager will negotiate equity in the new startup company and up to US$400,000 can be invested. The fund manager will then participate in the development of the company. The investment process is supported by high-quality board members with a breadth of business and scientific experience.

Lessons learned

Here are a few lessons that have helped Columbia University S&TV strengthen its technology transfer programme.

- Seek to work with investors that have commitment and vision. These people are far less likely to give up on an idea if it fails, as it always will. Visionaries believe in the concept, so they will push on in spite of mounting odds.
- There is no point in attempting to try to offer investors a 'full loaf of bread' when they can clearly see you can only really deliver 'half a loaf'. Making claims without proof of concept and proof of market to back them up only wastes their time and harms the spinout

Exhibit 4.1

The proof of concept funding process

Source: Dr Stéphane Méry, Bloomsbury BioSeed Fund, London.

team's own credibility. Acknowledge shortfalls and potential pitfalls, while simultaneously explaining how obstacles will be overcome.

• Avoid short-term thinking – it takes years for the efforts of the TTO to bear fruit. Do not quit on the inventor or give up on the important patents if the idea has merit. In some cases, the market simply needs time to catch up to the inventor's ideas. Encouragement given along the way is instrumental to continuing commitment from the inventors.

- The best opportunity the inventor has to raise a spinout's valuation and make it more attractive to investors is in the beginning. Proof of principle experiments accomplish both, saving significant amounts of time otherwise wasted on fund-raising. The potential for the scientists' contributions to create significant value is highest before the company has been funded.
- Time is the most valuable resource the TTO has: it should be allocated disproportionately to those inventors and ideas that have the highest likelihood of succeeding.
- University seed funds, if allowed to, can provide a very high return on investment, measured by new licensing income and sponsored research funds.

---

[1] This game should reside in the pantheon of proof of principle experiments. In 1949, Cambridge University scientists using the EDSAC machine (the first truly programmable computer) coded tic-tac-toe as the first computer game. Bill Gates' first computer programme was also a virtual tic-tac-toe game. Bill Gates and the Cambridge scientists still had years to go before developing commercial products, as is the case with the Columbia technology.

[2] A down round refers to a round of venture capital financing that is raised at a lower firm valuation than the previous round.

Chapter 5

From research to spinout and beyond – a venture capitalist's view

Dr Michael H. Gera
Pond Venture Partners, London and San Jose, California

This chapter looks at technology transfer through the eyes of a venture capital (VC) firm that specialises in investing in early stage European technology startups. It represents a VC firm's views on how technology transfer should happen. It then outlines the motives that an early stage venture firm is likely to have and what they should look for in spinout opportunities. Importantly, it then describes what universities and inventors can do to help to make a seed investment in a spinout happen. Some questions are posed to illustrate what universities should ask themselves before embarking on a spinout programme.

Navigating through the long journey

Exhibit 5.1 maps out typical steps in the life of a successful spinout commercialising information and communication technology. It is worthwhile examining it as it brings out some of the terms used in this chapter.

Exhibit 5.1
From birth to exit

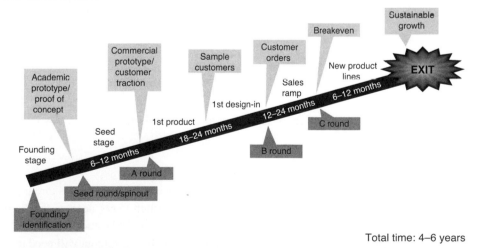

Total time: 4–6 years

Source: Pond Venture Partners.

What are the key stages and milestones?

- *Founding stage*. During this stage, a project with spinout potential is identified by the university. There is no external equity funding sought at this point. The founding stage aims to produce a proof of concept or academic prototype.
- *Seed stage*. During this stage, the group of founders gets a seed round of funding – typically not exceeding US$1 million. A separate company is set up. In the university context, this is the point of spinout. The objective of the seed stage is to produce a first commercial prototype and to have customer traction via direct meetings with potential clients. If these objectives are not met, the spinout should be shut down. The seed stage spinout is likely to benefit from staying close to the university.
- *Series A funding round and beyond*. During the series A round, the spinout get much more commercial. The A round is usually several million dollars in size. For a venture capital investor, the A Round is still very early in the spinout's life. There is still a long and hazardous journey ahead and failure remains a distinct possibility. For the university, the A round marks the end of the spinout process.

What are the criteria for achieving a seed round?

In most cases, the right way for a VC firm to first get involved with a university spinout is via a seed stage investment. Thus far, we have said that the VC firm should not expect a commercial team or product from a candidate university seed investment. However, what must be present to make it worthwhile for the venture capitalist? Clearly, there must be a kernel of technology within the university that has the potential to lead to a product that is significantly (say 10 times) better than competing technology in a large, growing market. The venture capitalist should also look for active and enthusiastic support from the inventors for as long as they are needed.

What is the objective of a seed round?

It may seem obvious, but the objective of the seed round is to start a company and take it to the point where it qualifies for a Series A funding round. Key requirements for the seed stage are:

- a sense that there is a significant and growing market that is partially understood;
- key inventors ready to be involved full-time for up to a year; and
- an academic prototype.

At most, the seed stage will last one year and up to US$1 million (but much less in certain sectors) will be spent.

What is important?
- *Inventors*. The inventors need to be full-time during the seed stage. 'Inventors' are the people who actually did the work and made the discovery, which is not necessarily the professor (for example, it could be a research assistant or a recent PhD student).
- *Intellectual property (IP)*. IP must be in place and, ultimately, the spinout will need to own it outright.

- *Proof of concept*. In reality, this is a prototype or a demonstrator. This is very valuable as it gives focus to those involved and facilitates thinking about the market potential.
- *Light legal agreements*. It makes no sense to spend US$100,000 on a legal document for a seed stage spinout that may not survive more than a year. Tighter agreements may be justified once an A round is reached, but until then keep it simple.
- *Staying sober*. The technology transfer office (TTO) can assist the process by attempting to keep inventors' expectations realistic. It is always worth remembering that most seed companies fail. Those that generate extraordinary returns will do so after a very long time. Avoid too much fanfare for now.
- *University premises and facilities*. The university can really help to keep things cheap and low-key by providing facilities during the seed stage. After an A round – if it happens – the spinout will want more independence and will be able to afford it.

What is not important?

- *A business plan*. A real business plan requires a market sizing, a competitive analysis and a description of a product concept. A business plan is not actually possible at the seed stage because the key elements cannot really be articulated at this point – as the following bullets explain.

   Attempting to plan things as much as possible is good. The danger of calling a 'plan' a business plan at this point is that it often takes on a life of its own. There is a danger in getting wedded to a non-business plan and travelling down poorly understood strategic paths.
- *Market sizing*. Without significant interaction with the marketplace it is hard to get a proper market sizing. Analyst reports are of limited value. The real market sizing comes from what customers say.
- *Competitive analysis*. A competitive analysis is not really feasible from publicly available information – especially if your competitors are also startups in stealth mode. The only real way to compare the business to a competitor is to ask customers.
- *A product concept*. A product concept – as opposed to a description of technology – must be driven by customer requirements and requires skilled marketing work.
- *An engineering plan*. This is another key element of a real business plan. Again, in the absence of a commercial prototype built by a commercial engineer, a realistic engineering schedule is simply not possible.
- *A CEO*. Without a clear understanding of target markets, it is impossible to recruit the right CEO for the job. At this point, the job has not been defined.

For university spinouts, business plans are often written and CEOs are often recruited before the seed round because some VC firms refuse to invest without them. This is unfortunate because it may well be riskier investing in the wrong business plan and CEO than investing when neither of the two are yet in place. In the latter case, precious time is not wasted undoing uninformed decisions.

   The spinout process is much easier if the university has a good working relationship with a set of good investors. 'Good' investors are those who are already aware of research projects long before they are ready to spin out, have relationships with the inventors, have given thought to the market opportunity, have held discussions with potential customers and have the ability to drive things forward.

What are the criteria for getting to the A round?

Some university spinouts get immediate A round funding and skip a seed stage. The three criteria needed for this are:

- a significant and growing market;
- an engineering team with significant commercial operating experience; and
- a commercial prototype that is significantly better than alternatives.

Some VC firms – notably Silicon Valley players – can take a simpler approach. They back proven entrepreneurs and they back them to the hilt. Their reasoning is that such people will get all key elements right most of the time – and with strong VC support they are able to take decisive action to fix things when they go wrong. So, if a proven entrepreneur is available, an A round is likely to be the right place to start a company.

Clearly, it is unusual to find an academic research group with an entrepreneurial superstar among its members. Neither is a team of academics likely to have a significantly commercial engineering team, or a commercial (as opposed to academic) prototype.

What technology transfer really means to investors

Technology is 'transferred' only when a head of engineering hired externally can build the technology unaided by the inventor.

As the head of engineering gets more familiar with the technology, he or she will start to consider the issues surrounding a commercial prototype. He or she will ask questions about yield and quality that the inventor might not have needed to ask. Eventually, he or she may design some prototypes of his or her own, taking engineering issues into account. This work may bring about questions about the underlying technology that were not previously asked. It is important that the inventor be involved in the spinout full-time during the seed stage to deal with such issues as they arise.

Failure is always a potential route to an early exit

Failure is an option, and sometimes a good one. If the seed company completely misses successive engineering or marketing milestones laid down at the beginning, it should consider shutting down. This is not a tragedy. It is an opportunity for talented people to do something more productive in other areas. If, during the seed stage, the inventors, engineering vice president, marketing vice president, VC firm and TTO developed a healthy respect for each other, always behaved ethically and truthfully, really gave it their best shot, and enjoyed working together, then the groundwork for a future seed company based on a new invention may have been laid.

All those involved in any kind of spinout – VC firms, entrepreneurs, employees and the university – must look at some VC statistics. VC returns are generated by a tiny percentage of the companies they invest in that are extraordinarily successful in terms of the value at which they are floated on a stock exchange via an initial public offering (IPO) or sold to a trade buyer.

A VC firm has fiduciary duties to its investors. If the choice arises between the firm investing another dollar in a new investment with good exit potential and making a further investment in an existing investment that is shaping up to be, at best, an average performer, the dollar is going to go to the former. The VC firm will view the latter company as a failure, whether or not it stays in business. Of course, lack of funds will likely lead to it having to close.

What can a university do to really help?

There is a tremendous amout that a university can do to aid the spinout process. Here are some of the key issues.

The university must know what it wants

If a VC firm wishes to invest in university spinouts, it needs to be fully cognisant of the university's point of view. This is only possible if the university is clear about what it wants from spinout companies.

Why does a university want to see spinouts happen? A university may have more than one reason for wanting a spinout to succeed. Different universities have different sets of reasons, including:

- *Money through exit*. A spinout that is successfully acquired or publicly listed can bring a large lump sum of cash to a university that has retained a stake in it.
- *Money through licence revenue*. If the IP is only licensed into a spinout, it may be possible to get a royalty stream.
- *Money via directed research*. A spinout may commission research work at the university from which it has spun out.
- *Good public relations*. Good public relations for a spinout may reflect well on the university.
- *Government approval*. The EU and the United States, among others, encourage spinout activity highly and offer various financial incentives to promote this activity.
- *Putting something back*. As a recipient of public funds, a university may feel it should 'put back' into society whatever it can.

One cannot achieve all of these outcomes simultaneously. The university has to prioritise, make a choice and stick to it.

Establish whether the inventor is truly committed

Academic inventors play a crucial early role. Thus, it is important that they examine carefully whether they are actually interested in spinout activity. If the answer is 'yes', is it to:

- get rich?
- get famous?
- find something to do on Wednesday afternoons?
- keep up with Professor Jones down the corridor who has his own spinout?
- make a permanent move out of academia?
- see their invention 'out there' in the market?

Each individual academic should be encouraged by the university to make up his or her own mind. Young researchers may see things differently to well-established professors. Biotechnology scientists may have different views to, say, computer scientists. The university

– as well as the VC firms later on – needs to understand all this. It takes a lot of thinking and preparing before a university can start a spinout programme.

Recruit specialists to operate the TTO

The university needs to do a considerable amount of preparation before embarking on spin-out creation and development activity. Typically, the first step is the appointment of an officer from the TTO. Similar to every step along the way, this appointment requires some care. The TTO is the nexus of spinout activity and interfaces with research teams, the university administration, commercial partners and VC firms. The TTO staff members need to be credible in the eyes of all these parties.

TTO staff members need a range of specialist skills. These include:

- understanding the academic research process, academic administrative priorities and the nature of research in different fields;
- being sufficiently technical to hold at least a high-level discussion with a researcher;
- having some commercial operating experience, which is necessary to hold a meaningful dialogue with potential commercial partners, such as VC firms, and vital when deciding which of the partners are better;
- maintaining independence from researchers and from the university administration, as it is important to ensure that short-term pressure does not lead to the wrong spinouts happening or the right spinouts happening in the wrong way; and
- displaying tact and diplomacy, as all spinouts go through some very tough times and the TTO that has developed good relations with all the counterparties is more likely to prevail.

Some tips for TTO officers are outlined in Exhibit 5.2.

University educational programmes

You cannot teach somebody to be an entrepreneur. Neither can you teach them to be a CEO, chief operating officer (COO), marketing vice president or engineering vice president. The goal of a university-run entrepreneurial-educational programme should be different – namely, to heighten awareness. The target audience is probably not primarily professorial. Professors are likely to know the TTO already and be familiar with the opportunities in commercialisation. The real target audience is composed of research students, research assistants, junior faculty members and, maybe, certain undergraduates. The programmes should provide answers to questions from inventors, such as:

- What is a spinout?
- What is needed for a spinout?
- Why should I be interested?
- Does my work have commercial potential? How can the TTO help me if it does?
- How can I enhance the commercial potential of my work without compromising academic quality?
- What are the steps to a spinout? What happens then? What will I need to do?
- What is venture capital? Should I care?

External speakers – such as venture capitalists – may sometimes be helpful.

A key objective is to encourage students and faculty members to come to the TTO with future candidates for spinouts.

Exhibit 5.2

Letter to a TTO from an early stage venture capitalist

Dear John:

Congratulations on your appointment as director of the university's TTO. I thought I would drop you a note with some suggestions on to how you might want to get things started.

- Communicate. Aim to produce a coherent statement as to why the university wants technology transfer and, in particular, spinouts. Do not just visit the Dean. Take this discussion to individual departments. You will find the motives in life science different to computer science – to pick just two examples.
- Consult widely. Organisations such as AUTM in the United States, UNICO in the United Kingdom and ASTP across Europe are full of people who have experience with spinouts. They will be happy to share experiences. Do not reinvent the wheel if you do not need to.
- Make friends. Identify which individuals at the university's administrative level as well as at the departmental level are receptive and prepared to help you lay the groundwork.
- Build relationships with venture capitalists. It is never too early for this!
- Understand what you have got. Understand the starting point. What research is being undertaken? By whom? Who is funding it? What is the level of receptivity to the spinout by the researchers?
- Create a research database. Once you have a growing list of research projects that you are tracking, build a research database. It does not have to be too sophisticated, but good enough to help you 'think outside the box'. This means that you should not fall into departmental/faculty compartmentalised thinking. I have heard of a great laser spinout that started in a Chemistry department and a billion-dollar biotech form that started in Chemical Engineering. Make sure your database helps you query creatively.
- Devise educational programmes. Make people aware of what commercialisation is all about as well as what the role of the TTO office is.
- Agree how to be measured. How will you be judged? Agree on this in advance with the university. Whatever you do, do not let them try to measure your success by counting the number of companies you register at Companies House per year. It is about quality and not quantity. Do not turn into a graveyard of dormant companies.
- Do not play professor. You are not an academic. You are not the best person to determine the academic value of a research project. Look to academics and their peers to guide you when trying to figure out what is of high academic value.
- Science is not business. Now let us be clear, great science does not necessarily mean you will get a great business. In fact, sometimes there is no commercial value to certain world-class research. For each research project, try to understand what is true.
- Do not play venture capitalist. Work with venture capitalists who can add value at an early stage. Do not try to write long business plans, hire CEOs or chase customers for your potential spinouts. Let the venture capitalists do this. Your time is too valuable and your real role too important to waste time trying to build companies.

Good luck!

Source: Pond Venture Partners.

Identifying candidates for seed rounds

The TTO should have an ongoing dialogue with key VC firms. The research database is a key tool in enabling the venture capitalists to identify projects where they could add value and spend time at suitable intervals holding discussions with the academics. The venture capitalist is ideally placed to identify projects with market potential. Through their own experience or via advisers, VC partners can perform some initial validation of this market potential much more easily than a university can. Obviously, these findings should be shared with the TTO and inventors and should of course be key factors in the decision to initiate a spinout and provide seed funding. Normally, the venture capitalist in question would be the seed investor.

Why should universities build relations with VC funds? The reason is simple. Good venture capitalists are much closer to the global market than either the TTO or the university will ever be. Also, a VC firm will have operational skills in-house that can be brought to bear.

Building relationships with venture capital funds

There is a plethora of VC funds out there. The TTO must be able to pick a few with whom to have ongoing dialogues. Some criteria for the TTO are listed below.

- *Seed-round venture capitalists.* The right stage for a spinout to happen is at the seed round. Therefore an investor that makes seed investments is the right one and a late stage only investor is a waste of time.
- *Venture capitalists who can follow-on.* Strong preference should be given to venture capitalists who can continue to invest in a spinout in later funding rounds. This ensures that the criteria for the seed round (see above) and A round are consistent. Also, it is a sad fact that seed-only investors often get so diluted in later rounds that they are 'washed out' and have no motivation to be in the driving seat of a spinout. Their motivation to make university investments may thus wane and the time invested in them by the TTO may end up wasted. Investors who can follow-on must have larger funds and therefore have more resources, global market contacts and influence that the spinouts can benefit from.
- *Venture capitalists who get to the 'dream' customers.* Which would you rather have before you spin a company out: a strong expression of interest from a medium-size potential customer company down the road or to be told by the head of business development at a US$50 billion market capitalisation industry leader that they are not interested and that there are five other stealth-mode startups with better technology. The latter feedback is hugely valuable, albeit negative. It could save the TTO and the inventors years of wasted effort. The venture capitalist who gets the spinout in front of the dream customers should get the vote.
- *Technically aware venture capitalists.* Similar to the TTO and its team, the seed venture capitalist needs to interface with the inventors. If the venture capitalist lacks the requisite technical background, this is much harder.
- *Operationally experienced venture capitalist partners.* Individuals who have started companies, taken them through growing pains, hired engineering and management teams in different countries, worked through crises, downsized and restarted, hunted for customers throughout the world and engaged with them, negotiated tough contracts, made mistakes, seen companies fail, and seen companies succeed are people who are credible partners.
- *Venture capitalists who are familiar with universities.* Look for partners in VC firms who understand academia and academic research.

- *Individuals of VC firms that you trust and like.* A VC firm that is chosen to invest in a spin-out will end up spending a lot of time with the TTO and several academics. It is best to pick individuals with whom you can work.
- *Venture capitalists who are prepared to invest time.* If a venture capitalist is prepared to invest time with a TTO before there is a spinout in the works, this is a good sign. Similarly, if a research project is obviously not yet ready for spinout, it is good to work with a venture capitalist who is nevertheless prepared to spend some time with the team looking to add value.

The changing role of the university–spinout relationship

The changing role of the scientist is part of an inevitable change in the role of the university during the spinout's life as it secures external funding. The change in personnel will lead to a far more commercial mood. Several new people in the company will have no links to the university. The company will want premises of its own and company employees will not be seen on campus quite so much.

The company will probably need to be seen by customers and investors to be reducing its dependence on university facilities, and either developing its own or using commercial sources. The university should not feel aggrieved by any of this. These steps are taken in the best interests of the shareholders – which will include the university.

Conclusion

By way of summary, here is a list of practical tips.

For inventors:

- be prepared for a full-time role during seed stage;
- do not expect a permanent full-time role; and
- be patient with the new hires and try to develop a common language with them.

For universities:

- understand the VC perspective;
- decide what your motives are;
- build the right foundations;
- choose your VC firms carefully;
- build for success, but prepare for failure;
- set the right expectations;
- do not over-incubate; and
- expect the spinout to move off campus.

For the investor:

- invest time getting to know universities and try to help, even if a spinout is not an immediate prospect;
- do not push spinouts to over-incubate by insisting on full management teams;
- understand the technology; and
- drive early customer feedback.

Chapter 6

From discovery to market opportunity

Dave Sands
START, Shell Global Solutions International BV,[1] *The Hague*

There is no such thing as a linear, step-by-step process for creating and developing a university spinout. There are sound guidelines available, however, and without these, early steps can be uncertain and challenging for the inexperienced entrepreneur. This chapter provides guidelines, hints and tips, and practical examples for part of the innovation journey – the path from initial discovery in the laboratory, to arriving at a market opportunity that shows adequate commercial promise to build a business.

Introduction

The case for change

Hindsight is a wonderful thing. Looking back, we can see that universities and other academic institutions have not always been very effective at translating academic discoveries into practical businesses.

Fewer than 3 per cent of academic spinouts in Europe make it to launch, let alone sustained success. That is a sobering statistic and, in itself, a powerful argument for a change of approach.

The root of the problem

In the author's experience, most problems arise in the early days of the journey from discovery to launch. A team attempting an academic spinout faces challenges similar to an adventurer about to cross uncharted territory. Although a spinout team may have some knowledge about the path to commercialisation, it can have little idea of the specific obstacles it will face or the best route to take. Just as the adventurer has no map and no road to follow, there is no linear, step-by-step guide to innovation. Dead ends, and having to go back to go forward, should be expected by the spinout team.

Improving chance of success

The author's view of the most likely causes of failure can be seen in the context of a journey:

- *Pursuing one path single-mindedly and ignoring other options to explore.* The spinout team creates a business concept, but it is not the best possible answer.
- *Not using the right navigational aids.* Without the right direction-setting and tracking

---

[1] Shell Global Solutions International BV gives no warranty and makes no representation as to the accuracy of the information conveyed in this chapter.

tools, the spinout team ends up going in circles, unclear about where it is trying to get to or where it has come from.

- *Ignoring advice*. The spinout team does not listen to innovation experts or appropriate industry gurus.

While a spinout team planning to cross unmapped territory to commercialisation cannot know the specific route to take, it must:

1. learn from the experiences of others about the different terrains it will have to negotiate, and the general rules it must follow in each terrain; and
2. apply the correct navigation techniques to ensure clear direction-setting and optimal route selection along the way.

This chapter starts at the moment when someone first believes that a discovery has the potential to be commercially successful. The end point of the chapter – the market opportunity – is less easily defined, but it is likely to be marked by the following.

- Each member of the team involved has reached a level of confidence that they have found the best way to get what they want from taking the discovery to the commercial world.
- A business plan is needed to communicate that confidence to other necessary parties – whether potential partners, financiers, management team candidates and so on.
- The risk for those involved is about to increase – whether that be in the form of money, reputation or time invested.

This chapter describes the one navigation aid the team needs and the two terrains the team must negotiate on their journey.

The innovation 'compass check'

The need for a navigation aid

The innovation journey requires the entrepreneur to pass through two forms of terrain. During the first – idea generation – the entrepreneur brainstorms all of the possible uses that the discovery could have. During the second – idea selection – ideas are tested and validated until one (or perhaps more) stand out as worthy of detailed business planning. These terrains are easily described, but difficult to navigate in practice.

Once ideas have been generated, the journey becomes one of knowledge-gathering, both through researching and testing the ideas. Each time the team gains knowledge, there are various possible outcomes. For example:

- some ideas under development no longer seem promising;
- ideas still seem promising but new questions need to be answered to validate the potential; or
- new ideas are sparked.

Thus, along the innovation journey, the team will frequently have to check and, perhaps, adjust direction. Stopping, questioning, planning and redirecting resources as new information arrives is critical. The crucial point is to adjust plans based on the changed perspective. Sometimes the best option is to retrace steps.

The spinout team faces a challenge that does not trouble a lone entrepreneur. Successful spinouts usually involve people from academia with different specialties, as well as business people with different expertise. The team must be aligned, so that all are pulling towards the same goal. This may appear simple, but the author's experience has shown that it is anything but. Regular team 'compass checks' including all the key members are therefore essential.

How the compass check works

The innovation compass check is a technique where the team asks itself three questions.

- Where are we now?
- Where do we want to be?
- How do we get there?

Each of these questions is answered by looking at different topics, and this chapter will look at each of the questions in turn.

Where are we now?

This question leads to little more than a review of the plan from the last compass check and should include assessment of:

- progress against current plan;
- any new information available; and
- stakeholders.

The last element, stakeholders, is critical but often overlooked by inexperienced teams. Understanding who is interested in progress and how much they can influence success is vital. The team will have to manage those individuals or bodies that have the power to block their efforts, and a sound communication plan is essential. Here are just a few examples of people or bodies that might need to be considered:

- *the inventor* – who may have most of the technical know-how;
- *the academic institution* – who may be providing facilities, salaries and so on;
- *trustees and government bodies* – who may be funding the research that led to the discovery; and
- *investors* – who may be interested in providing finance.

> Do not underestimate the effort required to manage stakeholders. You will need to identify your stakeholders, draw up a communications plan, and make the effort to follow it. Be aware that the effort needed will grow as the project develops and more stakeholders get involved.

Where do we want to be?

Setting the goal for the team consists of agreeing:

- boundaries; and
- the definition of success.

Boundaries are fundamentals that cannot be transgressed. They define the edges of the terrain that the team is set to explore. Examples of boundaries might include relevant national laws, or policies that the academic institution holds regarding the practices it will support.

Defining the criteria for success and checking against them are probably the single most important part of the compass check. Different individuals and different bodies involved will have different views about what success is. While the desired outcome is often a sustainable profitable business, there are many cases where it is not a top priority. Value means different things to different people.

- The academic institution might be interested in reputation – to attract more quality people and more money – and be seeking good publicity, papers being published and so on.
- The academic who made the discovery may only wish to secure more funding for his or her research projects.
- Some people involved may not be interested in making money – they may just wish to see the discovery put to good use in the world.

> Do not assume that all members of the team want the same thing. More often than not, at least one team member will have a significantly different view from the others.

How do we get there?

As stated above, once ideas have been generated, the innovation journey becomes one of testing and validating ideas until one (or perhaps more) stand out as worthy of a detailed business plan. In practice, the team follows a cycle of:

1. deciding which ideas to park and which to explore further (existing or new);
2. deciding which issues and uncertainties should be addressed by the next raft of testing and research;
3. conducting tests and research, and collating the information; and
4. running another compass check (in other words, back to stage 1 above).

The question 'How do we get there?' is therefore about:

- choosing which ideas to pursue (based on which look most likely to meet the definition of success);
- deciding which issues and uncertainties to address; and
- agreeing the plan of research and testing activities.

Time spent on issues is valuable because sound planning comes from focusing on the right issues at the right time. Some questions to consider when prioritising issues are:

- What could go wrong?
- What could affect our success?
- What can we control? And what can we not?

> To help generate issues, use the headings technical, economic, commercial, organisational and political (TECOP) as prompters. This will ensure that all angles are covered.

Practical application of the compass check

How often and how much of the compass check to use will depend on several factors, including the number of people involved, the extent to which ideas have been developed and the resources available.

> In general, a compass check is only needed when significant or surprising new information comes in, or when the team members are uncertain or at odds over what to do next.

The case study below provides a practical example of how the compass check is used.

Case study
Taking a new direction with a film technology

A spinout from a US university had developed a film that better managed and harnessed transmitted light in a liquid crystal display (LCD). The company was developing the technology with mobile phone and laptop manufacturers to improve screen performance when an encounter with a global energy company led to a new concept: using the film on solar cells to increase the amount of light they convert to useful energy.

The challenge was to decide if and how to pursue this new opportunity, given that the company had already made significant investments and commitments in the screen concept.

Using the compass check, the company's management team were quickly able to identify the constraints and issues they would face, and the success they needed to make it worthwhile. With this clearly understood, they could negotiate and agree to a joint development programme with the energy company, without compromising their other initiatives.

Having introduced the navigation aid, this chapter now examines the two terrains that will be encountered along the innovation journey.

Navigating the first terrain on the innovation journey – idea generation

When a discovery is first made, it is undefined and undirected. Potential is latent and everything is possible.

This creates both an opportunity and a threat. With a range of routes available and many apparently fruitful environments believed to lie ahead, the temptation is to trade focus for a fast start and analysis for a preconceived route forward.

Rather than objectively shape the innovation, the tendency for some academic entrepreneurs is to push subjective preferences in one or more uncharted directions. To avoid falling into this trap, two key questions should be answered.

1. What exactly is this discovery that we have got?
2. How can it be useful?

Free and creative thinking, often termed brainstorming, is needed here. There are many texts available that describe brainstorming techniques, so, rather than describing them in detail, this chapter highlights the most important rules for the team at this stage.

- Be aware of the team's own preconceptions, and actively try to challenge them.
- Question the obvious: the way forward is highly unlikely to be the first one that the team identifies.
- Assessment comes later. Any idea at this stage, however seemingly far-fetched, should be included.
- Do not be constrained by the team's own knowledge. The temptation is to follow paths that are better known than others.
- Do not assume that the customer is an end-consumer. An idea's greatest potential may arise through its role as a component or enabler within a wider product or process.

When the well of ideas has dried up, the team should have a long list of very different possibilities to explore. They are ready to move into the next terrain.

The team members should not, however, be surprised to find themselves returning to this first terrain at least once, and perhaps more often. They may discover that the paths that seemed most promising are dead-ends, but knowledge gained along the way may well have revealed entirely new avenues to be explored. Every time such a new world of possibilities is unveiled, the team should again allow time for brainstorming and creative thinking.

> Going back to the idea-generation terrain should not be seen as a failure. Instead, it should be viewed as successfully avoiding a doomed venture and creating more promising opportunities.

The case study below provides a practical example of how this can occur.

Case study

Re-thinking the application of intelligent polymer technology

A research team had created an intelligent polymer that could 'detect' substances in water. Originally, they were considering developing it commercially as a product to monitor water pollution. This application of the technology seemed to be the most obvious and was based upon preconceptions of likely demand in this sector for such a product. In practice, the team's approach to commercialisation was met with resistance as they sought to gain access to this market.

At this point, the team was encouraged to stop and think more broadly before moving forward. The process of idea generation was purposely separated from the process of idea assessment and idea selection.

Many ideas were generated that were then used as possibilities to be explored in greater detail. Focus was applied to analysing the range of environments in which the technology could be applied. Potential routes to commercially exploiting the technology in each environment were explored.

The possibility of using the same polymer technology to detect impurities in gases had not previously occurred to the team. Examining this possibility opened the eyes of the team members to applying the technology to industrial processes using gases. The knowledge that the team gained about this possibility greatly increased the chances of finding a 'killer application' – where the need for a solution is desperate, and the path to money is much, much faster.

Navigating the second terrain on the innovation journey – idea selection

Having generated a long list of ideas, the next task is to assess them and validate their potential.

The idea or ideas that make it through this stage will have convincing answers to the following questions:

- Who is the customer?
- How does this idea help to meet that customer's needs?
- How much value does this idea create?
- How much of that value will the innovators be able to take?

This chapter will take each of the questions in turn, describing how each can be answered. Remember, though, that this sequential explanation will not be reflected in a spinout team's journey towards a validated idea. Instead, they will have to cycle through the questions, refining and fine-tuning the answers as more knowledge is gained. The innovation compass check is invaluable, because the team must continually decide which ideas to explore and where to focus their efforts.

Who is the customer?

Understanding the customer and knowing what his, her or its needs are is critical. One of the core assumptions in any business case is how many people or businesses will find a product or service attractive. This requires an intimate understanding of customers' behaviour and needs.

For example, consider a new medical device product. Different customers have different priorities on their needs: price, performance, ease of use, quality and interoperability. There are also different behaviours to understand: those who buy devices for an entire hospital, those who buy a single unit for their own use, those who are already used to buying existing technologies and devices from competitors, and those who buy devices to be integrated with their own technologies and systems.

Identifying precisely the target customer group is critical. Only then is a realistic estimate of the target market size possible.

Broad-brush customer data can often be found in publicly available market research reports, but real confidence in understanding is only achieved by talking to customers. Some good ways to get the detailed understanding needed are interviews, surveys and involving customers in the development of the idea.

How does this idea help to meet that customer's needs?

Customer needs come in many forms – reduced price, better performance, enhanced reputation or even something for which the customer had never explicitly stated a need.

With intimate customer knowledge, the team stands a good chance of refining the idea into a product or service that exactly matches the needs of the customer. The surest way to gauge the potential of that product or service, however, is to test it with the customer and then to measure the response.

> In the author's experience, a test that proves the product/service does not work is obviously disappointing, but it is invaluable – it is better to have to rethink at this stage than after launching a business. A compass check to reset direction is advisable in such cases.

How much value does the idea create?

For an idea to be a viable business, it must create value for someone. This can come in many forms, such as:

- the idea improves something so that an end-consumer is willing to pay more for it;
- the idea helps a company reduce its costs;
- the idea helps a company win more customers; and
- the idea helps a company improve its image.

Estimating and validating how much value the idea creates will lie at the heart of the business case. Optimism has no place here. The potential value for a non-invasive blood glucose level monitor is not the global annual sales of all glucose level monitors. Its non-invasive feature has obvious potential benefits – less patient discomfort, faster patient turn-around, or even allowing patients to monitor their glucose level at home – but these benefits will not apply everywhere. Private healthcare organisations may decide that reduced patient discomfort outweighs the cost of changing from one system to another, but public healthcare organisations may not. On the other hand, patient turn-around may be far more appealing to public than private healthcare organisations.

> In the author's experience, overestimating the commercial value of a scientific discovery is a common mistake. A good question to ask is: where is the money coming from? There must be absolute confidence that someone, somewhere, is willing to pay.

Note that only a portion of the value created will be available to the spinout. How much is the topic of the next question.

How much of the value created will the team be able to take?

To answer this question, the team will need to understand the position of a potential market opportunity within the industry value chain. A value chain describes all the activities needed to take a product or service from its beginning right to the end-customer. It also shows the different kinds of companies that carry out the activities in the value chain. A simplified example is given for the bioscience industry in Exhibit 6.1.

Exhibit 6.1

Simplified value chain for the bioscience industry

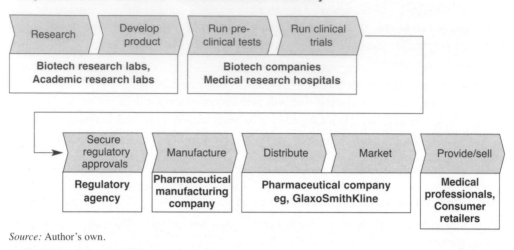

Source: Author's own.

The members of the spinout team need a detailed understanding of the appropriate value chain for their idea. They must then decide which part(s) of the value chain they want to be in, and how they will achieve that.

There are many possibilities for capturing value:

- sell intellectual property (IP) to another company;
- licence IP to another company;
- partner with another company;
- form a joint venture with another company;
- retain ownership but contract out activities; and
- carry out activities in-house.

Each of the possibilities named above will carry a different risk. Note that those players in the value chain who take most risk will want the lion's share of the total value available. Selling a patent, for example, carries little risk. On the other hand, creating a company to buy the patent and sell products involves taking significant risks in the marketplace. The company that buys the patent, not the original patent holder, will therefore take most of the value available.

The best fit for the spinout team members will depend on their definition of success, the level of risk they are prepared to accept, where their capabilities best match those needed in the value chain, and the strengths and weaknesses of those companies already present in the value chain.

> Success for the team may only be cash in hand. For example, if long-term success of the business is unimportant then selling the IP rights may be the best strategy. Another team (or its stakeholders) may see value in the reputation gained from a successful business, making an IP sale less appealing.

The importance of covering the four questions rigorously is illustrated in the following case study.

Case study

Constructing a business model for a new kind of building material

A spinout company has developed a new building material that can outperform cement in many applications. Although it cannot compete with cement under heavy structural loading, it has other attractive performance characteristics: it is faster-curing, more crack-resistant, waterproof and more environmentally friendly.

The technology team planned to create a new spinout company that sold the building material to high-value niche applications. The team's original approach to commercialising the technology was based on preconceptions of what the market wanted, based on the team's development work done. Most importantly, the team assumed that they could not compete with cement on a price basis for use in similar applications. To do so, they would have to scale the business up to a certain size quickly to benefit from economies of scale.

The team also failed to generate alternative options or assess the economics of different business models. This was partly due to the team's desire to keep control and ownership over the development of the company. Pursuing alternative options would almost certainly involve entry of new team members and collaboration with new partners. In hindsight, the team's reluctance to use knowledge beyond its own boundaries meant that they lacked the commercial know-how to scale the business up quickly and get costs low enough to compete on price.

The original approach pursued by the company limited the maximum potential value of the business. In fact, the team was struggling to attract external investment for opportunity they had defined. Potential investors viewed the company as a sustainable business, but one that did not offer sufficient growth potential for an attractive return on investment.

At this point, the spinout team started a detailed review by asking the four simple yet powerful questions.

1. Who is our customer?
2. How does our idea help to meet that customer's needs?
3. How much value does the idea create?
4. How much of that value will we be able to take?

These questions challenged the team's perceptions over the best route to market. The answers provided important insights into what customers really wanted, and where the opportunities and risks lay in the value chain. Most importantly, the assumption that the spinout should not compete on price was challenged.

This re-analysis revealed that the team lacked the skill-set for accelerating the development of the business. If the technical know-how of the existing team members could be complemented with business development skills from new team members, the spinout could form alliances with partners elsewhere in the value chain and put together a business offering a highly competitive price model.

> The team developed a model with far greater potential value than their original model – to compete directly with cement on price rather than performance in selected applications, and use a joint venture model instead of a wholly owned subsidiary. The 'industrial flooring' sector was identified as the first market sector to target, because it would generate healthy profits quickly. This would allow the spinout to scale up and compete in the larger market of paving, where even more value could be captured.

What next?

Only the team can decide when one or more opportunities have withstood examination to their satisfaction, but it is the rigour of that examination that determines their chances of success.

Nevertheless, in the team's view the discovery is now a contender, ready for its IP to be protected, a management team to be put in place and detailed business plans to be established. The journey from discovery to market opportunity is over.

As a market opportunity, the idea has real potential value. That potential now needs to be realised.

Tips for entrepreneurs

For those new to the innovation journey and unfamiliar with the terrain, always remember the following.

- There is no such thing as a linear step-by-step process to creating and developing a university spinout that someone can follow. Dead ends, and having to go back to go forward, should be expected by the spinout team
- Perform a compass check whenever significant or surprising new information comes in, or when the team is uncertain or at odds over what to do next.
- Use the TECOP headings – technical, economic, commercial, organisational and political – to be sure that all the angles are covered.
- Do not underestimate the effort required to manage stakeholders. It is essential to identify stakeholders, draw up a communications plan and make the effort to follow it. Be aware that the effort needed will grow as the project develops and more stakeholders get involved.
- Do not assume that the team members all want the same thing. More often than not, at least one member will have a significantly different view from the others.
- Things often start to go wrong whenever the spinout team:
  - pursues one path single-mindedly, ignoring other options to explore;
  - does not use the right navigational aids; and
  - ignores advice from experienced experts.
- Arriving back at a point where you have been previously should not be seen as a failure. View it instead as successfully avoiding a doomed venture and creating more promising opportunities.

Chapter 7

Intellectual property management

Renee Rottner

Graduate School of Management, University of California, Irvine

Intellectual property (IP) protection ensures that inventors have rights to their ideas. This chapter discusses the IP building blocks and the management of the disclosure process.

IP can be managed through several mechanisms, such as copyright protection or material transfer agreements. However, the main focus in this chapter is on patents, due to the large role they play in the valuation and financing of spinouts.

Patents are a sign to investors that something is novel about the technology and hint at new market opportunities. In addition, patents can buy time before competitors emerge and impede commercialisation efforts. If there is a research development that has commercial promise, then it pays to protect that IP before disclosing the invention in public.

The protection of IP is a shared responsibility of the researcher and the university technology transfer office (TTO). It describes the steps that a typical researcher and TTO might take to identify, evaluate and, when applicable, patent a university invention. Some of the pitfalls and conflicts common in this process are highlighted. The chapter ends with a discussion of the commercialisation process.

IP building blocks

In the academic environment, the distinction between IP and research discoveries is often blurred. After all, both are valuable results from the application of knowledge. However, there are critical differences between the way IP is viewed by TTOs and researchers. Take, for example, a generalisation of how different parties value IP: to the TTO an idea is most valuable before it is published, while to the researcher, an idea has its greatest value after publication. This may sound like an irreconcilable situation, but with a little cooperation it can be resolved. A common understanding of invention and disclosure is needed to address the following concerns:

- What makes an idea an invention?
- Which inventions are patentable?
- When should an invention be made public?
- How should an invention be disclosed?

The invention

A research breakthrough can take many forms, such as a new theory, or the transfer of knowledge from one field of research to another. However, an invention refers to an idea that has been conceived and reduced to practice, such as a new process, mechanism or compound. Sometimes, such an invention is patentable: it must be shown to be useful, novel and non-obvious (see Exhibit 7.1). The first two conditions are examined more carefully below.

- 'Useful' means that the invention has real world utility, for example, merely combining chemicals is not useful, but it might be if there are industrial or therapeutic applications.
- 'Novel' refers to an invention that has never been described before by anyone in public, including the inventor – an act known as 'public disclosure'.

Exhibit 7.1

Qualities of patentable inventions

Patentable inventions are useful, novel, non-obvious:

- processes;
- machines;
- manufactured items;
- compositions of matter; or
- improvements on the above.

They are not:

- an abstract idea;
- a law of nature; or
- a physical phenomenon.

Source: Author's own; based on information provided by the US Patent and Trademark Office (USPTO).

Two types of disclosure

Public disclosure is a threat to patentability, confidential disclosure is not. Unfortunately, almost every non-confidential discussion about an invention is considered a public disclosure. This is significant because, once in the public domain, inventions are typically barred from being patented. Patent rights can be lost in the rush to publish or share research results.

Exhibit 7.2

Confidential and public disclosures

Confidential disclosures that help patentability	*Public disclosures that hurt patentability*
<ul><li>filling out an invention report at the TTO;</li><li>secrecy agreements or non-disclosure agreements (NDAs) with sponsors; and</li><li>private discussions with members of the same research group as the inventor.</li></ul>	<ul><li>informal discussions outside of the inventor's department/organisation;</li><li>talks at meetings;</li><li>poster sessions;</li><li>prototype demonstrations;</li><li>chats with colleagues;</li><li>abstracts;</li><li>publications;</li><li>advertisements;</li><li>offers of sale;</li><li>trade show demonstrations;</li><li>posters;</li><li>slides;</li><li>letters;</li><li>e-mails;</li><li>web postings; and</li><li>beta tests.</li></ul>

Source: Author's own.

When a patent is being considered, it is better to talk with the TTO before making a public disclosure. Reporting the invention to the TTO is a confidential disclosure and is used to assess the invention's patentability and plan for public disclosure (see Exhibit 7.2).

Disclosure is easy, sometimes too easy. A public disclosure is almost every oral or written description of the invention made, even if it is made to just one person outside of your own research group or organisation. It includes obvious communications such as publications in books and journals, but also advertisements, conference presentations, posters, slides and e-mails. If you teach someone 'of ordinary skill in the art' how to actually duplicate the invention, such a disclosure is 'enabling' and serves to bar patentability.

Do not immediately despair if a chalk doodle made of the invention is witnessed by the next group to use the conference room. The TTO or a patent attorney might determine that the 'public disclosure' was not enabling, or that it left out some valuable information that can be used as the basis for a patent application.

There are many subtleties about patents and disclosure rules vary by country. For example, in the United States, disclosures that bar patentability are limited to written materials or offers of sale, while in Europe only those offers of sale that 'enable' another person to duplicate the invention will bar a patent. The intent of this chapter is simply to increase your awareness of the complexity of IP management and offer some practical advice.

Invention and ownership

University as owner

In many countries, it is common practice for a university to require that the rights to any inventions made by its employees belong to the employer. The reason for such a policy is that the university provides and manages the resources necessary for research, without which the inventions might not occur. In exchange for access to funds, equipment, labour and other resources, research personnel assign their IP rights to their employer. Exceptions are often made for inventions that occur without the use of university resources or by personnel not explicitly hired to conduct research, such as undergraduate students.

Individual as inventor

Regardless of ownership, a crucial step in protecting IP is to identify who contributed to the invention. Inventorship is a legal standard that, when properly applied, can strengthen a patent against future challenges. For the scientist familiar with publishing research results, the legal standard of inventorship is not the same as that of co-authorship. Only those who have made unique contributions – without which the invention would not have occurred – are inventors (see Exhibit 7.3).

Inventorship is the combination of conception and reduction to practice. In conception, an innovation must be definitively formed in the mind of the inventor, as well as a complete idea of how to obtain it in practice. The reduction to practice is not necessary to claim inventorship, unless the process itself requires inventive skill. If the reduction to practice can be performed with adequate instruction by someone of ordinary skill, then the inventor must merely exercise control over the process. An inventor does not need to know if the invention will work for conception to be complete, just what it will do if it does work.

Exhibit 7.3

Determining inventorship

Common contributions	Am I an inventor?
I am a co-author on a research publication related to the invention.	Not necessarily
I performed research tasks or supplied materials or resources.	Not necessarily
I made an intellectual contribution to the invention.	Not necessarily
I made a contribution that no other person could easily have made.	Not necessarily
I suggested what should be done, but not the means of accomplishing it.	Not necessarily
It was just an idea someone had, and I made it work.	Not necessarily
Without my contribution, this invention (or the means identified to reduce it to practice) would not have been conceived, in the same time period.	Highly likely

Source: Author's own.

Ask the question: 'Without my contribution, would this invention (or the means identified to reduce it to practice) have been conceived in the same time period?' This will help identify those inventors who conceived the necessary ideas. For example, a scientist who identifies a new material and the technician who invents a new method of producing a critical component of its composition might both be inventors. However, a technician who was simply following orders, however time-consuming, complicated or expensive, is not an inventor; neither is the scientist who conducts dozens of experiments in the hopes that something useful will result. Only the results of activities that have a clear objective in mind and the means for achieving it are inventions.

Another constraint on inventorship is the patent itself. A patent is defined by the claims within it, and only those individuals whose contributions appear in the claims of the patent are inventors. It is common during the review by the patent office that certain claims are rejected. Therefore, the inventors themselves might be removed from a patent if the claims they contributed are eliminated. Whoever is an inventor must be named each time a filing is made and formally notified of the filing.

Notebook as proof of invention

As any scientist knows, good record-keeping is essential to research work. However, it is also essential to protecting inventions. Good records serve as important references in both the patent application and possible future litigation and defence. Furthermore, in a collaborative research project where IP rights are pre-assigned to the sponsoring organisation, the notes will ensure that only those inventions due the collaborator will be assigned.

A well-written research notebook can establish the date of invention, the breadth of the claims, the inventorship of the researcher and the methods used to reduce the invention to practice. A model notebook should include the following information, which is helpful in obtaining and defending a patent:

- use a bound notebook;
- date each page;

- describe work sequentially;
- do not add information to the page after the date;
- separate items (signed and dated) may be affixed or the location indicated;
- electronic data (backed up and secured) should be noted and location indicated;
- mark out blank pages or sections;
- inventor's signature; and
- witness (expert and non-inventor) signature.

Managing the disclosure process

In managing IP, the TTO has many tasks. It must:

- clarify who owns the technology;
- characterise its uniqueness;
- assess its value; and
- select a path for commercialisation.

While the emphasis is on spinouts and patents in this book, the TTO does not exclusively rely on these mechanisms. An innovation might be suitable for licensing, whether or not it is patented. While these outcomes are very different, the first step is the same: disclosure – by which is meant the confidential, non-public report of the invention to the TTO or patent attorney.

The disclosure of an invention to the university by the researcher starts the process of commercialisation (see Exhibit 7.4). The challenge is to make this as easy as possible, given all the other demands on a researcher's time. There are several creative approaches that TTOs might take to raise awareness of the need to disclose and to make it easier to comply. TTO staff have been known to drop by research labs to learn of the latest results, hold lunches for researchers who have been granted patents, and host seminars and guest speakers to address commercialisation topics of interest to researchers. These are all done to build the trust and relationships upon which prompt disclosure depends.

Exhibit 7.4

The process from disclosure to commercialisation

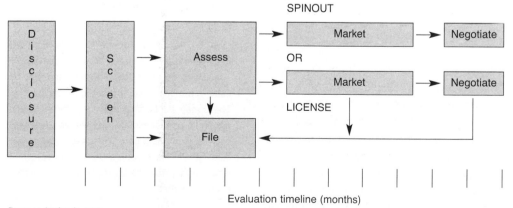

Source: Author's own.

In addition, some TTOs have found ways to streamline the disclosure process, by posting administrative forms online, and even enabling them with live data fields that can be directly submitted. A demonstrated interest in the researchers' work and respect for their time are not just good manners; they increase the rate and quality of disclosures, making the process more effective.

Tracking disclosures

The strength of the TTO's ties to the researchers will depend on how it follows up on the disclosures it receives. The TTO might begin with a database in which to log the disclosure, assign a tracking or docket number, and assign a specific TTO associate for all of the follow up. This last point is particularly important, as inventors often complain about the lack of responsiveness by TTOs. By having a main contact at the TTO, the line of communication with the researcher is stronger and both parties can manage the disclosure better, from general expectations of the commercial potential to the particulars of the technological uniqueness of the invention.

When to disclose

As soon as a researcher thinks that he or she has an invention, they should disclose to the TTO. This should happen, for example, where there are interesting research results, or a proof of principle, or partially supporting data or models. While the science might not be ready to write up for an academic journal, it may be sufficient to establish statutory IP protection. Then, when the research is ready to publish, the invention rights have already been claimed.

While it is generally acceptable for findings to be revealed to others in the research group or organisation, disclosure to outsiders should only take place after safeguarding the IP, through confidentiality agreements, disclosure forms, patent applications and the like. In the case of accidental disclosure, the TTO can help decide what protection is necessary (see Exhibit 7.5).

Disclosing the invention

To capture the information needed for patenting and assessing the market opportunities for the invention, an Invention Disclosure Form should be prepared. It is best for the lead investigator or the person with the greatest knowledge of the invention to complete the form. A sample Invention Disclosure Form can be found in Annex A.

A complete description is essential to an enforceable patent, so include any key technical elements and contributors of the invention. In general, a manuscript that has been

---

Exhibit 7.5

What to do after an accidental disclosure

If an invention has been disclosed accidentally, speak with the TTO or patent attorney. There may still be protective actions to take.

- Ideally, have the person or company that received disclosure sign a confidentially agreement before further disclosures are made.
- There may be undisclosed aspects that can be used in a more limited patent application.
- There may still be time to file a patent, depending on location. In the United States, it is possible to file a patent one year after public disclosure. This is not the case in Europe, while Japan provides six months (under some circumstances).

Source: Author's own.

prepared for submission to a journal will satisfy this requirement. State the utility of the invention, the advantages derived from it, how it may be put to use, and why this differs from the current state of the art. Quantitative measures and specific patent and literature references are extremely useful.

Describe the chronology and disclosures of principal events in conception and development of the invention. Indicate any additional resources (such as expertise, proprietary materials or other contractual resources) that were involved in making the invention. Be sure to note any resources or obligations beyond the research group or institution. Summarise any experiments or prototypes that demonstrate the invention's validity and functionality.

Describe the industries, companies, applications or specific customers that might be interested in this invention or are doing similar research. List any keywords that would be helpful in a literature or patent search (for example, list the type of discipline, technique, compound, diagnostic, device, research tool, therapeutic, and so on). With the invention's shortcomings in mind, describe the current stage of development, anticipated work and alternatives to the invention.

Evaluating the invention

The next step is to conduct an initial assessment of the invention being disclosed. As the languages of science are often very obtuse, it is helpful for TTO personnel to have some educational or professional experience in the technical fields they are representing. Many TTOs will have some personnel that manage life science disclosures, while others handle the physical sciences. The assigned TTO associate will meet with the inventor(s) to gather background information, as this is a critical step between the initial disclosure and obtaining patent protection.

A sample Invention Evaluation Worksheet can be found in Annex B. The questions it includes are meant to guide the decision of whether to place additional resources on the invention, for the purposes of marketing, patenting and/or a more in-depth assessment.

Commercialisation considerations

Only those inventions that are novel, non-obvious and useful are patent candidates. Even when these criteria are met, the TTO must still decide whether it is worth the time and expense to patent. Generally, at this point the TTO or the inventor will hire an attorney to assist in preparing the patent application. Seek an attorney who is not only experienced in patent law, but can offer guidance in how patents can enhance your commercialisation strategy (see Exhibit 7.6).

- Is there a need for the invention and in which countries will it be sold?
- How effective is patent protection in the selected markets?
- To what end will the invention be used: as the basis for a spinout or a technology licence?

Deciding to patent

The decision to pursue a patent depends on market proof – is there demand for applications of the technology? Is there anyone who would want to commercialise this invention? A common practice at most universities is to identify an interested potential licensee before a patent is filed. This validates the market demand for the invention and identifies external funds for the patent filing fees.

Exhibit 7.6

Think of patents as business tools

Introduction

In many circumstances, thinking of a patent merely as 'a way to protect an invention' is too nebulous to be useful. Patents are not the right tool for advancing academic research or disseminating knowledge to a research community. It is more practical to think of a patent as a business tool. Valuable patents are those that can be used to support or achieve business objectives. Keeping in mind throughout the patent process that patents are business tools, leads to more valuable patents.

Increase your valuation

Technology-based startup companies, such as spinouts from universities, typically seek funding from outside investors such as venture capital firms. Investors always evaluate the patents, including pending patent applications, of a startup company prior to investing. The investors will be looking at the patents in order to analyse a collection of issues. The results of that analysis can have a great impact on the investor's valuation of the company. The investor's valuation of the company determines the share of ownership in the company the investor expects to receive in exchange for their investment.

Strengthen barriers to entry

Investors want to know what will prevent competitors from entering the company's market or from competing effectively in the company's market. One of the most basic and important tools provided by a patent are barriers to entry. A patent grants its owner the right to legally exclude others from practising what falls within the scope of the patent. A patent that is properly aligned with the business plan of a company will deter competitors from effectively competing in the market. Investors place a high value on such patents.

For example, if a semiconductor memory company has a patent on technology that allows it to increase greatly the speed at which a computer can access the memory, competitors will not be allowed to copy that patented technology during the life of the patent. Therefore, competitors will be forced to compete in the marketplace with slower technology or incur the time and expense of trying to develop an alternative technology that is outside of the scope of the patent. Both of those effects provide a competitive advantage to the company with the patent.

Increase your negotiating leverage

Investors recognise that technology-based startup companies often become involved in transactions where they can benefit from the leverage provided by a patent. In many cases, the scope of a company's patents should extend into areas beyond the company's products to provide the broadest range of possible leverage. For example, it is inexpensive to include in a patent claims to the methods of making the product, methods of using the product and systems which include the product, even if the company only plans to sell the product itself.

Such patent claims can provide leverage when forming a strategic alliance and making agreements with value-added resellers and original equipment manufacturers. Such claims can also be used as bargaining chips to obtain cross-licences from other companies that own patents covering a company's product. In order to obtain these advantages it is critical to think beyond the company's own product when obtaining patents.

Exhibit 7.6 continued

Think of patents as business tools

Provide proof of ownership

Investors want to see proof that the company owns its technology. Patents typically include an assignment of rights from the inventors to the company. When the patents are aligned with the business goals of the company, the clear assignment of the patent to the company provides the investors with a high level of confidence that the company has strong ownership rights in the technology. For example, a business formed by a group of inventors without any patent assignments or other proof of ownership of the technology underlying the company introduces the risk that the company may not own the necessary rights to the technology. Patents with properly executed assignments greatly reduce that risk and therefore increase the valuation of the company.

Define the technology

A well-drafted patent gives the investors a working definition of the technology underlying the company. Though not often a complete or perfect definition of the technology, a patent does provide a concrete technical description. The claims of the patent also indicate the extent to which the company can lay claim to the technology. For example, reviewing a patent can indicate whether the company owns the rights to a new class of antibiotics or only a specific application of a member of an already known class of antibiotics.

Meet investors' expectations

Finally, sophisticated investors expect that a company will have taken reasonable steps to protect its technology. Having filed one or more well-drafted patent applications with the assistance of a reputable patent attorney increases the likelihood that an investor will seriously consider investing in the company and will justify a higher valuation of the company.

Source: Richard E. Campbell, Procopio Cory Hargreaves & Savitch, LLP.

A typical university will handle hundreds of disclosures each year, therefore only those that have a clear path to market usually justify the time and expense of patenting. The typical cost for filing a patent in the United States is US$10,000 and to obtain protection in the countries participating in the Patent Cooperation Treaty (PCT) it is often more than US$100,000. Costs to maintain the patent can add hundreds of thousands of dollars to the initial filing cost.

The TTO may revisit these issues throughout the patenting process. Patents take several years to obtain, during which time new information about the commercial opportunities will become available, possibly changing the commercialisation plan and the patent strategy. Moreover, feedback from the patent office reviewer will indicate which claims will be allowed. If key patent claims are disallowed or are too narrow, the patent might be of little commercial or strategic value (see Exhibit 7.7).

Exhibit 7.7

What is a patent?

- A patent is merely the right to exclude others from making, using, selling or exporting an invention.
- Permission to exploit the invention is at the discretion of the patent holder.
- The term of a patent is generally 20 years from the application filing date.
- If patent protection is being sought in more than one country, additional patent applications are required.

Source: Author's own.

Do not be discouraged – even without a patent, there might be a motivated licensee or entrepreneur who is more interested in getting the invention to market than in patent protection. The TTO will be searching for an interested party while it is considering whether or not to patent. These activities are not mutually exclusive. However, as patents are strong indicators of commercial value and are likely to be considered at some point, it is worth looking at how they are granted.

Patent process

Obtaining a patent is both a long and dynamic process. Although the process is much more complex than shown in Exhibit 7.8, patenting is marked by several major milestones and decisions. The details will vary depending on the type of patent being filed and in which country patent protection is being sought. Inventors should consult with their TTOs and patent attorneys to determine the best approach for a specific invention. In general, the patent will be reviewed and modified several times during the course of the patent process. Claims will be examined to ensure that the inventor has provided sufficient support and that no other patents are infringed.

Disclosure

The clock starts to tick as soon as a public disclosure is made (although in some countries this can entirely eliminate the chance to patent). Regarding disclosures to the TTO, which do not affect patentability, the clock may also be ticking, but for a different reason – many TTOs close the file in a year's time if no commercial opportunities are identified. In any event, a

---

Exhibit 7.8

The patent process

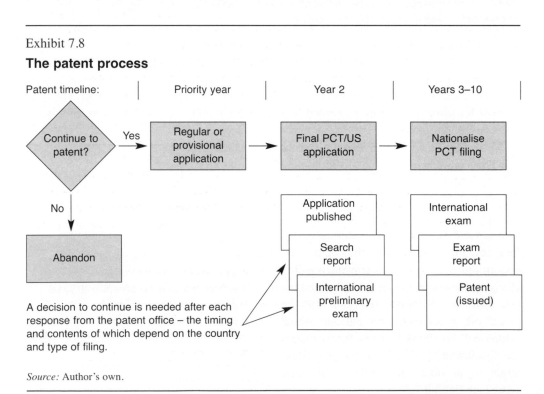

Source: Author's own.

---

thorough disclosure can be used to formulate the patent application. The consulting attorney or TTO will describe why the invention is unique and useful, and specify ways in which it can be used ('patent claims').

Application

Claims are then submitted either in preliminary or full form. Specific types of applications are available, some of which afford limited or temporary protection, such as the PCT and US provisional patents (see Exhibit 7.9). A professionally devised patent strategy can take into account the best way to apply.

The priority year

During the first 12 months after an application has been filed (known as the 'priority year'), the application is not available to the public. The inventor may submit additional supporting documentation or revise (but not add) claims during this time. Any new claims must be made on new patent applications. This means that the initial application (including provisional patents) must be well crafted in order to obtain the desired protection and establish claims.

Exhibit 7.9

Types of patent applications

US provisional patent

The provisional patent offers a way to establish an early effective filing date without a formal patent claim or information disclosure (prior art) statement. It is cheaper than other patent applications, but it is ony temporary. After 12 months, patent protection will end unless a regular patent is filed. During this time, the words 'patent pending' can be used in reference to the invention; however, provisional patents are not examined by the patent office and do not ensure that a patent will be granted. The provisional application establishes the priority date and scope of the invention, and can serve as a useful place-holder while the inventor comes to understand the market and applications for the invention.

US patent

If patent protection is sought, an application must be filed within 12 months of the date that the invention is publicly made known, used or sold. This deadline is extended by the duration of the Patent Cooperation Treaty (PCT), if one was filed. Generally, most applications will be for utility patents, which offer 20 years of protection, if granted. The value of a patent will be determined by the quality of the claims, which define the invention and are what are legally enforceable. The US Patent and Trademark Office will review the claims and typically require a few modifications before granting a patent. This process can take several years.

Patent Cooperation Treaty

If international protection is desired, foreign patent applications must be filed within 12 months of any US patent application. For temporary coverage in over 120 countries, a PCT application can be submitted. PCT protection lasts 18 months, in which time inventors must file a regular patent application for each country in which full patent protection is sought, a proccess called 'nationalising'. Of course, patent laws vary widely by country, and it is important to be aware that even the most benign public disclosures (such as conference presentations or proceedings) prior to filing can void one's patent rights.

Source: Author's own.

If a PCT application is desired, it must be filed in the priority year. Later on, at the end of the PCT process, consideration should be given to 'nationalising' the PCT application, by submitting a separate application to each country in which long-term protection is being sought.

Revise and respond

Approximately 18 months after the initial application submission, it will be made public and the patent office will provide a preliminary review of the claims. Selected claims will have been questioned or rejected. The inventor may wish to prepare a response to refute the examiners' conclusions or answer questions. This process can go on for many years, depending on the speed of the country's patent office and the complexity of the patent claims.

Patent office decision

The application will be complete when the patent office either issues a patent or rejects the application. This whole process generally takes three to 10 years. Note that the time the patent was under review counts toward the 20-year period of patent protection.

Additional legal actions

Once a patent has been issued, the inventor might wish to license the invention or may need to defend it against competitors infringing on the patent claims. The maintenance of a patent is an expensive proposition and it would be useful to evaluate at the time of disclosure which party will be responsible – the TTO, the licensee, the spinout or the inventor.

Prior art search

Proactive inventors can speed patenting efforts by conducting a 'prior art search' (see Exhibit 7.10). This is simply a search of existing patents that might be related to one's own invention in order to determine if it is truly novel and non-obvious. Understanding the prior art, or what

---

Exhibit 7.10

Useful sites for prior art searches

- US Patent and Trademark Office (USPTO) (www.uspto.gov/). Full text copies of patents are available online at no charge. As the name suggests, the list is limited to US patents. To broaden your search to patents filed in Europe and Asia, you might visit another patent database.

- Delphion (www.delphion.com/). Users can obtain a free account to search several international databases and view the first pages of such patents. A TTO might opt for a paid subscription to Delphion, which provides access to additional search and analysis tools.

Other Patent Offices include:

- Europe (www.european-patent-office.org/index.en.php)
- Japan (www.jpo.go.jp)
- United Kingdom (www.ukpats.org.uk)
- World Intellectual Property Organization & the Patent Cooperation Treaty (www.wipo.int/index.html.en)

Source: Author's own.

---

is already known, will allow the inventor and the TTO to identify the ways in which the new invention might be best represented in a patent application.

Deciding to licence or spinout

Historically, universities have relied on licensing as the main path for commercialising inventions. While this remains a common method, spinouts are an attractive alternative for some technologies. There are pros and cons to each approach, with the tradeoffs being primarily the length of time until revenues are received, the uncertainty of such returns, and bureaucratic and cultural constraints. The differences between large and small companies highlight these issues, which are summarised in Exhibit 7.11.

The TTO is typically responsible for choosing the best commercialisation path for an invention. It must balance the needs of the researcher, the university and perhaps the local community in its decision to license or spin out. The success of a technology may involve many stakeholders that are in the TTO's charter to accommodate. While the following list merely touches on the critical questions, it is intended to show how many perspectives the TTO must balance in the decision between licensing and spinning out a technology.

- *Return on investment.* Are the university's financial, collaborative research, or regional development goals being met?
- *Technology.* Is the invention robust and broadly applicable and/or is the market need large enough to warrant a spinout company's full attention to its commercialisation?
- *Team.* Is there a team with the technical and managerial skill needed to make a new venture succeed?
- *Alternatives.* Are there no readily available licensees or portfolio companies who could commercialise the invention?
- *Time.* Is the university prepared to provide more intensive assistance that the spinout company is likely to require?

Conflicts of interest

As universities have become more active in commercialisation activities, the worry is that the main mission of research and education might be compromised. While studies have not shown that commercialisation leads to such a compromise, the concerns about conflicts of interest remain.

In a proactive move, Stanford University's Office of Technology Licensing has taken an innovative approach to align its mission with that of the research units. A Research Incentive

Exhibit 7.11

Tradeoffs between working with established firms and new ventures

Likelihood of:	*Established, large firm*	*New, small firm*
Equity	No	Yes
Royalties	Yes	No
Near-term revenue stream	Yes	No
Internal or bureaucratic barriers to deal-making	Yes	No
Conflicts of interest	No	Yes
High workload regarding contracts and negotiations	No	Yes

Source: Author's own.

Fund was recently established to channel royalty income from licensing back into 'research innovation' at Stanford. Funds are intended to provide seed grants to junior faculty staff to 'support new, innovative research initiatives, especially projects that are not currently funded and/or for which funding may be difficult to obtain from traditional sources'. In this way, the TTO can actively support the research (and non-profit) activities of the university.

Even if the multiple roles of the university are not a concern, the roles of the individual researcher might be. It is now common for a faculty member to be an inventor, a consultant, a board member and a company owner – all it takes is one especially useful invention.

To keep separate the research and commercial activities of its employees, many universities have developed conflict of interest policies. These rules are intended to ensure that researchers do not have a conflict of interest between their university research and any legal obligations or economic incentives they may have with a firm. In the event that a university researcher is also an equity holder or board member in a company (especially a licensee), the employee is typically asked to affirm that he or she will:

- not employ students at the firm or use them at the university on projects for the firm;
- not impede access to information or withhold invention disclosures resulting from university research;
- not take funds or resources from the firm to conduct research at the university; and
- differentiate between the roles and activities at the firm and the university.

Summary

This chapters offers a number of the ways in which IP can be managed to meet the needs of the inventor, the university and the wider community. To balance these interests is a challenge. However, the reward is when the IP reaches the public – through new products, new firms and new opportunities.

Tips for entrepreneurs and scientists

- It is better to talk with the TTO before making a public disclosure.
- A public disclosure is made in almost every oral or written description of the invention made, even if made to just one person outside of the research group or organisation.
- Regardless of ownership, a crucial step in protecting IP is to identify who contributed to the invention.
- Good record-keeping serves as an important reference in both the patent ownership application and possible future litigation and defence.
- The disclosure of an invention to the university by the researcher starts the process of commercialisation.
- As soon as an invention could have arisen, it should be disclosed to the TTO.
- It is best for the lead investigator or the person with the greatest knowledge of the invention to complete the Invention Disclosure Form which is necessary to capture the information needed for patenting and assessing the market opportunities for the invention.
- While obtaining a patent is both a long and dynamic process, it is marked by several major milestones and decisions (details will vary depending on the type of patent being filed and in which country patent protection is being sought).

- Think of patents as a business tool that could increase the value of the company as well as increase leverage in forming strategic relationships for the invention.
- Do not be discouraged: even without a patent, there might be a motivated licensee or entrepreneur who is more interested in getting the invention to market than in patent protection.

Annex A

Record of Invention & Disclosure Report ('Disclosure')

This form should be **submitted at least two weeks prior to public disclosure**, such as at scientific meetings, conference presentations, poster sessions, article submissions and the like.

Case Number (Assigned by University): _____

Title of Invention (4–8 words): _____

Designated Inventor:* _____

* One inventor is asked to assume primary responsibility for interacting with the University on all matters related to this Disclosure and to keep all other inventors named on this Disclosure informed of the status of such matters.

Inventor List. Please provide information for all University employees, students and any non-University personnel who have worked on this invention by conceiving or elaborating on the idea, designing experiments, evaluating experimental results, contributing features while first building a device or performing a method, or otherwise directly contributing to the invention beyond merely providing funds, work space, or entirely directed labour. If any person holds a joint appointment with any other university, a company or governmental agency, or any other institution, please note that fact.

Full Name	Full Name
Title	Title
Department Address	Department Address
Other Affiliations (incl. % appointment)	Other Affiliations (incl. % appointment)
Home Address	Home Address
Email Address	Email Address
Work Phone	Work Phone
Fax Number	Fax Number
Citizenship	Citizenship
Social Security Number	Social Security Number
Percent Contribution to Invention	Percent Contribution to Invention
Nature of Contribution	Nature of Contribution
Inventor Signature	Inventor Signature
Date	Date

Additional Inventors. Use copies of this page to list all inventors (contributions must total 100%). Do not list inventors gratuitously, as the rules for inclusion are not the same as a scientific publication.

Witnesses. The Disclosure must be signed and dated by all inventors, read and understood and signed by technically qualified non-inventor witness(es), and read and signed by appropriate University officer(s).

Name of Witness	Name of University Officer
Signature of Witness	Signature of Officer
Date	Date

Abstract of Invention. Describe the invention in a few sentences, without disclosing any proprietary or unique unpublished details. This abstract may be used for reporting to funding agencies or for marketing purposes.

Detailed Description of Invention. A complete description is essential to an enforceable patent, so please do not withhold any key elements of the invention. In general, a manuscript that has been prepared for submission to a journal will satisfy this requirement if it addresses the following issues:

- *Purpose:* State the purpose or utility of the invention. For example, is it a new product, process, or material? Or is it a new use for or improvement to an existing product, process, or material?
- *Solution:* Describe the problem solved by this invention, new applications achieved, or other advantage.
- *Current State of the Art:* Briefly describe the current practice or knowledge (prior to the invention). A list of literature references or related patents is helpful in the evaluation of the invention.
- *Novelty:* Identify the elements of the invention believed to be new, unexpected or critical and explain how these differ from the closest known methods (current state of the art).
- *Reproduction:* Describe how to make the invention in sufficient detail so that one skilled in the same discipline could reproduce the invention. Include drawings or photographs illustrating the invention, structural formulae if a chemical, procedural steps if a process, schematics if a device, etc.
- *Feasibility:* Describe any prototype or working model and/or any data pertaining to the invention or other evidence of the feasibility or operability of the invention.
- *Practice:* Describe the best way of practising the invention, emphasising the new features or improvements over the known methods.

Record of Invention. Describe the chronology and disclosures of principal events in conception and development of the invention. (Please note that public disclosure before patent rights are granted may compromise the granting of a US patent and may bar the granting of any foreign patents. Preparing this Disclosure is not the same as the filing of a patent application, although US law generally allows inventors up to one year to file for a patent after first public disclosure.)

- *Earliest Conception Date:* Indicate the date and describe what substantiating evidence exists, such as a notebook or witness.
- *Oral Disclosures:* List the dates and the names of people to whom the invention was initially and orally disclosed.

- *Written Disclosures:* List the date first written record and location of such written record, such as a notebook, letter, proposal, drawing, etc.
- *Test:* List the date(s) and result(s) of the first test of invention and the first successful test.
- *Pending Disclosures:* List any plans to submit a report, publication, presentation, poster or abstract that mentions or describes the invention as disclosed herein. Indicate the date on which these disclosures are expected to be made public (include conferences and sponsor meetings).
- *Public Disclosures:* List any disclosures to non-University personnel (such as research sponsors), date and a copy of any publications, presentations, posters or abstracts (oral or written) that mention or describe the invention as disclosed herein. Separate and identify general, non-enabling publications from those which disclose the critical elements of the invention.

Resources for Invention. Describe the resources that were used in the invention and what further resources may be necessary to develop the invention. Please address the following issues:

- *Funding:* List the funding source(s) for the project under which this invention was made. If applicable, identify by contract or grant number and name the Principal Investigator/Supervisor of each. If any funds are from federal sources, indicate which is the primary source of such funds.
- *Obligations to Third Parties:* Please indicate any additional resources, such as expertise, proprietary materials or other contractual resources, that were involved in making the invention. This includes any materials transfer agreements (common in biological research), consortia agreements, consulting agreements, confidentiality agreements and any external expertise, if any, that led to the conception or first actual reduction to practice of the invention.
- *Development Status:* Please indicate the current stage of the invention (concept, laboratory tested, prototype, clinical trial and so on).
- *Ongoing Development:* Describe nature of anticipated work, if any, and the sources of funding for the work that is planned.
- *Alternatives:* Describe possible modifications and variations on the invention or practice. Indicate any alternate embodiments, procedures or methods of construction on the invention. If possible, estimate the funds necessary to implement such improvements.
- *Future Development:* Describe any disadvantages or limitations of the invention and explain how they might be overcome. If possible, estimate the funds necessary to implement such improvements.

Next steps. After receipt of this Disclosure, the appropriate University office will notify any applicable federal funding agency of the invention and will initiate an evaluation of the invention for patentability. To assist in this, please address the following:

- *Potential Commercial Use:* Describe industries, companies, applications or specific customers that might be interested in this invention or are doing similar research.
- *Keywords:* List any keywords that would be helpful in a literature or patent search (for example, list type of discipline, technique, compound, diagnostic, device, research tool, therapeutic and so on).

84

If you would like assistance in completing this Disclosure, we would be happy to help and ask that you contact our office. Upon completion, return the original signed document to the University's office of _____ (insert address of appropriate record-keeping office.) All signers retain a copy.

Annex B

Initial Invention Assessment Report ('Assessment')

Case Number (assigned by University): _____

Title of Invention (from Disclosure Form): _____

Designated Administrator*: _____

* It is good practice for one administrator to assume primary responsibility for interacting with the inventor(s) on all matters related to this Assessment and to coordi-
nate all related marketing and legal activities, as appropriate.

Abstract of Invention (from Disclosure Form) Attach a short description of the invention
(a few sentences), without disclosing any proprietary or unique unpublished details. This
abstract may be used for reporting to funding agencies or for marketing purposes.

**The following questions are meant to guide the decision of whether to place additional
resources on the invention, for the purposes of marketing, patenting and/or a more in-
depth assessment.**

Invention Appeal

❑ Is the invention still state of the art?

❑ Does it confer a sustainable competitive advantage?

❑ Is the invention easy to demonstrate?

❑ Is there a demonstration, sample or functioning prototype available (in other words, reduction to practice)?

❑ How long before the invention is ready for market entry?

Inventor Appeal

❑ Has the inventor(s) previously obtained a patent?

❑ Does the inventor own competing or infringing patents?

❑ Has the inventor(s) previously commercialised an invention?

❑ Is the inventor(s) available to help patent or market the invention?

❑ Does the inventor have relevant market/industry connections?

Market Appeal

❑ Does the invention fill an identifiable market need?

❑ Is the market large and/or growing?

❑ What is the upside potential?

❑ Are there directly competitive products?

❑ Does it conform to relevant industry standards?

❑ Is there a market niche or accessibility to the larger market (no monopoly)?

Patentability Appeal

❑ Are there dominating patents?

❑ Are these dominating patents available for licence?

❏ How great is the strength or breadth of claims?
❏ Has the invention been publicly disclosed?
❏ Are there competing claims?

Investment Appeal

❏ Can a prospective licensee be identified?
❏ Is the invention the basis for a spinoff company?
❏ Does the invention represent a 20 per cent improvement in a critical aspect, such as cost or performance?
❏ Is a major investment needed to bring the invention to market?
❏ Is the invention in an emerging market?

Economic Appeal

Is the invention _____ than the alternatives?

❏ Easier to Use or Repair?	❏ Lighter?	❏ More Efficient?
❏ Easier to Produce?	❏ Smaller?	❏ More Aesthetic?
❏ Longer Lasting?	❏ Safer?	❏ More Precise?
❏ Higher Quality?	❏ Quieter?	❏ More Compliant?
❏ Cheaper?	❏ Faster?	

Programmatic Appeal

❏ Is the invention based on basic or applied research?
❏ Is the invention related to ongoing research projects?
❏ Is the invention part of a long-range university research plan?
❏ Could this invention form the basis of a new research program?
❏ List potential sponsors for future work.

Return the original signed document to the University's office of _____ (insert address of appropriate record keeping office.) Signer retains a copy.

Chapter 8

Selection, recruitment and development of the spinout management team

Dr Claire Baxter
Business Liason Office, University of Sydney, Sydney

Dr Phillip Wing
Technology Venture Partners, Sydney

Ben Anderson and Sebastian Kayll
Renoir Christian & Timbers, London and Menlo Park, California

Introduction

This chapter covers the selection, recruitment and development of a management team. It is one of the critical factors in the success of any spinout company. The chapter covers different stakeholder perspectives – investors' requirements and expectations, the university's role in facilitating the process, how professional search firms can accelerate the process, and finally how the spinout itself must develop and evolve. The chapter also provides insights for entrepreneurs in what to do, when to do it and who to turn to for help and assistance.

Financing university spinouts can be challenging, given the dynamic link between the provision of funding by investors and the quality of management. In what is a frustrating cycle, the availability to the spinout of venture capital funding often depends on the existence of good quality management, and the attraction of quality management depends on funds being available.

In some cases, academic scientists do not to want to play a direct role in the commercialisation of their technology. In other cases, the inventor might not have the appropriate skills or experience to take the new company forward. As a result, entrepreneurial management and talent must be recruited.

Spinout management teams evolve and are not simply assembled at the outset. The process of designing, recruiting and developing management teams requires intense relationship-building, good communication and regular consultation. Therefore, at different stages of development, it is not uncommon for technology transfer offices (TTOs), investors and executive recruitment firms to provide entrepreneurs and spinouts with valuable assistance.

This chapter examines these activities and is based on three primary propositions.

1. The design of spinout management teams is driven by an understanding of the capabilities required.
2. Capabilities are dependent on the nature of the technology and potential business model.

3. The management team capabilities that are needed change over time as the spinout matures from inventor craft mode, to commercialisation, to startup venture and eventually into a high-growth technology-based company.

Understanding management capabilities

Although the initial, and primary, interest from venture capitalists in university spinouts is intellectual property (IP), it is the formation and development of the management team that will directly influence whether the commercial opportunity that the IP presents will be exploited.

Typically, the academic scientist has deep technology-focused subject expertise. This know-how is crucial to product development, prototyping and market validation. Beyond this know-how, the venture capitalist (VC) will look at the potential to attract a management team as a qualifying factor when making an investment decision. It is important for the academic scientist to be able to articulate both the idea and the potential value of that idea in order to attract the necessary talent to supplement his or her capabilities. The academic scientist's personality is also a crucial factor. Investors may choose not to fund research because the academic scientist's objectives are not well aligned with those of investors or if it is highly likely that the founder will not be open to constructive suggestions or take advice from others with more experience in commercialisation or market development.

Turn-ons

Professional investors assess spinout management teams on two key dimensions: their commercial awareness and their engagement style. In the best case, investors would be turned on and excited about backing and building a spinout management team that:

- is attuned to the real world problem they are solving;
- understands the fundamental value proposition for customers they plan to serve;
- knows the importance of engaging with potential customers;
- is responsive, enthusiastic and willing to listen; and
- has objectives that are reasonably aligned with those of the VC.

Turn-offs

The reality of venturing is that a great percentage of spinouts are neither investment-ready, nor show signs of ever being so. Major turn-offs for VCs are management teams that:

- are driven by a blind belief in the technology or product;
- lack clarity over why their technology, approach or solution is better, faster, cheaper or unique;
- have achieved little or no market validation or reference points to potential customers;
- are unable to interact with a VC in a timely and focused fashion;
- are overly focused on 'perfect', over-engineered responses to questions;
- project feelings of rejection or believing they have been misunderstood;
- show little empathy with the need for cultural alignment with investors; and
- expect decisions to be made immediately – or sooner if possible.

Defining management capabilities

The process of building initial startup teams is dependent on the nature of the technology, the business idea and the proposed business model. At one extreme, the commercial value may be in the patenting of research science-based algorithms, gene signatures, or industrial or medical compounds. Where the opportunity is to create unique and defensible IP within an obvious window of opportunity, then the team will initially be focused on the technical product development and on ensuring that the IP strategy is well thought out and executed. A CEO, in the traditional sense, may not be needed immediately. The founder may be better supported by a resource that has general commercialisation experience and an ability to keep research efforts focused on producing intellectual assets. This capability may even be provided on a contract basis or via a mentor-style non-executive director.

Where a spinout opportunity is addressing a known market problem and must get fast engagement with potential customers and build immediate access to commercialisation partners, a very different management team is required. Clearly, the CEO will need to be market-facing, and preferably have strong networks in the target customer segment. The spinout will also require a resource that has experience in assessing alternative routes to market and business models such as licensing, original equipment manufacture (OEM) and channel arrangements will also be required. If the technology needs to be included in engineering designs for next release products, knowledge of these processes, the lead times and the ability to deal with both the engineering and commercial arms of potential partners is essential. This often creates tension with the founder/inventor, who typically has a propensity to over-engineer the prototype or design and is often not willing to release technology for external review until it is 'almost perfect'.

Where a spinout opportunity is addressing new markets (such as nanotechnology materials or plastic electronics with potential applications in many markets) engagement with potential customers in the chosen target markets must be achieved quickly. In this case, the CEO must either have experience of choosing the initial priority target markets to focus upon or should come from the specific target markets and have strong networks into the target customer segment.

Ideally, a founding team will have:

- a subject matter/technical leader;
- product development and commercialisation experience;
- someone that can engage the market in meaningful business development, (either with potential end-customers or with partners); and
- a blend of commercial or financial skills.

These capabilities can be built via a combination of the management team and the board or outside advisers. Sometimes academic scientists have a natural commercial flair and can grow into an entrepreneurial manager role. In other instances, they have neither the aptitude nor interest and will often migrate towards a chief technology officer's role (CTO). However, the CTO is often required to provide a commercial perspective on the technology development and, if the founder cannot provide this, he or she is often moved into a chief scientist, technology evangelist role.

At each stage of development for a spinout, a practical approach to defining the capabilities of the management team is to think about the choices that need to be made for the enterprise and the drivers that create value in the venture.

Strategic issues driving these choices for the spinout will include:

- What is the role and position of the spinout in the industry value chain?
- What is the basis of competition in the industry value chain?
- Does the spinout have a business model for generating sustainable returns?
- Does the spinout have operational excellence?
- Are team dynamics leading to productive activities?

As the spinout develops, typical value drivers will include:

- the number and quality of market engagements with partners, influencers and potential channel customers;
- developing a unique defensible offering;
- achieving customer references; and
- developing scalable business routines and processes.

By having the spinout team think about the issues surrounding strategy and value creation, the challenges facing management become clear. As a result, the depth and breadth of the spinout team's capabilities can be translated into gaps in knowledge, skill and experience that need to be addressed.

The case study below describes the successful use of an entrepreneur-in-residence programme to create a management team from a spinout from the University of Sydney.

Case study

Medsaic Pty Limited: involving the technology transfer office to recruit entrepreneurs

The University of Sydney through its Business Liaison Office (BLO) frequently uses the spinout route to commercialise its technologies. Through the Entrepreneur in Residence (EiR) programme, the BLO delivers a founding CEO to the shareholder and board. It is not always easy to find the right entrepreneur who can work independently and also work closely with the team of commercialisation managers, academics and, in time, investors, and who also has the right technical and business background. It is worth putting as much effort as possible into recruiting the right person. Medsaic Pty Limited is a spinout that serves as a successful example.

Medsaic was formed by the University to commercialise a body of patented intellectual property (IP) from the Faculties of Science and Medicine. Medsaic uses a protein nanoarray platform for diagnosis and treatment of disease. The first product is for the diagnosis of leukaemia but the company is more than a diagnostics company and represents a global health care opportunity, focusing on a vertically integrated approach to personalised medicine. Seed funding grants from the University of Sydney supported the development of the company. The company also received Government grants for business development and research.

A key aspect of the successful development and fundraising for Medsaic was the University's EiR programme at the BLO. The recruited entrepreneur, Dr Jeremy Chrisp, was known to BLO staff through local business networks. Jeremy proved to fit the ideal profile for an entrepreneur in residence:

- relevant technical qualifications;
- specific market knowledge, or the ability to source this knowledge effectively;
- relevant business expertise;
- experience in small and large companies, although not all have both and one or the other can be acceptable;
- ability to take ownership but also to work in a team; and
- ability to prepare business plans and to pitch to investors.

Jeremy was funded initially through the University seed fund. He was provided with a work-station in the BLO and worked closely with the New Ventures Unit Team, particularly with Dr Brenton Hamdorf, together with the Office's IP and legal experts, and the inventors. During the 18-month long pre-incubation phase six new patent applications were filed.

Given the complexity of this development, it is difficult to see how Medsaic would have been launched in its current form without the EiR programme. Jeremy brought to the team a deep understanding of the market and an ability to draw information from all members of the team as the business model evolved. Through the University's funding, and some unpaid and at-risk time contributions of his own, he was able to work full-time on the project, unlike other members of the team who were involved in many projects.

A comprehensive business plan was developed and the investment fund Symbion, backed by ABN AMRO, became the first-round investor. Jeremy became the CEO and was then in a position to implement the plan that he played a central role in developing. The company is seeking further investment funding as rapid progress has occurred. In addition to the CEO, the early-stage team was made up initially of active inventors, technology commercialisation managers and later hands-on investor-appointed board members who collectively support the efforts of the CEO.

All of the inventors wished to remain within the University, but collaboration has continued through research contracts and through the appointment of a director nominated by the inventors. As for many university spinouts, the key inventors, senior and successful researchers, did not want to leave the university or their chosen careers in academia. Their continued input through contracted research and representation on the board has been essential for the early stages of the company's development.

The EiR model has proved a highly successful boost to the formation of spinouts at the University of Sydney. Key factors that have led to its success include:

- careful and serendipitous recruitment of the entrepreneur;
- the availability of seed funding from the university and/or other sources, and where possible access to supportive government granting programmes;

- the ability of the BLO to apply dedicated expertise and resources to each opportunity;
- care to ensure that all payments are based on achieving pre-agreed milestones;
- close involvement and engagement with inventors; and
- effective communication to all stakeholders involved in every company.

The concept appears to be attractive to entrepreneurs, with the carrot of being able to get involved from the outset and the opportunity to be responsible or closely involved in assembling the rest of the team, with a possible job as CEO at the end.

The evolution of management capabilities

As the spinout enterprise develops, the emphasis on each core capability changes, although a base level competence across all dimensions is needed for resilience and ultimate commercial success (Exhibit 8.1). The initial focus is on transforming the technology into a prototype product or achieving scientific proof of concept. The focus of management then shifts to commercialising the technology so that it solves a compelling problem in a tangibly better way and to identifying and design in the needs of the potential customers. Another shift can then often occur when management decides what part of the value chain to play in, defining the value proposition and achieving market and customer validation. The research and development (R&D) continues, but is now driven more by the agreed entry product and market strategy. At this stage, significant tradeoffs begin to occur. Preserving capital, making resource allocation choices and deciding on the product and geographic portfolio come into the foreground. It is not uncommon for fresh expansion capital to be needed, and the management team then needs capital-raising skills and experience. The process of raising this finance can occupy half of management's focus for up to six months.

The practical value of having a life cycle view of the spinout venture is that it helps the team to identify key points where change in the business will occur. This builds awareness of

Exhibit 8.1

The development of spinout company capabilities over time

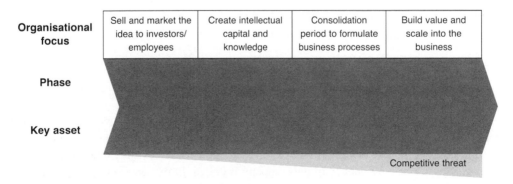

Organisational focus	Sell and market the idea to investors/ employees	Create intellectual capital and knowledge	Consolidation period to formulate business processes	Build value and scale into the business

Phase

Key asset

Competitive threat

Source: Dr Phillip Wing.

Exhibit 8.2

Drivers of new capabilities

Type	Organisational changes driving new capabilities
Investor's perspective	• Technical proof of concept • Commercial proof of concept • Move from pilots to full-scale deployment in customers • Potential exit points
Management's perspective	• Additional capital requirements • Headcount moves to new plateaux – 20, 50, 80, over 100 – which implies differing organisational and operational models • Geographic expansions • Need for outside consultants or advisers • Scale up points for design, manufacture or distribution • Contracting out or outsourcing • Engagement with channels or partners

Source: Dr Phillip Wing.

the business plan and allows for new and extended management capabilities to be grown or hired into the business and for non-valuable management capabilities to exit the team. Exhibit 8.2 sets out the indicators of key changes in the stages of a spinout.

The requirements at each stage of a spinout company's development are so different that it is very unusual to find one person who can effectively lead an organisation through more than two or three of those stages. It is equally unusual to find one person who truly enjoys the issues related to both a very early stage startup and a much larger, more mature organisation. In addition to the fact that the skills required for each stage are different, the personality types that are attracted to different stages of company growth are quite distinct. The only individuals that tend to remain passionately involved across all stages of a company's development are the founders. Ironically, they often lack the skills necessary to be an effective CEO.

How can board members and investors help?

The role of the board and investors is to help guide the management team through developmental transitions. Guidance will often point to:

• adding new capabilities to the team;
• reconfiguring roles; and
• taking existing people out of the business (sometimes this includes the founder).

In more than half of all investments made by Technology Venture Partners, the founder was not in the business on exit. For spinouts the original founding CEO is replaced more often.

Studies in the venture capital industry indicate that strategies shift three or four times from the original spinout idea until the company is exited. In this environment, the management team must be able to adapt and deal with high levels of uncertainty and ambiguity. The investor and boards have a crucial role in trying to relieve the organisational stress that emerges in these environments, and to assist the management team in delivering and executing to the best of their ability. This also involves early recognition and remedial action if those abilities are not sufficient to meet the business's needs.

VCs have a crucial role in spinouts to ensure that talent is focused on the main game – building value in the business. These objectives can be achieved by:

- defining, agreeing and monitoring business milestones;
- developing a functional partnership between the management team and the investors;
- keeping focused on the main game and avoid distracting low-value activities; and
- continually adapting to the market and flexibly adjusting the strategy.

It is highly unlikely that the VC can add any real value to the management team if the team displays:

- no discipline or gives lip service to meeting agreed milestones;
- a 'take the money and run' attitude;
- demonstrate little strategic thought about the constant re-positioning and refining of the strategy; and
- no clear path to value creation.

Finally, the management teams of spinouts should expect VCs to aggressively help them win the war for talent. Good VCs have the leverage and influence to:

- build a bank of talented people who are looking for opportunities in spinouts and startups;
- source talent internationally;
- influence talented people to join the spinout because of the potential the VC sees in the venture and because of the commitment to fund that business; and
- provide flexibility in remuneration including equity and options.

Partnering with the VC to attract and retain talent is a crucial ingredient of success in spinout ventures.

Getting the most from professional search firms

Fast-moving technology companies require the highest possible quality of technical and managerial talent to have the best chance of success. One approach to reaching into the global pool of this talent is to appoint a search firm.

Choosing the right search firm

How can a company hire one from the hundreds of search firms that are out there? There are a number of factors to consider and a process to follow.

- Get to know the search firms by researching their size, client base, areas of expertise, performance record, list of clients and candidates and experience in your industry and geographic area. What other services does it offer? How many early stage engagements have they completed?
- Decide what sort of firm you want. Large multi-national search firms have strong brand recognition and deep industry relationships. Small firms may have excellent personal contacts, but lack global reach.

- What is their approach, what are their methodologies and processes?
- Who is your recruiter? Impressive client lists are one thing, but what about the executive you will be working with? Consultants can handle anywhere between four and eight searches at a time. Will they have time to focus on your search?
- Who is really doing the work? Will the executive who pitched the job to you also be running the search?
- What technology is being used and how will it affect your search? How is it used to find candidates and keep clients and candidates informed of progress in the search?
- What qualifications do they have to assess candidates? How is the interview process managed and how is leadership measured? What references are checked?
- Finally, is the firm committed to client satisfaction? Clearly, all firms will say they are, but beware of firms that celebrate after being retained. This is just the start.

Preparing for the search process

It is important to select a search firm that understands what the company is, where it is in the development process and what its vision is. The search firm needs to have real clarity around the business, on where it is going and what its human capital strategy is for the next 12–18 months, because that is the window in which things must be completed.

Good search firms will talk to analysts and experts to understand the market, industry and the technology. What problem the company is solving – how unique it is and the size of the opportunity. The market for talent is highly competitive and if the search firm does not fully understand the opportunity they will not be able to position it to a prospective candidate (see Exhibit 8.3).

Managing the transition

The appointment of a CEO is not the end of the process. There is almost always a transition, usually from company founder to new professional CEO. It is a complex process. The founder is the person that gave life to the company, who believed when few others did and who got the company to where it is now. Why should he or she be replaced?

Everyone wants the process to be quick, smooth and voluntary. Of course, this is easier in theory than in practice. Even among founder CEOs that recognise the need to bring in new blood, some tend to hang on for longer than they should.

Spinout companies bring an extra set of complications when managing the transition. There are cultural differences and potential complications when a university owns some of the business. This means that potential candidates have to be able to handle working with university people and understand the politics involved.

What can be done to smooth the process?

- Be clear about what the leader is expected to provide. If there is a clear set of attributes, requirements and a specification of what the leader is required to achieve, it will be easier to 'sell' the transition to all stakeholders.
- Enlist support. It is important that everyone buys into the need for a new CEO, and that includes the founder, as well as the board, management team, employees and investors

Exhibit 8.3

The search, selection and recruitment process

Search	Selection	Recruitment
1. Determine client strategy and culture, position responsibilities and qualifications	1. Conduct preliminary research to develop initial candidate list I. Renoir network II. Desk-based research	1. Consult with client to review candidates and assist in the selection process
2. Develop position profile	2. Meet and assess potential candidates through telephone and personal interviews	2. Assist in structuring the compensation package
3. Prepare candidate briefing document		3. Provide counsel to both client and candidate when an offer of employment is made
4. Work with client to develop search strategy including target industry sectors and companies	3. Identify qualified candidates for recommendation and conduct preliminary reference checking	4. Provide ongoing follow-up with both client and successful candidate to ensure satisfaction
5. Benchmark interview	4. Prepare confidential candidate assessment report for each qualified candidate	
	5. Optional use of behavioural profiling	
	6. Present recommended candidates to client and assist with interviewing process	

Source: Renoir Christian & Timbers.

(who are usually the ones driving it). Many founders find it exceptionally difficult to relinquish control.

- Give the founder a new role. The most suitable role will depend on the skill-set of the incoming CEO, but technical founders can often be moved to chief technology officer. Making the founder non-executive chairman can be a way of moving them out of an executive role, while keeping them on-side – however, very few founders have previous chairmanship experience and there is a very good argument to retain the chairmanship role for a seasoned board operator.
- Monitor the transition period and stay close to the new CEO. Open communication, after the appointment, is vital between founder, CEO, management and investors. This is where a good board comes into its own.

The case study below illustrates the management issues faced by many spinout companies. The company had great technology, but its academic-orientated management team had overestimated the scale of the opportunity, expanded too fast and lacked managerial control. For the company to survive, it needed to raise further venture capital funding and change its senior management team.

Case study

Celoxica: lesson learned from the move to a new CEO

The move to a new CEO is fraught with difficulties, but it is not impossible. The experience of Celoxica is typical of many spinout companies. Founded in 1996 as Embedded Solutions Limited, it was spun out of the University of Oxford in the United Kingdom in 1998 through its technology transfer arm, ISIS Innovations.

The company operates in the field of system-level electronic design automation (EDA). It is a world leader in software-compiled system design, a process that accelerates design productivity by using high-level languages to directly drive design verification and implementation. Target customers include big electronics systems companies, from aircraft and weapons manufacturers Boeing, Lockheed Martin and Northrop Grumman, to electronics products companies such as Canon and HP.

In October 2000, Celoxica raised £11.8 million from private investors. The investors hoped for a quick listing on the stock market and appointed an investment bank to establish interest and handle the process. Vast sums of money were spent developing products and building the corporate infrastructure of a company that was going to take over the world. Then the internet bubble burst, dragging the whole technology sector down with it, and hopes of a flotation were dashed.

Strengthen management team

Celoxica, advised by UBS Warburg, needed more money and turned to venture capitalists. Jeremy Milne of UK venture firm Quester liked the company, but felt the management team needed strengthening.

'It was a management team that had been brought in to do rapid startup and float. They had more general business experience rather than specific EDA industry experience,' says Milne. 'The company was moving into a phase where it needed to be very careful with its cash and had to be very focussed with its approach. It was important that we had a team in place that would be able to execute in the tougher environment of 2002 onwards.'

But the underlying technology was still attractive. 'There was an element of truth in the way the old management team were talking about revolutionising the way electronic circuits are designed,' says Milne. 'But there was hyperbole as to how big the immediate opportunity was, how quickly it would come about and the speed of response that would be seen from customers.'

Quester participated in a US$30 million round in October 2001, alongside Advent Venture Partners, Cazenove Private Equity, Isis College Fund, Intel Capital, Wind River Ventures and Xilinx Inc, a US-based designer and developer of programmable logic solutions.

'At the first board meeting post-investment our suspicions that the management team needed to be changed were confirmed,' says Milne. The board initiated a search to find a new chief executive. After beauty parading a number of executive recruitment firms, the decision was taken to engage Renoir Christian & Timbers, the London-based trans-Atlantic technology search firm. Milne says: 'Renoir had done a lot of work for us upgrading the management teams across our portfolio. They had a particularly good guy in EDA on the West Coast and were able to demonstrate their expertise.'

The search

Renoir Christian & Timbers started the search, digging deep into the industry to find prospective candidates and draw up a long list (as described in the main text). After whittling down the candidates, a clear favourite emerged. Phil Bishop was a senior executive at Mentor Graphics, a NASDAQ-listed EDA company with 3,600 employees and annual revenues of US$650 million.

Ben Anderson, managing director of Renoir Christian & Timbers, says: 'This is a typical example of our global candidate pool and the depth of our research. When we referenced him, his boss asked how we had found him, because he was being fast-tracked through Mentor.'

Bishop fitted the criteria that many early stage companies are looking for in a CEO. He was 41 years old, with a technical and business background, experience in a global technology company. He had recently completed an MBA in international business from Duke Business School and was looking for an assignment at CEO level. In the highly-competitive technology sector, 'alpha' managers such as Bishop have plenty of options and need to be courted.

'I had a very solid job,' says Bishop. 'I met with Renoir in San Jose. They sent me a placement document for Celoxica, which I felt was very big of the company. It had a lot of detail on the history of the company, shareholdings, financial structure. There were 250 pages of it. I got a very good feel for the investors, financials and status of the company.'

A series of meetings were held with the investors and then the company. 'I was trying to qualify everything, analysing the business plan,' explains Bishop. 'I made a presentation of my strategy for Celoxica, worked it and reworked it and it evolved into the business plan.' Milne and the other VCs were impressed: 'He saw some value in the business that we had not seen. The big thing about Phil is his ability to talk at the very highest level to customers and persuade them to do things that they do not normally do – like hand over purchase orders for services that Celoxica had done for free previously. They buy his vision of how the future is going to be.'

Other team members

The contract was signed in May 2002, but it was by no means the end of the process. Other management positions needed to be strengthened. Bishop brought along two former

Mentor colleagues, Jeff Jussell to be vice president of marketing and Tony Vittuci as vice president of consulting. 'Many successful executives have a team around them,' says Anderson. 'We call them the pit crew and they tend to be brought in pretty fast because with early stage companies you don't have a lot of time up your sleeve. You need to execute very, very quickly.'

It was not a total clearout, with CFO Bernard Morgan and general counsel Stephen Dyde continuing in their roles. Similarly, the engineering function, under Matt Aubury, had developed great technology, but as Bishop explains. 'They were quite brilliant but overloaded with processes that were not really necessary and without a functional head.' Bringing in that discipline has been a key part of Bishop's job.

The new CEO usually brings a different culture and Celoxica was no exception. The main change was to the sales approach. 'Prior to Phil arriving, Celoxica produced a lot of nice marketing material and thought the product would just fly off the shelves,' says Milne. They were, of course, mistaken. 'We focussed on specific markets and customers,' says Bishop. 'We go and partner with our customers. We are selling them a solution. We went from being a company that is product-led to one that is market-led.'

Part III

Financing the spinout

Chapter 9

Developing winning business plans

Keith Arundale
PricewaterhouseCoopers Global Technology Industry Group, London

Introduction

The main purpose of a business plan when raising finance is to develop and market the venture. It should show potential investors that if they invest in the business, they will have a unique opportunity to participate in making an excellent return on their investment. As Exhibit 9.1 shows, the business plan of a university spinout has many differences from that of a traditional company. This chapter provides entrepreneurs with advice on producing a winning business plan for spinouts and offers a suggested outline for its contents and practical guidance on style and presentation. Finally, the chapter considers how to use the business plan – both as a sales tool to attract investment and as a constantly evolving document.

Essential areas to cover in the business plan

It is essential for the business plan to be written by the spinout team, rather than by the university's technology transfer office (TTO) or by professional business plan writers or other advisers. Investors want to learn what management is planning to do, not see how well others can write for the team. Professional advisers can provide a vital role in critically reviewing the draft plan, acting as 'devil's advocates' and helping to give the plan the appropriate focus. However, it is the team who must research and write the plan.

The business plan should cover the following areas before an investor is approached:

- executive summary;
- the market;
- the technology and key products;
- management team;
- business operations;
- financial projections; and
- amount and use of finance required and exit opportunities.

Each of these areas is covered in the following sections.

Executive summary

Investors receive hundreds of business plans each year and most only have time to skim the executive summaries of these plans to determine whether to give the plans further consideration. It is

© 2004 PricewaterhouseCoopers LLP. All rights reserved. 'PricewaterhouseCoopers' refers to PricewaterhouseCoopers LLP (the limited liability partnership registered in England) or, as the context requires, other member firms of PricewaterhouseCoopers International Limited, each of which is a separate and independent legal entity.

Exhibit 9.1

Differences between a traditional business plan and an early stage spinout business plan

Traditional business plan	Early stage spinout business plan
Usually prepared to obtain major financing	May be used initially for relatively small amounts of seed/startup finance, but also needs to show longer-term requirements to attract investors.
Can take several months to prepare	Will need to be prepared quickly to capture the competitive/technological advantage, but still needs to be fully inclusive.
Often involves most of management team in preparation	Likely that academic founder will be mainly involved in preparation, with input from others.
Details full development over life of venture	Involves many more 'unknowns' than a typical venture, more difficult to chart out path.
Product may be easy to understand by reader	Product will need careful explanation in non-technical language.
Intellectual property (IP), if any, likely to be owned by company	IP may be owned by university – link with spinout and technology transfer company will need explaining.
Industry may be well established – relatively straightforward to obtain market data	Market data likely to be sparse and needing separate customer questioning to project likely take-up and sales.
Market need may be clear to understand	Market need for innovative new product must be demonstrated. Product likely to be either creating an entirely new market or fundamentally disrupting an existing market.
Project likely to be beyond development stage, and at commercialisation or expansion stage	Project likely to be at prototype stage. Commercial development will need to be addressed.
Management team likely to be fairly well in place	Focused on founder/researcher. Gaps in management team will need to be addressed.
Financial projections likely to be based on some historic financial data	No track record, so projections will be more speculative. Assumptions used must be capable of independent review.

Source: Author's own.

vital to give this summary significant thought and time, as it may well determine the amount of consideration the investor will give to the detailed proposal. It is often best written last.

It needs to be convincing in conveying the spinout's technological advantage and intellectual property (IP) protection, its commercial potential, whether it is addressing a real need in the marketplace, its growth and profit potential, and the team's skills and experience. It needs to encapsulate the unique selling proposition (USP) of the venture – why customers should buy the product as distinct from any available from competitors.

The summary should be limited to no more than two to three pages (that is, around 1,000 to 1,500 words) and include the key elements from each section of the plan.

Other aspects that should be included in the executive summary are the spinout's 'mission statement' – a few sentences encapsulating what the business does for what type of customers, the management team's aims for the business and what gives it its competitive edge. An overall strengths, weaknesses, opportunities and threats (SWOT) analysis also should be included. This summarises the key strengths of the business and its weaknesses, and the opportunities for the business in the marketplace, together with competitive threats.

The legal structure of the business should also be included here, in other words the company's incorporation, and how it is linked to the TTO, incubator and/or venture capital fund.

The market

The spinout team will need to convince the investors that there is a real commercial opportunity for a viable business in a large and expanding marketplace, following the development of the technology. This is where previous work done to achieve 'proof of market' can really pay off. Having evidence to convince investors of the commercial potential for applications of your technology is important. Using research and market analysis data to demonstrate how the team plans to penetrate and develop the market is crucial. Real numbers can make a real difference to your investment case.

Market analysis

Existing data on the market, if available, can be obtained from government sources, business libraries and the press, company literature and the internet.

However, existing market data on the specific new technology may not be readily available. The team may therefore need to carry out, or commission, original research.

Points to cover include:

- size of market;
- growth rates;
- government regulations;
- legal and ethical issues;
- is market developing, growing, maturing or decreasing;
- impediments to market entry;
- potential customers and individual purchase rate;
- who makes purchase decision; and
- what percentage of market will spinout capture.

Marketing plan

The primary purpose of the marketing section of the business plan is for the team to convince the investors that the market can be developed and penetrated.

The marketing plan should include an outline of plans for pricing, distribution channels and promotion.

Pricing

Explain the key components of the pricing decision – that is, technological leadership, competitive advantages, supplier costs and gross margins, and any discount structure for different distribution channels. Address to what extent suppliers can control the cost of key components or services, and to what extent customers' attitudes can influence the selling price.

Distribution channels

If the company is going to manufacture the technology, as opposed to license it, then the business plan should clearly identify the distribution channels that will get the product to the end-user. Distribution options for a manufacturer may include:

- direct sales;
- original equipment manufacturers (OEM), integration of the product into other manufacturers' products;
- distributors or wholesalers; or
- retailers (including on-line).

The plan should explain the reasons for selecting these distribution approaches and the financial benefits they will provide.

Promotion

The marketing promotion section of the business plan should include plans for product sheets, potential advertising plans, internet strategy, trade show schedules and any other promotional materials.

Competition

Even if the spin out company is first-to-market for the new technology or product, it is necessary to explain how the market's need is currently being met and how the new product will compete against the existing solution. The business plan should analyse the competition (who are they? how many are there? what proportion of the market do they account for?). The strengths and weaknesses of competitor products relative to the spinout's product should be addressed and likely competitive responses to the product predicted.

The technology and its applications

The spinout team will have already considered different commercial applications for the invention that may usefully be documented in the business plan. Investors will also be looking at the overall industry in which the technology resides and the attractiveness of the applications. Points to consider include:

- *barriers to entry* – is it easy or difficult for companies to enter the industry?
- *supplier power* – do suppliers to this industry have the power to set terms and conditions?
- *buyer power* – do buyers (customers) have the power to set terms and conditions?
- *threat of substitutes* – is it easy or difficult for substitute products to steal the market?
- *competitive rivalry* – is competitive rivalry intense or genteel?

The competitive edge of the product (its USP) will need to be set out clearly. For example, is the product:

- totally at the leading edge without any direct competitors?
- available at a lower price than competing products?
- of higher technical specifications?
- of higher quality?
- of greater durability?
- faster to operate?

- smaller in size?
- easier to service and maintain?
- offering additional support products or services?

State whether the product is vulnerable to technological advances being made elsewhere. Include a brief summary of the current state of these advances globally, without getting into too much technical detail, and how the spinout plans to keep its technology ahead of other developments.

If the product is still under development the plan should list all the major achievements to date as well as remaining milestones. Is a working prototype available? Better still, have trials of the actual product been carried out such that manufacturing costs are better understood and potential customers have actually sampled and tested the product? Specific mention should be made in the business plan of the results of both internal and external product testing.

Most importantly for a spinout company, the legal protection on the product, such as patents attained, pending or required must be documented. These considerations are addressed in the Chapter 7, 'Intellectual property management'. Investors will assess the impact of legal protection on the marketability of the product and will always ask the following.

- Who owns the IP?
- Is the IP owned by the university or by other academic organisations or by industrial companies?
- How is ownership of IP to be transferred to the spinout company?
- Is IP licensed in return for a share of royalties or assigned in return for an equity stake in the spinout company?
- What happens if the spinout doesn't work out and becomes insolvent – does the IP revert to the university or remain as an asset for the investors?

Management team

This section of the business plan should introduce the team and what each member brings to the spinout company. The attention that investors pay to this section of the business plan should not be underestimated. After all, investors will be relying on the spinout management team to execute the business plan successfully.

At the point at which proof of concept and proof of market have been achieved, the 'team' may of course be fairly embryonic, comprising the lead members of the university research team and representatives from the TTO. External resources will need to be brought in as soon as possible to help with the assessment of the market and development of the financial projections. Someone must take the lead with the spinout, however. Often this is the founding researcher. This early leader may not necessarily remain as the CEO of the spinout company. He may not have the skill-set that will be needed to turn the technology into a successful business.

The management team should ideally be experienced in complementary areas, such as the technical side, strategy, finance and marketing, and their roles should be specified. The prior experience and capabilities that each member brings to the spinout venture should be explained. This is particularly the case with technology companies where the combination of technical and business skills will be important to the backers.

Venture capital firms and TTOs can often assist in locating experienced managers and other skills gaps. A concise curriculum vitae should be included for each team member.

Details of keyman insurance (personal accident insurance) for the key members of the team should be included.

A key consideration will be whether to bring in an external CEO to run the company, leaving the founder to focus on technology and product developments, and maybe technical support for the company, and at what stage in the company's life cycle to bring in the CEO.

An alternative to bringing in permanent members of the team is to outsource key tasks, for example, by using consultants to help with marketing campaigns or deal with patents. A member of the management board will need to accept overall responsibility for any outsourced areas.

The plan should also address how the management team will be incentivised. Bringing in people from outside into a startup can be difficult as potential new recruits will be taking a risk in doing this, maybe even leaving the relative security of long-term employment. They need to be compensated for this, usually in terms of stock option plans.

The business plan should include an explanation of what performance measures will be implemented to review the performance of management and employees.

The appointment of a non-executive director (NED) should be seriously considered. NEDs can add significant value to the companies with which they are involved. Many venture capital firms at the time of their investment will wish to appoint one of their own executives or an independent expert to the board as a NED. Many university spinouts will have a NED appointed by the TTO, particularly if it has an equity stake in the spinout or a continuing interest in the IP.

The TTO can usually provide access to legal, financial and tax planning experts. The office can also help spinouts to find appropriate premises and technical and office equipment.

Auditors, lawyers, bankers and other advisers should be listed in the plan.

Consider the use of an advisory board in addition to the legal board of directors. The advisory board may even be set up ahead of the main management team to provide initial guidance to the founder/scientist at the earliest stages of commercialisation of the technology.

Business operations

This section of the business plan should explain how the spinout company will carry out its operations, including:

- how applications or products will be developed;
- how applications or products will be manufactured;
- how applications or products will be delivered to customers or end-users; and
- the spinout's approach to ongoing research and development.

Having achieved proof of concept and proof of market for the invention and decided on which commercial exploitation route to take, the steps needed and time taken to produce a prototype and develop the final product should not be underestimated. Many university researchers naturally focus on the technical aspects of the product. How the invention will be transformed into a commercial reality both from the marketing and operational viewpoints are not considered in sufficient depth. It is likely that a vice president of engineering or a clinical director experienced in product development or something similar, will need to be recruited to the team at an early stage.

Key issues to be considered include:

- timetable and budget for completion of a prototype and then final product;

- whether manufacturing is to be outsourced;
- location and size of the planned manufacturing, production and research facilities;
- availability of labour;
- accessibility of materials;
- proximity to distribution channels;
- government grants and tax incentives;
- equipment needed and cost;
- flexibility and efficiency of the facilities;
- safety and employment laws;
- quality control of production; and
- requirements for information technology systems.

Financial projections

The financial projections need to demonstrate that the spinout company offers enough growth potential to deliver the type of return on investment that the investor is seeking, and that the projections are realistic enough to give the company a reasonable chance of attaining them. Of course, with some spinouts the business will be at too early a stage for numerical projections to be all that meaningful.

Notes to the projections that explain the major assumptions used to develop the revenue and expense amounts in the projections are essential, as is an explanation of the research that has been undertaken to support these assumptions.

Investors will use the projections to determine if:

- the spinout offers enough growth potential to deliver the type of return on investment that the investors are seeking; and
- the projections are realistic enough to give the company a reasonable chance of attaining them.

Investors will expect to see a full set of cohesive financial projections, including a balance sheet, income statement and cash-flow statement, for a period of three to five years. It is usual to show monthly income and cash flow statements until the breakeven point is reached, followed by yearly data for the remaining timeframe.

The team should have regard to the following when considering the assumptions in preparing the projections.

Sales

Typically, the plan should state an average selling price per unit along with the projected number of units to be sold each reporting period. Sales prices should be competitive, depending on the uniqueness of the product in the market, and should take into consideration the cost to produce and distribute the product.

Cost of sales

Investors will expect accurate unit variable cost data, taking into consideration the labour, material and overhead costs to produce each unit. There should be a good grasp on initial product costing so that it is protected against price pressure from competitors. The fixed costs should also be documented.

Product development

Product development expenses should be closely tied to product introduction timetables else-where in the plan. These expenses are typically higher in the early years and taper off because product line extensions are less costly to develop. Investors will focus on these assumptions because further rounds of financing may be needed if major products are not introduced on time.

Other expenses

A detailed set of expense assumptions should take into consideration headcount, selling and administrative costs, space and major promotions. It is useful to compare final expense projections with industry norms. All expense categories should be considered.

Other areas where care is required in preparing the projections are as follows.

- Realistically assess cash flow and working capital requirements.
- Assess the value attributed to the company's net tangible assets at each projected year-end.
- State the level of gearing (in other words, the debt to shareholders' funds ratio). State how much debt is secured on what assets and the current value of those assets.
- Include all costs associated with the business. Sales and marketing costs should be split.
- Provide budgets for each area of the spinout's activities. What are the controls in place to ensure that management keeps within these or improves on these budgets?
- Present different scenarios for the financial projections of sales, costs and cash flow for both the short and long term. For example, what if sales decline by 20 per cent, or supplier costs increase by 30 per cent, or both? How does this impact on the profit and cash flow projections?
- If more than one round of financing will be required (as is usually the case with technology-based spinouts), the projections should identify the likely timing of these and any associated progress 'milestones' that have been specified by the investor as needing to have been achieved before additional funding is granted.
- The plan should be kept feasible and a tendency on the part of entrepreneurs to be over-optimistic avoided. Any key challenges and how these will be met should be highlighted.

The team might wish to consider using an external accountant to review the financial projections and to act as 'devil's advocate' before presenting them to an investor.

Amount and use of finance required and exit opportunities

The plan should include the team's best estimate of how much finance is required by the spinout to complete prototype and commercial development, and to set up the manufacturing operations and distribution channels. The sources from which the finance is hoped to come should be set out (for example, founder and management team members, seed funds such as the university seed-corn funds, government research and development (R&D) grants, regional venture capital funds, business angels, venture capital firms, banks and others).

The use that will be made of the finance raised, whether for capital expenditure or working capital, should be spelled out clearly. An implementation schedule, including capital expenditure and production timetables, should be included.

Consideration should be given as to how the investors will make their return, in other words by realising their investment in due course, possibly through a stock market flotation or trade sale. The options for exit will need to be considered and discussed with the investors.

Risk management aspects: a note of caution

Legal and regulatory issues

Raising finance is a complex legal and regulatory area and this is not intended to provide legal advice or substitute for the team taking its own professional and/or legal advice. Sending a business plan to, or discussing it with, potential investors is a financial promotion and this may require the management team or other persons involved in the process to be authorised or regulated in certain jurisdictions. There are usually exemptions available if the plan is to be communicated to investment professionals, such as venture capitalists.

Care also needs to be exercised to ensure that there are no misleading statements in documents that are designed to induce or persuade people to enter into investment agreements or to buy or sell shares in companies.

It may be necessary to verify any statement, promise or forecast contained in any communication document, including a business plan, private placement memorandum, information memorandum and so on, made available to potential investors. However, if the plan is being sent to an authorised venture capital firm then it may not be necessary to have the verification process undertaken. Nevertheless, the plan should not contain any misleading statements. In case of any doubt, if the team is seeking equity or debt finance, other than ordinary banking facilities, they are recommended to obtain legal advice before making any communications (whether written or oral) with potential investors, including the circulation of the business plan.

Warranties and indemnities

The spinout company directors will be asked to provide warranties and indemnities to the venture capital firm. If the information later turns out to be inaccurate, the venture capital firm can claim against the providers of the information for any resulting loss incurred. A disclosure letter, containing the key information disclosed by the directors to the venture capital firm and on which the investment decision has been based, will be required.

The team must be able to support the assumptions used to prepare the financial projections in the plan. Vague or unsustainable statements should not be made. Statements should be substantiated with underlying data and market information.

The business risks inherent in the company and its industry should also be clearly set out in the plan. Credibility can be seriously damaged if existing risks and problems are discovered by outside parties.

Any material contracts, not being contracts in the ordinary course of business, would need to be disclosed, as would any litigation or arbitration proceedings of material importance, actual, pending or threatened.

Tips on the presentation of the business plan

Readability

Make the plan readable. Use plain English – especially as technical details are being explained. Aim the plan at non-specialists, emphasising its financial viability. Avoid including unnecessary detail in the main body of the plan and prevent the plan from becoming too lengthy. Put detail into appendices. Ask someone outside the company to check the plan for clarity and 'readability'.

Length

The length of the business plan depends on individual circumstances and on whether it is prepared to attract potential investors or used for internal management purposes. If the latter, it may well be more detailed. It is probably best to err on the side of brevity – if investors are interested they can always ask for additional information. Unless the business requires several million pounds of venture capital and is highly complex, the body of the business plan should be no longer than, say, 20 pages.

Appearance

Graphs and charts should be used to illustrate and simplify complicated information. Ensure it is neatly typed or printed without spelling, typing or grammatical mistakes – these have a disproportionately negative impact. Yet avoid very expensive documentation, in terms of binding and cover design, as this might suggest unnecessary waste and extravagance.

How to use your business plan

Raising finance from investors is a sales process in which the business plan is a strategic tool. Hitting them with a business plan the size of a telephone directory straight off will not get the spinout company very far along this process. To begin with, investors are being sold a vision.

The executive summary or a 2/3 page 'teaser' should be used as bait to get a potential investor hooked and interested to learn more about the opportunity. This teaser should whet the investor's appetite by describing a compelling opportunity.

* *The customer's point of pain:* how important a problem is this to the customer?
* *The proposed solution:* how does the product meet the customer's need?
* *The market:* what is the size of the market and the timing of the opportunity?
* *The rewards:* how and when are customers, investors and stakeholders rewarded?

When investors can relate to the 'vision', they are more likely to be persuaded to take the next step, which is an initial meeting.

If a meeting with an investor can be successfully arranged, all the preparation in producing the business plan will provide most of the material needed for the presentation. Copies of the business plan should always be taken along, but the presentation should not be simply a word for word replication of the business plan in PowerPoint format.

At the end of the meeting, make sure copies of the business plan are left behind – if investors are interested they will read it, if they are not they will 'file it'.

Finally, the business plan should never remain static. It should be constantly evolving to account for every new development, meeting or event that is relevant to improving the chances of getting your spinout funded. As progress is made along the fundraising journey, gain feedback from every advance and setback. The lessons learned should be reflected in the current version of the business plan.

Final advice

- Be realistic, especially with the revenue projections.
- Do not underestimate the costs – especially of commercial development and achieving consistent quality expectations and standards .
- Focus on the customer – no matter how good the technology.
- The business plan is a selling document, but it needs to be robust and statements need to be defensible with facts, since this is the document against which due diligence will be carried out.
- Do not present the ideas too early, in other words before basic technical flaws have been ironed out.
- Ensure that there is some contingency for slippage built into the business plan, to allow the company to take action if plans are delayed.
- Take care not to disclose any information to the public before a patent application is filed.
- Do consider using a professional adviser, with experience of helping spinouts to raise finance, to act as 'devil's advocate' in reviewing the plan. Also rehearse presentations of the plan to investors. The TTO may well be helpful here.
- Do not use a 'scattergun' approach when sending the plan to potential investors. Select them carefully so that their investment preferences match the spinout's needs.
- If the plan is turned down by an investor, do find out the reasons why and correct any issues as far as possible before presenting to the next potential investor.
- Constantly update the business plan. Use it to monitor progress with the company's milestones and targets. Incorporate what is learned from meetings with potential investors.

Chapter 10

The role of business angels

Kjell Nace
Library House, Cambridge, United Kingdom

Charles Cotton
Library House and business angel, Cambridge, United Kingdom

Introduction

This chapter explores the important role played by business angels in providing seed or early stage finance and advice to nurture university spinouts. The chapter explains what value good business angels can offer to an entrepreneur, the types of business angels to look out for and how best to interact with angels to develop your spinout company.

Investor types: a reminder of the different stages and roles of financing

Successful spinout companies can expect to have to navigate through multiple financings and encounter many different kinds of investors. Exhibit 10.1 summarises the main sources of external finance.

Exhibit 10.1

Key financing sources by company stage

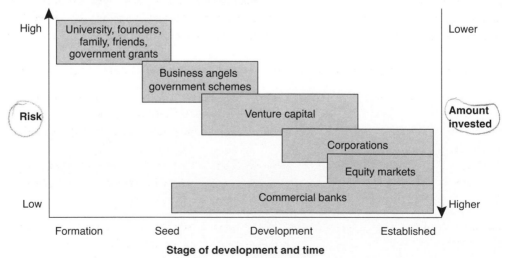

Source: Library House.

Many universities and colleges offer funds that aid the transition of a newly born spin-out from the shelter provided by their internal departments into the harsher external world. In addition to accessing university seed-corn funds or 'challenge' funds, entrepreneurs traditionally reach into their own pockets and reach out to family and friends to fund their nascent companies. This is frequently the stage where governments also offer grants aimed at assisting research and development of a company's products.

Business angels are the next port of call, supplemented and complemented in some countries by further government initiatives such as the Small Business Investment Company (SBIC) model in the United States, which has been in operation since 1958. These government schemes are designed to bridge an equity gap between business angel and venture capital funding.

Successful fast-growing businesses reach the stage where capital investment over US$1 million is required to fund further development, marketing and production. At this stage the investment baton passes to venture capital firms. Typically, venture investments are conducted in a series of rounds that reflect the growing maturity of the business through its development stages. As the investment risk falls further, commercial banks and non-financial corporations are attracted to the opportunity.

For the very successful businesses that are able to navigate their way through the private company development and funding maze, the opportunity may arise to secure further investment through listing the company's shares on a publicly traded financial market.

What is a business angel?

Business angels are high net worth individuals who invest their own funds in private companies, typically at the formation or seed stage. A typical business angel is an older, high net worth individual with an entrepreneurial background. Business angels are more likely to invest in other investing activities, such as the stock market and property rather than consumption activities, such as racehorses. While business angels are motivated by financial return, this is not their sole motivation. Many seek an active role in the development of a company where they can add value beyond their financial investment. In this context, it is worth noting that business angels are more likely to argue that constraints on their time, rather than finance, limit the number of investments in which they engage, indicating their propensity to get involved in the business.

According to the MIT Entrepreneurship Center, business angels fall into four categories.

1. *Guardian angels* bring both entrepreneurial and industry experience. Many have been successful entrepreneurs in the same sector as the new companies they back.
2. *Entrepreneur angels* have experience of starting companies but come from different industry sectors.
3. *Operational angels* bring industry experience and expertise, but generally from large, established companies, and may lack first-hand experience with the travails of a startup.
4. *Financial angels* typically invest purely for the financial return.

The ranking of these four categories of business angel is significant. In terms of their desirability for spinouts, guardian angels are the most, and financial angels the least attractive.

As a class, business angels exhibit one common trait – they actively seek opportunities at the risky, early stage of a business and are the most important source of 'smart' money available to spinout companies. Not only do they invest their own money, many also get actively involved in the development of the business, applying their own domain knowledge and operational experience. Fledgling technology-based companies face a steep learning curve as they grapple with the multiple demands of evolving a business. For the entrepreneur, having an experienced business angel to turn to for advice will ensure that many pitfalls are avoided, and development of the business can be made more rapidly and efficiently.

The significance of business angels

It is important to realise the significance of business angels as investors in early stage companies. As an investing class, business angels are more important than venture capital for early stage companies. Exhibit 10.2 illustrates the percentage of investments made at different stages in the United Kingdom.

According to recent research in the United States, the number of companies that business angels fund is greater than that funded by venture capital, while the capital invested by business angels approaches half the amount invested by the venture capital industry (see Exhibit 10.3).

Exhibit 10.2

Distribution of angel and venture capital investments by stage (%)

Stage of finance	Business angels	Venture capital	Others
Early	65	30	5
Expansion	30	50	20
Management buy-in/buy-out	5	20	75

Sources: Mason (2002) and BVCA, Mason and Harrison (2002).

Exhibit 10.3

Comparison of activity levels in the United States between angels and venture capital (2000)

	Business angels	Venture capital
Number of participants	400,000+	1,010
Number of deals financed	50,000	5,485
Total invested (US$ billion)	40.0	89.8

Source: Sohl, J.E. (2003), 'The US Angel and Venture Capital Market: Recent Trends and Developments', *Journal of Private Equity*, 6(2), pp.7–17.

It is clear from this exhibit that the typical amount invested by a business angel is much less than a venture capital firm invests. In the United Kingdom, the median amount invested is around £50,000 (US$92,000), with a range from less than £10,000 (US$18,000) to over £250,000 (US$460,000). The median total deal size is around £75,000 (US$138,000) for an angel round.

Business angels are a key element of the financing spectrum for technology-based businesses. They span the funding divide between founders, friends and family and venture capitalists. Not only do they plug a funding gap, they also bring experience and expertise to bear, thereby plugging a knowledge gap as well.

From the perspective of an entrepreneur spinning out a new innovation-based company, business angels and venture capital investors can be compared as shown in Exhibit 10.4.

The different kinds of business angels

There are many different types of business angel. For the spinout company, the most valuable are those that offer specific technology, industry and/or market experience. The good news is

116

Exhibit 10.4

Key differentiators between angels and venture capitalists

Attribute	Business angels	Venture capitalists
Behaviour	Entrepreneurs	Money managers
Accessibility	Local	Local/national
Approach	Friendly	Formal
Time to investment	~ 3 months	6–12 months
Diligence	Limited	Exhaustive
Documentation/contracts	Simple	Extensive
Financial instruments	Common shares	Preference shares
Funds invested	Own money	Fund provider's money
Investment/round individually (US$000)	10–250	500–10,000
Investment/round syndicated (US$000)	50–1,000	1,000–25,000
Involvement in day-to-day management	Hands on	Strategic
Exit clarity	Less important	Very important
Rate of return	Important	Extremely important

Source: Library House.

that over the last two decades, the success of information technology and life science companies means there is a very large number of wealthy entrepreneurs with a wide range of domain and operational experiences looking for new and exciting opportunities in which to invest their money, time and expertise.

There are also 'good angels' and 'angels from the dark-side'. The vast majority of business angels fall into the first category, but there are also angels from the dark-side who are distinguished by the havoc they cause – in the worst cases actually causing a business to fail. In some instances, the havoc results from ignorance. Unfortunately, there are also the rare cases where the angel from the dark-side attempts to wrest control of a company through deception or other wilful actions.

There are several morals for the spinout company executive.

- Exercise great care and undertake extensive diligence in selecting a business angel.
- Talk to people they have worked with, employees who have worked for them and their friends. Build a rounded picture of the kind of person they are and, importantly, how they behave when the going gets tough.
- Ask yourself: 'do I respect this person, do they share my vision for the company? Can they help me make the company successful and will the experience of working with them be enjoyable?'

Business angel networks

Some business angels prefer to operate as loners. Others operate as members of groups varying in size from as few as 10 to more than 100 investors. These groups operate in a variety of different ways, from loosely aligned to those that require members to complete legal documentation confirming their status as an 'accredited investor' or 'qualified investor' to meet regulatory

117

requirements. Some angel groups invest in a joint fund which is managed and administered by a professional investment manager. Others prefer to invest on their own account and participate in syndicates according to their appetite and interest in a particular deal.

The concept of angels coordinating their efforts as part of a group or club means that they can assemble syndicates to enable larger investments than typically can be supported by one individual. Where an individual business angel might invest US$10,000–250,000, a number of angels acting together might invest up to US$1 million. For certain types of spinouts, being able to access this level of investment is an important element of success, particularly when it is supported by the cumulative expertise of the syndicate members. Other reasons for angels to band together include:

- exchanging their experiences of angel investing to avoid repeating mistakes;
- sharing due diligence where individuals focus on their areas of competence;
- assembling 'standard' deal documents which have been generated by lawyers in accordance with the practices favoured by the angel group, as a starting point for negotiations; and
- the opportunity to socialise with a group who share common objectives but with different backgrounds.

One of the best-known angel groups is the Band of Angels in California, which was formed in 1994, grew to 100 members and developed an original and successful format. The group meets monthly for dinner. Selected entrepreneurs are invited to make a presentation if they pass an initial test – find a Band member who is willing to act as a sponsor and to lead a syndicate if members of the group determine, after due diligence, that this is a promising opportunity. Since 1994, Band members have invested more than US$110 million into more than 140 startup companies.

Cambridge Angels in Cambridge, England was formed in 2002 and operates along similar lines. Six times a year, 20–25 angels meet at a University of Cambridge College to hear two pitches from entrepreneurs. Each of the presenting companies is sponsored by one of the Cambridge Angels, who is then subjected to a barrage of detailed questioning over dinner from which the entrepreneurs are excluded. The group is then invited to nominate their interest in joining syndicates to research, analyse, undertake due diligence and potentially invest in the opportunities. As an example, the Cambridge Angels' model and investing criteria include:

- an outstanding, clearly defined business or technology opportunity;
- an enthusiastic, capable entrepreneur;
- an identified, under-served market;
- a clear route to cash generation or further funding;
- the support of at least three angels; and
- the opportunity for one angel to go on the board.

In its first two years the Cambridge Angels received presentations by 23 companies and invested in 10. The total invested by the angels across the 10 deals was £2 million (US$3.7 million). Interestingly, the 10 deals also pulled along an additional £2 million (US$3.7 million) from other investors. The impact of an additional £4 million (US$7.5 million) investment in early stage companies in the Cambridge Cluster was significant and made the Cambridge Angels the largest seed investor in the Cluster. The Cambridge Cluster, as defined by Library House, encompasses those innovation-based companies that make up the significant technology and life sciences cluster in the geographic area of Cambridgeshire, based around the city of Cambridge. Innovation-based companies in the immediate surrounding areas that have a strong affinity to the cluster, but fall outside the geographic definition of Cambridgeshire are also included.

Of the 10 companies, one has ceased trading and two have progressed to receive venture capital funding of more than £7 million (US$12.9 million). An additional three are expected to receive A Series funding, the first venture capital funding round.

The Cambridge Angels successfully engaged 25 business angels, all of whom had previously started, grown and sold an innovation-based company. None of them was engaged with a business angel group prior to the formation of the Cambridge Angels, and as a result they were an untapped resource. None of these individuals had seen the value in joining existing groups, mostly because the other groups were open to anyone, frequently run for the profit of the administrator and did not permit the angels to meet behind closed doors with a group of peers.

The best angel syndicates offer several advantages for spinouts including:

- potential for larger investments;
- access to multiple business angels with specific domain and operational experience;
- halo effect of the association with 'known' business angels; and
- smoother transition to venture investment stage.

Motivations of business angels

Having cashed out of their own businesses, entrepreneurs are faced with choices including, 'doing it all again' by becoming a serial entrepreneur or a more vicarious existence as a business angel. Aside from the desire to make money through application of their skills and experiences, surveys of business angels indicate the following wider motivations:

- personal satisfaction;
- having fun with some of their money;
- supporting a socially beneficial product or service;
- helping friends set up in business;
- encouraging the next generation of entrepreneurs;
- opportunity for current or future income (through fees, part-time salary);
- participating in a spinout or startup without the day-to-day responsibilities;
- enjoying as active an involvement in the company as the team and they agree is appropriate – potentially creating a full- or part-time job for themselves;
- securing many of the satisfactions of the successful development of the business without the daily challenges and crises that the entrepreneur inevitably faces;
- acting as mentors and having their advice and counsel valued; and
- reliving formative stages in their own business life, renewing old acquaintances and demystifying a critical step in the development of a business while preparing the team for investment by venture capital firms.

Interaction of business angels with other investors

Business angels interact with earlier stage investors – the so-called 3F investors: founders, friends and family – as well as with the later stage venture capital investors. Interaction between the business angel and earlier stage investors tends to be reasonably straightforward, at least for the business angel, because they generally understand and control the investment process. The value delivered by the business angel is easily grasped based on their business track record, their fluency with the development of an innovation-based company and their mentoring. However, it is frequently the case that the entrepreneur's lack of experience leads to over-ambitious valuation expectations which take time for them to come to terms with. The due diligence and investment process, including legal agreements, is often conducted on a one-to-one basis between the entrepreneur and the business angel and as a result is discussed and understood at each step.

For many entrepreneurial companies, investment by business angels only satisfies the funding needs of the business for a limited time. Although multiple angel rounds are possible, they are not common with fast-growth companies. For those companies seeking more capital to expand and develop their businesses, the next stage involves venture capital.

Only fast-growing businesses addressing large markets are likely to attract venture capital. Some businesses may bypass angel finance and go straight to venture capital – this is usually associated with a company founded by a serial entrepreneur who invests his or her own money to kick-start the business. That being said, where angel funding precedes venture capital investment, this is generally viewed as a positive signal for the quality of the investment by the venture capitalist. For a number of reasons, it is commonplace for a business angel and a venture capitalist to want to continue alongside each other following the funding.

- It takes time for the venture capitalist to become accustomed to the operation of the company and the interactions between the key players.
- Encouraging the business angel to remain engaged with the company diminishes the potential for misunderstandings and disruption.
- The business angel may have relationships with customers, suppliers and partners that are important to the company's success.

However, post A Series funding, the interests of the business angel and the venture capitalist are not fully aligned. Typically, the business angel has invested alongside the founders and other first stage investors in common shares whereas the venture investor will in most cases demand preference shares. Only in a minority of cases do business angels invest alongside venture firms in A series and subsequent institutional rounds.

Assuming that the first venture capital round is at a valuation above prior angel round(s), it is generally the case that business angels would like to be able to recycle their initial investment from the company into their next venture, while leaving the balance to participate in any future upside. This opportunity is rarely forthcoming from venture capital firms.

Role played by business angels in developing institutional investor readiness

'Been there, done that' are the benefits that experienced business angels bring when the time comes to seek investment by venture capital firms. Their understanding that venture firms will be an order of magnitude more thorough in every element of the investment process by comparison with an angel investor ensures that the management team embarks with the necessary appreciation of the rigour and time demands of the process. Where the business angel has recent venture funding experience, the value is even greater as they have relevant personal contacts in target venture capital firms and are attuned to the current deal expectations of the venture industry. Other benefits that the business angel brings in preparing the company for its first venture capital investment include:

- encouraging the entrepreneur and their team to be comfortable presenting and explaining the salient facts about their company at conferences and with other audiences;
- explaining the expectations venture firms will have and how they will approach key aspects of a deal;
- helping construct a presentation underpinned by a business plan and financial projections that will capture the interest of the target venture capital audience;
- deciding which venture capital firms to approach and providing personal contacts in these firms;
- anticipating the critical questions venture capitalists will ask; and
- comprehending the need for the entrepreneur to engage with suitably experienced professional advisers – accountants and lawyers – and personal contacts with suitable candidate firms.

Summary – advantages and disadvantages of business angels

Exhibit 10.5 illustrates that, for spinout companies looking to business angels as a source of funding, the advantages outweigh the disadvantages.

General points

The following general points apply when seeking funding from business angels.

- Research who can provide money for the company and at what levels they provide funding. Pitching to investors who traditionally invest at other stages than where the company is will inevitably lead down a blind alley.

Exhibit 10.5

The pros and cons of business angels

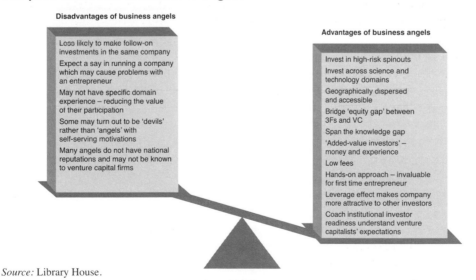

Disadvantages of business angels

Less likely to make follow-on investments in the same company

Expect a say in running a company which may cause problems with an entrepreneur

May not have specific domain experience – reducing the value of their participation

Some may turn out to be 'devils' rather than 'angels' with self-serving motivations

Many angels do not have national reputations and may not be known to venture capital firms

Advantages of business angels

Invest in high-risk spinouts

Invest across science and technology domains

Geographically dispersed and accessible

Bridge 'equity gap' between 3Fs and VC

Span the knowledge gap

'Added-value investors' – money and experience

Low fees

Hands-on approach – invaluable for first time entrepreneur

Leverage effect makes company more attractive to other investors

Coach institutional investor readiness understand venture capitalists' expectations

Source: Library House.

- There is a big difference between 'money' and 'smart money'. Smart money means finding investors with background and industry experience that really can contribute to building the business. This is especially important at an early/seed stage where key decisions and strategic business trajectories are being decided. Smart investors contribute significantly above and beyond money in terms of general experience, industry insight and relevant contacts.

- If funding is sought or obtained from an angel group, it is important to understand how the group interacts. If the structure if flat and informal and the group has a number of members this can make it difficult to identify 'one voice'. This can again make it difficult to manage expectations.

- Be completely open and honest with investors and the board. They must be on your side 100 per cent, and complete transparency means they are able to help and assist at every step of the way.

Early stage companies rarely appreciate the difference in experience and attitude between business angels. The following case study highlights how a savvy group of business angels provided not only mentoring and education for a fledgling CEO, but also how they helped the company gain early market traction.

Case study

NaturalMotion, a spinout from Oxford University: from research to the creation of virtual characters in Hollywood movies[1]

There may not appear to be much overlap between the fields of complexity theory and evolution and the technologies applied in 3D animation software. However, endorpin, the first product launched by the Oxford University spinout company NaturalMotion in mid-2003, not only successfully applied these techniques to 3D animation, but also managed to see endorpin being used in the creation of one of the blockbuster movies of 2004 – *Troy*, directed by Wolfgang Petersen.

Background

For Torsten Reil, the founder and CEO of NaturalMotion, the journey started in 1995 when he first came to Oxford University. Two years before enrolling at Oxford, Reil read *The Blind Watchmaker* by the evolutionary biologist Richard Dawkins and developed a deep fascination with biology. When Torsten arrived at Oxford the big questions of evolutionary biology were hotly debated and at this point it was asked if computers might help to solve some of the riddles. After graduating with a Bachelor's degree in biology from Oxford, Reil received a Master's degree from the University of Sussex in artificial intelligence in 1999 where his thesis specifically aimed to combine complexity and evolution by developing a computer program relying on neural networks and genetic algorithms.

Advanced research, germination of product leading to questions of financing

Returning to Oxford for a PhD, Reil continued his research into computer-based modelling of biological phenomena based on complexity theory and neural networks. By using neural networks that simulate groups of nerve cells he had a mechanism that would produce new emergent properties. The genetic algorithms, mechanisms for selecting between versions of a program based on their performance, would choose adaptations that worked best. By creating artificial 'generations' of two-legged figures with slightly different neural circuits, an evolutionary approach was created by copying the 'fittest' members into new generations while adding new mutations to their neural networks and running simulations over and over again.

After 20 generations, Reil had simulations that could walk but not in a very human-like fashion. At this point Reil collaborated with Colm Massey, mathematician turned software developer, who helped write an engine designed to apply natural laws such as gravity to the simulated environments. The two also decided to give their simulated creatures distinct human features such as kneecaps that prevented the lower legs from hyperextending and muscles that resist being overstretched. The result was human-like beings and behaviours that could be created in artificial environments with a significant degree of accuracy. Reil also knew that existing techniques in this area (3D animation) were slow and often very costly as they were primarily created by pre-producing images that were then added together into the film or game to create a 'moving' image. Reil and Massey strongly believed they could change how this worked and decided to pursue the commercial opportunity this represented.

Identification of financing sources leading to angels

As Reil's early concept gradually became more tangible, he became increasingly concerned about protecting his ideas and the body of work that had already been developed. By the end of 2000 this had led him to ISIS Innovation, the technology transfer arm of Oxford University, which helped him initiate a patent filing that, by early 2001, secured him a patent with close to 100 claims, covering everything from the basic components to the build of the underlying technology.

A few months later, ISIS Innovation again proved very helpful by facilitating Reil's first introduction to business angels, and in November 2000 he made his first ever investor presentation to the Oxford Investor Opportunity Network (OION).

'The response was very good and we had a number of calls and enquiries over the following weeks,' recalls Reil. 'Rather than talking too much about the technology details which were still at an early stage we focused on the opportunity, the business potential and what we believed we could do.'

Participants from the OION meeting had in the meantime talked to George Brown and Robert Helms, two other business angels, to whom Reil presented a few months later. Both Brown and Helms liked the idea and were interested in coming in as potential investors. Both realised however, that it would be crucial to build knowledge and expertise around the fledgling company and subsequently contacted David Gardner (UK managing director of Electronic Arts, the computer games company) and Nick Alexander (former CEO of SEGA Europe, founder and former managing director of Virgin Games and Virgin Mastertronic).

Interaction, choice of angels and experience of working with angels

Towards September 2001 the initial financing round started coming to a close when the tragic events of the 11 September bombings of the World Trade Center in New York made the world stop in its track. For Reil this delayed closing the round, but only for a short while. In the middle of October 2001 he incorporated NaturalMotion and closed the financing round in November the same year, with George Brown and David Gardner coming in as investors in addition to Simon Murdoch (founder of Bookpages, which later was sold to Amazon.com) and others. Nick Alexander subsequently joined the board as chairman.

As Reil stated: 'Initially I had seen applications for the NaturalMotion technology in 3D markets, robotics and biomedicine. Following the incorporation of the company and the close of the financing round, my board emphasised the importance of focus and we saw the 3D animation market as the most immediate opportunity.'

'One of our first-round investors was Alan Shiach, the film producer, and this combined with the contacts and network my existing investors had really opened a lot of doors for us. We rapidly hit the road and started having meetings with games developers and animators. It was not only that our technology at that point was at a very early stage, or flaky if you want; but we really saw the importance of talking to people in the industry, the people who would be potential users, about what they wanted and their needs as part of our product development process.'

Meanwhile George Brown and Robert Helms had been recruiting an interim management team that would be in place for the Spring 2002.

Reil stated: 'It really was extremely useful and such an important part of the development of the company and myself. You have to realise I had come straight from academia and had a very limited knowledge about how to run a company. The interim management team and my investors showed me how to run a company as well as details such as how to prepare for a board meeting. This process is far from over, probably never will be, but in May 2002 I assumed the formal role of CEO for NaturalMotion.'

On the technical side, the chief technical officer of GorillaPark (another investor) continually monitored NaturalMotion's technology progress (this role is now filled by Colm Massey). At this point Reil started advertising, primarily through trade press to build up a core technical team. Product development picked up pace significantly over mid-2002 and by early 2003 the NaturalMotion Active Character Technology (ACT) was in beta testing and the endorpin product range based on ACT was subsequently released in mid-2003. The endorpin product range won a Computer Graphics World 2003 Innovation Award in November 2003 and Reil also saw the product being used by Weta Digital to make *Lord of the Rings – The Return of the King* in late-2003.

Early-2004 finds Reil spending more time on planes and in California talking to potential customers and working on setting up a US sales office than in Oxford. He is also looking at closing a new financing round in late Spring 2004 and believes the lessons imparted by his angel investors over the past two years are crucial in securing new finance as well as accelerating the growth of the company.

Key lessons learned

Looking back, Reil believes he has been very lucky in involving angel investors with crucial skills and industry knowledge at an early stage of the formation of NaturalMotion. Summing up his experience he believes there are a number of elements that could be invaluable for entrepreneurs in similar situations.

- Getting the 'right investors' is far more important than getting any investors. Right investors are people who can contribute significantly above and beyond money in terms of general experience, industry insight and relevant contacts.
- Reil also believes location has been critical: 'given the networks, the availability of money and people, and angels and mentors with crucial skills and knowledge I really don't believe NaturalMotion would have been a company today if I had set it up outside Oxford, Cambridge or London.'
- Be completely open and honest with your investors and board. You want them on your side 100 per cent, and complete transparency means they are able to help and assist at every step of the way
- Make sure you proactively seek advice – coming from a pure academic setting, Reil realised from the outset he needed significant help in building his commercial acumen and knowledge about running a company.
- Get in touch with potential customers as early as possible. This can lead to early revenues, but more importantly to early and often vitally important insight into customer needs and subsequent design and technology choices affecting your product.[2]

---

[1] The authors would like to acknowledge Torsten Reil, CEO of NaturalMotion, for his time, insight and permission to use NaturalMotion as a case study.

[2] An element of this case study is based on O. Morton's article 'Attack of the Stuntbots' which appeared in *Wired Magazine* in January 2004. Torsten Reil, co-founder and CEO of NaturalMotion, has been interviewed and given significant input in the writing process. In addition, publicly available information on NaturalMotion, including press releases and websites has been used.

Chapter 11

Approaching, presenting and selecting investors

Hazel Moore
First Stage Capital, London

Introduction

Selecting an investor is one of the most important decisions that a young company makes. In addition to providing financial support, investors must be able to add real value through a detailed understanding of the industry and experience in helping to build successful companies. The process of raising money from investors will always take longer and be more difficult than anticipated. Most venture capitalists (VCs) fund only a tiny percentage, around 1 per cent, of the businesses that approach them for money. What can a company do to secure funding?

Fund raising is a sales process that can be split into five stages:

1. preparation;
2. contacting investors;
3. first meeting;
4. initial due diligence; and
5. securing a term sheet.

This chapter covers the first four stages and explains what investors are looking for in a spin-out investment opportunity (term sheets are covered in Chapter 14). It describes what is involved in the process and what investors are looking for to help a company prepare accordingly and increase the chances of success.

Preparation

The first thing to do is to take a long, hard look at the business. The founder may think it has the potential to be an attractive business, but does it have the characteristics that make it an attractive investment opportunity for a VC? They are not necessarily the same thing.

The crucial raw materials for a venture capital investment are people, market and technology, probably in that order. VCs are looking for a talented and experienced management team exploiting a very large and rapidly growing market with a strongly differentiated product of high commercial potential. Does it sound like something the business could be?

- If the answer is no, then the different funding options should be explored.
- If it requires a large leap of faith to reasonably predict that the business can achieve this, then it is too early to approach VCs.
- If the answer is yes, then read on.

What are VCs looking for?

Investors want to make money. It is as simple as that. An investor will hand over their money in the expectation that at some point in the not too distant future it will be given back to them with a (substantial) profit. Keeping this core principle in mind will greatly help the fund-raising process.

How to increase the chances of success

Do not go too early

By and large, if an investor is approached too early, before the company is ready, the answer will be 'no'. The entrepreneur should make sure, therefore, that he or she is fully prepared and that the business is suitably far advanced before the process is started. A key aspect of the preparation falls to the technology transfer office (TTO).

As Dr Maire Smith, chief executive of Manchester Innovation Ltd (MIL) the commercialisation company of the University of Manchester, says: 'Manchester Innovation exists to create value from technology which has viable market potential. It is the application of the technology that holds the value and MIL has a role in identifying how best to extract this value. This role cannot be underestimated as most potential entrepreneurs need assistance to advance beyond the basic technology concept. The most common blind spot for entrepreneurs is a failure to evaluate realistically the market value of future products.'

Understand an investor's appetite for risk

It is a common misconception that VCs are paid to take risk. They are not. VCs are paid to take risk only where the rewards justify the risk. A very significant part of their job is to manage and reduce risk. Therefore the risk/return tradeoff in the business needs to be considered from the point of view of the investor. The sorts of risks related to spinouts that an investor will be thinking about include:

- *Market risk:* what if the market opportunity is not big enough or the customer does not want to buy the product?
- *Execution risk:* what if the management team cannot deliver?
- *Investment risk:* what if the investment does not generate enough value, or cannot be sold?
- *Technology risk:* what if it does not work, or does not scale in a commercial environment?
- *Financial risk:* what if the company needs more money and cannot raise any?

Courses or action that can be taken to mitigate these risks are set out in Exhibit 11.1. The more that can be done to mitigate the risks and/or to select investors who have the ability or appetite to accept the relevant risks, the better the chances of raising money.

The experience of Dr Maire Smith shows that university spinouts can minimise risks if they do not spin out too early. Early fund money is generally the most expensive when the young company is at its lowest valuation. The more that the universities and entrepreneurs can develop the business proposition by achieving proof of concept and proof of market, the further the move towards a point where external investment can be sought for better terms.

Deal with the cultural mismatch before meeting investors

The need to shift the culture of the spinout to a commercially focused entity is an important one. There is almost always a big cultural mismatch between university spinouts and investors. Too

Exhibit 11.1

How to mitigate risks

Type of risks	Actions to take
Market	1. Conduct thorough market research and reference trusted external sources to validate the size of the market.
	2. Demonstrate commercial engagement with the customer by asking potential customers what they want and/or by involving them in the product design and development.
	3. Have customers trial or buy the product and collect positive feedback.
Execution	1. At the earliest possible moment get a businessman on board, preferably one who understands and has experience of the market being entered (this could be a non-executive director or an angel investor).
	2. Prove that the product can get into the market and be sold. Do not waste too much time on product development, refining the product and adding extra features. At some stage, enough is enough – the product has to be marketed, customers engaged and sales generated.
	3. Hire a sales and marketing person instead of that extra engineer.
Investment	1. Choose an appropriate business model that will build value within the company. Relatively few venture capitalists, for example, will invest in a business that starts out by licensing technology or selling technology consulting services because the returns are generally low.
	2. Point to companies that have used the chosen business model and been successful.
	3. Try to identify a potential exit strategy by understanding who might want to buy the company and why (for example, complementary technology, market access and so on).
Technology	1. Select investors who have made prior investments in this area.
	2. Get as far down the development path as possible before raising money so that the time to product launch is as short as possible and the remaining technology risks are as low as possible.
	3. Provide evidence of customers who can talk about the benefit of the product and how much they are willing to pay to gain access to it.
Financial	1. Develop robust financial models that give reasonable visibility of how much money will be required in the future and when.
	2. Develop the correct funding strategy that ensures enough money is raised to take the company far enough down the line (at least 12, if not 24 months). This must deliver against significant milestones before the company comes to the market for more funds. Each milestone achieved will reduce risk and increases the valuation.
	3. Have a realistic idea of how much equity in the company must be sold to raise the money.
	4. Have a realistic idea of how much money can be raised given the company's stage of development and sector.

Source: Author's own.

128

many spinouts have been handicapped by the 'founder effect' – whereby the inventor-academic wants to play a controlling role in the management of the company and is reluctant to engage with other talented and experienced business people. As the following case study highlights, the 'founder effect' is typically at work in funding negotiations when some inventor-academics can be unrealistic in their valuations and in their unwillingness to dilute their equity.

Case study

Overcoming the 'founder effect' – turning scientists into commercial team players

Paul Field, Australia Technology Park Innovations, New South Wales

E-Nose Pty Ltd is a spinout from University of New South Wales (UNSW), Australia, that has addressed the 'founder effect' with the assistance and coaching of Australia Technology Park Innovations (ATPi). E-Nose was formed around 'electronic nose' technology for the detection and monitoring of odours. The technology has applications in meat processing plants, water treatment plants, multi-storey buildings and other facilities that are subject to the environmental controls laid down by government.

The Enterprise Workshop run by ATPi has been a major catalyst in this transition – exposing the founder to the full range of business issues and challenges that lie before E-Nose. The Workshop runs for a number of months and includes seminars on finance, marketing, corporate governance and other non-scientific or technical aspects to building a company. The business plan that is required from Workshop participants must address all operational and management issues. By going through the Workshop as part of a team, the E-Nose founder gained a full appreciation that his company required a multi-skilled management team and that non-executive strategic advice could be powerful. ATPi has a significant 'sweat equity' stake (ie, share of company in return for labour or services) in E-Nose and is providing high-level advice and working with the company founder to consolidate the business plan, secure investment and lock-in the first customers for its odour detection system.

Based on ATPi's experience, it is worthwhile for universities to consider supporting their academics through programmes such as the Enterprise Workshop before they set out to raise funding. The process challenges incorrect perceptions that many academics can have. In particular, it provides them with an opportunity to realise that good science is not enough to sustain a new business and that the worth of the company is not based solely on the technical excellence of the research.

Contacting investors

There are two points in the process where an entrepreneur gets to choose between investors: firstly, when he or she decides who initially to approach, and secondly, when the choice is made between two or more potential investors who have actually offered to invest. This section looks at who to initially approach. Choosing between investors is covered later.

What type of investor to approach?

Exhibit 11.2 indicates the principal different types of investors and their typical investment size and stage.

As an aside, do not forget, especially in the early stages when the company is raising relatively small amounts of money, to leverage this to draw in as much other non-equity funding as possible. Friends and family can be asked (begged, pleaded with) to provide some capital to get the company up and running. It is possible to attract matched funding in the form of government grants. University seed funds should be used to get as far as possible down the road by achieving proof of concept and proof of market. All of these sources of funding get the company further down the line, and avoids parting with expensive equity.

Furthermore, external investors are much more likely to provide capital if the company exists and is moving ahead with plans. It demonstrates commitment and progress, which is always viewed more positively by investors than someone who is sitting in a job and is not prepared to take the plunge unless someone else finances it.

Business angels and university seed funds are covered in great detail elsewhere in this book (see Chapters 10 and 4 respectively). However, corporate investors and venture capital funds deserve closer examination here.

Corporate investors

Corporate investors are companies (generally large companies, such as Intel, Siemens, BASF) who have a commercial interest in what the business is doing and are prepared to invest cash in return for taking an equity stake. The more active corporate investors usually have dedicated venture arms, which are relatively easy to identify. Corporate investors can be very beneficial to a young startup and might really help accelerate a company's development in a number of ways. They can provide:

- additional resources;
- valuable knowledge, for example, of markets; and

Exhibit 11.2

Different investor types

	Typical amount	Stage	Comment
Seed:			
Friends and family	<£50,000	Startup	Can cause sleepless nights!
Business angels	<£250,000	Early stage	Invest own money, often in sectors they know well
University/other seed funds	<£500,000	Early stage	Specialised funds
Development:			
Corporate investors	>£1 million	Prototype or beyond	Interested in access to technology, may provide revenues
Venture capital	>£1 million	At or near commercialisation	Take board seats, value add depends on track record and experience

Source: Author's own.

- endorsement, which may be of assistance in establishing credibility for the company in its supplier and customer relationships, or in raising further finance.

When considering potential corporate investors, it is important to recognise what their motives are. These might be to:

- grow the market demand for their own products;
- give a window on new technologies which are potentially important to them; and
- access new markets.

The presence of a corporate investor in the company is usually positive, but any such investment needs to be carefully matched to the objectives of the company management team and shareholders.

A note of caution on corporate investors is that making venture capital investments is usually not core to their business. Therefore a spinout company can be vulnerable in a business downcycle to decisions completely outside its control. If a further funding round is needed, it is usually important that existing investors also participate. If there is a prominent corporate (especially one that is there for endorsement purposes) who is not participating in the round it generally raises difficult questions in due diligence, and can impact on the success of fund raising.

Venture capitalists

VCs, even early stage VCs, do not fund research and will only rarely fund product development. The exceptions arise in certain sectors such as biotechnology or semiconductors, where the amount of capital required to bring a product to market is very substantial, but the rewards are correspondingly large for the winning propositions.

This means that a product must be a substantial way down the road towards being ready for market before the majority of the venture capital community can be approached. The reason for this is that their time horizon for the investment is generally three to five years, and rarely more than seven. Therefore, an entrepreneur should be honest about the business plan and ask:

- How far developed will the business be in five years?
- If at that stage the product has just been introduced to market, and the business has only small revenues, then how will the investor achieve an exit?
- Who will buy the company at that stage of its development and for how much money?

The next section looks at different types of VCs, and provides greater detail on how to work out which ones to approach.

Screening criteria

With the probable exception of friends and family, the same basic principles apply to each category of investor, in terms of how to screen them and how to approach them.

Time spent researching potential investors to select targets carefully is time well spent. Check national industry associations such as the British Venture Capital Association (BVCA), the European Venture Capital Association (EVCA) or, in the United States, the National Venture Capital Association (NVCA). These will give directories of investors and usually a brief description of their fund. Armed with a list of potential candidates, next go to the individual fund websites and investigate each one in more detail.

Websites are a great source of information, and will give some guidance as to the fund's investment criteria, which will include, at a minimum:

- stage of company development;
- sector focus;
- size of investment; and
- geography.

However, the main pages of the website are probably fairly generic, so do not just look at what they say they do, look at what they actually do.

Drawing up a shortlist of investors to approach

After having done some basic research into potential investors and matched that against the business's characteristics, a shortlist of targets must be drawn up. The kinds of additional criteria to consider include:

- What is the size of their fund and how much capacity for further investments do they have left?
- What is the fund's track record in developing substantial businesses?
- Has the investor had any notable exits?
- Does this investor have the expertise, contacts and reputation to attract other potential investors in future rounds of funding?
- Look at the individuals in the fund and identify who is the most relevant person to be speaking with about the particular proposition. What experience does this person have in the sector? What deals have they done? What boards do they sit on that can assist the business?
- What kind of return does the investor need to make on the investment?
- What is the investor's time horizon for exit?

Do not forget to ask around and get a feel for who is doing what and how they are regarded.

Raising capital on the right terms, with the right valuation, from the right investors is a fine balance. An entrepreneur needs to balance how much the business is seeking to raise against the time taken to raise it and the impact that this will have on the company. Going to a wider pool of potential investors increases the chances of success but also increases the workload. The business needs to talk to enough investors to generate sufficient momentum in the fund-raising process to close the deal, but it is difficult to be prescriptive about how many that is – it depends on market conditions and the sector. The tougher the market conditions, the more investors the business needs to approach. If the business operates in a specialist field, it needs to talk to the specialist funds. If it is in a more widely recognised field, there is more choice as to who to approach.

Approaching investors

Once the list of targets has been determined, do not waste it by sending off unsolicited e-mails. Never email a business plan blind-copied to a list of people.

An entrepreneur must get on the radar screen of the potential investor. As a general rule, business plans from people an investor does not know are treated as junk mail. They get auto-deleted, or thrown in the bin. Therefore, an entrepreneur should never send a business plan to someone he or she does not know without either:

- getting an introduction from someone he/she does know and then telephoning; or
- if it is impossible to obtain an introduction, even after having explored all six degrees of separation, calling him/her up to ask whether he would be interested in receiving the business plan before sending it.

It is always preferable to get an introduction to a potential investor, rather than telephoning out of the blue. A referral from a trusted source is much more likely to get a favourable review than an unsolicited approach. Places to look for introductions include the TTO, professional advisers (lawyers, accountants and corporate finance advisers), former portfolio companies (which have already been checked in the business's research) or by assiduous networking at various events and conferences.

The telephone pitch (or the pitch in person to the VC that an entrepreneur happens to run into at an event or conference) is vitally important. First impressions count. One of the key factors in the investor's decision about whether to invest in the business proposition is the entrepreneur. The better the entrepreneur's selling skills to potential investors, the more confidence they will have in the entrepreneur's ability to sell the product to the customers, and that helps to reduce the perception of the risk. The sales process starts the minute the investor picks up the telephone or engages in conversation with the entrepreneur.

The elevator pitch

An entrepreneur needs to prepare a very short elevator pitch. An elevator pitch is a concise summary of the investment proposal, so called because an entrepreneur should be able to give it if he finds himself riding in a (short) elevator with an investor, before the investor steps out and his attention is lost.

The elevator pitch should say, in plain English:

- what the product does;
- why that is important to the customer;
- how big the market opportunity is;
- why the business can do it better than anyone else;
- why the management team is qualified to do this; and
- how much money is needed to achieve that.

The entrepreneur should be able to deliver it in no more than two minutes. Above all, do not confuse the investor by talking about technology, using jargon and trying to tell him/her everything – keep something in reserve.

The purpose of the elevator pitch is to grab the investor's interest and make him/her want to know more. It is not a sales pitch for the product, it is a sales pitch for the investment opportunity.

The elevator pitch, as with every stage in the fund-raising process, is designed to get the business to the next stage. Therefore, do not forget to ask for next steps. This might be one of the following: 'Can I get your card? Can I send you my business plan? Can I come in and introduce the plan in more detail?'

Finally, and most importantly, do not forget to follow up. Send the plan, give the VC a few days to read it and then call him/her up to ask whether he/she is interested and to arrange the next step (a meeting).

Presenting to investors

At this point the business will have prepared a shortlist of investors, called or been introduced to the relevant individual, and sent off the business plan. What is the next step when someone comes back with a request for a meeting?

The first meeting

The first meeting is an introduction to the business.

Always prepare a presentation to provide structure to the meeting. This should be clear, concise and tell a story in a logical and easily comprehended manner. Do not present too much information and do not waste time with fancy graphics or animation. A common problem with university spinouts, in particular, is a tendency to talk about the technology and how it works, and show reams of technical results. At this early stage, what investors are interested in is how the entrepreneur will build a business and create value, so make sure the focus is on presenting the business case for investment.

In delivering the business case to potential investors, the entrepreneur should have already:

- analysed the audience:
  - who exactly from the investor's team will be there?
  - what is their background?
  - do they have any special areas of focus?
- decided who should attend from the spinout team and what their roles in the meeting will be. All speakers must come across as convincing and professional;
- anticipated likely questions;
- organised visual aids and handouts and set up necessary equipment. Avoid PowerPoint overplay; and
- rehearsed the pitch fully, using a panel of colleagues or advisers to act as the investors if possible.

At the end of the meeting:

- make sure the investors are left with a copy of the business plan – if they are interested by then they will read it, if they are not, they will 'file it'; and
- ask what the next steps are – how long will it be before the business can expect feedback?

What should the presentation cover?

Prepare a presentation of 12–15 slides that takes no more than 30 minutes to give. Take it on a laptop (preferably) or in hard copy. Assume the meeting will last one hour, which gives time for introductions and for questions, and do not outstay your welcome. A basic outline of the kind of topics to be covered in the slide presentation is as follows:

1. Introduction – a brief summary which encapsulates what the business is all about.
2. Management team.
3. Problem – describe the customer's problem, and how important it is to him.

4. Solution – describe how the product meets the customer's need.
5. Market – identify the size of the market and the timing of the opportunity.
6. Sales and marketing – describe how the product, will be sold, to whom and for what price.
7. Competition – identify how customers are currently solving this problem.
8. Financials – talk about the forecast revenues and profits and when the business can be expected to reach breakeven.
9. Funding requirement – specify how much money is needed and what that will deliver, as well as any expected funding requirements in the future.
10. Summary slide – remember to ask for the money!

Presentation style

Charles Irving of Pond Ventures, an active early stage technology VC in the United Kingdom, has several tips on presentation style and meeting etiquette.

Do:

- Research the VC. Make sure they invest in the business's space.
- Be upbeat but be honest.
- Show clearly how the business will ramp revenues.
- Be prepared to give references.
- Be prepared to admit that the entrepreneur is not the right person to run the company as it grows. In other words, a hired CEO can come in if needed.
- Check the VC out. Is he/she likable? Ask for references and conflicts of interest. Ask for examples of what they have done.
- Ask for the money!

Do not:

- Drone. Start the meeting with a few key points that capture the audience's attention, and stay brief and punchy.
- Try to impress by having notable but irrelevant people on your board.
- Forget to check the allotted time and stick to it.
- Ask for too little money because you think it will be easier to raise more later. Ask the VC what percentage of the company they need to make it worth their while.
- Forget to ask for next steps.

What questions to expect?

Most VCs will not sit quietly waiting for the presentation to finish before asking questions. They will dive right in and ask. This can be off-putting.

- Listen to the question, and answer clearly and concisely.
- Do not get flustered and put off.
- An entrepreneur should be patient, even if he or she thinks the question is stupid or the answer is blindingly obvious. Explain the answer.

The non-disclosure agreement

The author of this chapter does not ask a VC to sign a non-disclosure agreement (NDA) before a first meeting (or, worse, before receiving the business plan). The first meeting is an introduction and should be conducted on a non-confidential basis. If it is made difficult for the investor then he/she probably will not even bother to consider the proposal.

Learning from rejection

VCs invest in only a very small percentage of the businesses that apply to them for funding. The first meeting is only the beginning of the process and typically only 10–25 per cent of first meetings progress on to second and subsequent meetings. It is very important to learn as much as possible from all the meetings so that the business can improve its chances for the next one.

Always solicit feedback from each meeting. Ask for their initial impressions at the end of the meeting. If the business does receive an email saying that they are not going to proceed, a follow-up phone call should always be made to ask for the reasons behind the decision. Do not be aggressive, or defensive, but use it as an opportunity to listen and learn. Ask for suggestions as to how to increase the chances of success next time, and ask if they know of anyone else who might be suitable for the business to talk to.

If no changes are made to the presentation and slides after each meeting, then the business probably has not been listening to what the VCs are saying.

What happens next?

Once the hurdle of the first meeting is over, initial due diligence will commence. Subsequent meetings will be arranged to introduce the entrepreneur to other members of the VC's organisation. The entrepreneur needs to facilitate this, while at the same time protecting referees, especially if they are important to the business, until he or she is sure that the investor is serious about wanting to make an investment.

It is extremely important to keep the business moving forward during the time that it is engaged in fund raising.

Selection of investors

The business has gone through the process, found a couple of investors who want to invest, and they have put offers on the table (this is known as a term sheet). How does an entrepreneur select who to go with?

It is not necessary to choose the deal that puts the highest price on the company. Valuation at this stage is just a paper valuation, whereas the price paid at exit is real money that you can bank. Therefore the business needs to choose the investor who will help develop the company into the most highly valued business at exit, and with whom it can work successfully. A good investor can provide:

- valuable strategic input into the development of the company;
- advice to the management team based on their previous experiences of success and failure;
- introductions to members of their network to break into a new customer market or forge important partnerships;
- help with recruiting members of the management team and board; and
- further capital if needed, either from their own funds or by introducing new investors.

They might do none of the above. Worse, they might actually hinder the development of the company, for example, by blocking the company's ability to raise new capital if they cannot themselves provide it and do not want to be diluted.

Before making any choices the business needs to establish whether the offer that is on the table is so called 'smart money' or 'dumb money'. Perform due diligence on the potential investor. Call up the CEO of a portfolio company and ask them what they think. Ask around the market and find out what kind of a reputation the investor has (the individual who will be working with the business, as well as the fund). Ask for references and take them up. Key questions to seek answers to are:

- Are the investor's goals in line with what the business can realistically offer?
- What do other founders in the VC's portfolio companies think of him/her (especially those which failed)?
- How active was the investor in those firms?
- When things got tough, did the investor provide constructive contributions or criticise?
- Did the investors prepare well before board meetings?
- How has the VC treated founder entrepreneurs in the past?
- Is the investor's personality compatible with mine?
- How helpful will the investor be in trying to obtain future rounds of financing?
- Would the VC be willing/prefer to work with other firms and which ones?

Aside from the quality of the management team, the investor syndicate is one of the most important variables affecting the success of a new startup. As the case study below highlights, the founders and management team of a spinout should select a high-quality investor syndicate and engage the investors throughout the company building process.

Case study

Selecting investors: looking for an investor or a partner who adds real value

Kim Kamdar, MPM Capital, Boston

MPM Capital has extensive experience investing in life science companies and helping them flourish. The approach MPM capital takes is to build and sustain a close relationship with the management of its portfolio companies. The case of Genpath Pharmaceuticals illustrates the value of choosing experienced investors that are able to do more than just bring financial muscle to the spinout. The experienced investor syndicate assisted in bringing in the right management team and has helped shepherd the startup into a viable and sustainable company.

GenPath Pharmaceuticals, Inc. is a biotechnology company based in Cambridge, Massachusetts. It employs powerful, proprietary genetic model systems to discover and develop drugs against essential targets critical to the origin, maintenance, and spread of malignant tumours. GenPath is a spinout from the Dana Farber Cancer Institute and Harvard Medical School. The company began with the breakthrough of leading cancer researchers, Ronald A. DePinho MD and Lynda Chin MD, and was supported in the scientific and business arenas by luminaries in the fields of drug development, cancer genetics, cancer models and genomics.

GenPath raised its first financing round of US$15.5 million in March of 2002 by an investor syndicate group lead by Nickolas Galakatos, MPM Capital. Additional investors were Anthony Evnin, Venrock Associates, Russell Hirsch, Prospect Ventures, Greylock, Kenneth E. Weg and A. Grant Heidrich.

The founders – including Drs Ron DePinho and Raju Kucherlapati – knew from the start that they wanted more than one investor so that they could get a balanced perspective, but it was also important that there was compatibility among the group of investors that were selected. They were looking for a team with a good working relationship and mutual respect to help move Genpath towards a productive path. The founders also felt it was critical to have top-tier investment groups with a proven track record. The VC syndicate needed to be scientifically sophisticated so that they could understand the platforms and approach that Genpath would undertake, but also creative on the business side to help lead the company in the right directions. The investors needed to have tremendous experience in building companies. The Series A GenPath investors have been involved in the founding and growth of companies that have made a lasting impact on the biotechnology sector, including Genetics Institute, Caliper, Millennium, Vertex and so on, and the collective wisdom gives Genpath a lot of experience to draw from.

Since the founders knew that this was not simply a financial investment, they wanted a group with a philosophy that emphasised the long-term view. On a practical level, the founders wanted to ensure that the venture's funds were large enough to provide downside protection for the company in difficult financial market environments. It was also important for the investors to be able to help bring about corporate deals, which would provide non-dilutive revenue.

From the MPM perspective, there were several reasons to lead the investment and help create Genpath. The most significant was the outstanding quality of the founding team. The founders and their scientific advisers are leaders in cancer biology, genetics and mouse model systems, and they are uniquely positioned to discover, validate and develop antibodies/drugs against novel cancer targets. In addition, the founding team had strong intellectual property associated with their inducible-tumour assay systems. MPM was certain that the strength of the team of founding scientists and their technology would also allow the VC syndicate to attract a top management group to Genpath Pharmaceuticals. This came to fruition in June of 2002, when Tuan Ha-Ngoc and Dr. Steven Clark, former senior executives at Wyeth and Genetics Institute joined Genpath as president and CEO, and as chief scientific officer, respectively.

GenPath raised a second round of financing of US$42.7 million in August 2003 at a significant step-up in price to the initial round of financing. It has continued to recruit world-class talent, growing to a total of 65 employees. CEO Tuan Ha-Ngoc feels that one of the major reasons for the continued success of the company has been a very active group of blue-chip investors. These investors provided a strong commitment to support the base case strategy, and the vision and capacity to go beyond base case and create exceptional and rapid value through strategic transactions.

Investors working with management have been instrumental in establishing a collaborative agreement with Merck & Co., Inc. Merck is one of the leading global research-driven pharmaceutical product companies. Collaboration with Merck provides great validation for the importance and uniqueness of the Genpath technology. This will also facilitate a route to commercialisation since the deal is not just about discovering the right targets, but also about utilising Genpath's technology to ensure that the most appropriate compounds move into development, and are tested in appropriate patients. Total payments to GenPath by Merck – based on the successful commercialisation of multiple products resulting from the collaboration, exclusive of royalties – could exceed US$100 million.

Tuan Ha-Ngoc feels that his role, and the best strategy for Genpath, is engagement of the Board of Directors in the decision-making process. The investors are more than willing to lend support, assist in the recruitment of top talent, secure further rounds of financing in a timely fashion and offer operational experience. Only with the combined efforts of company management and intelligent investors can Genpath navigate through the hurdles of biotech development to turn a university spinout into a market leader.

Lessons learned: what should entrepreneurs look out for when selecting, approaching and presenting to investors?[1]

- Be patient and deliberate when seeking investors. It takes time to make an investment decision. The due diligence process can take a long time. However, it also does not hurt to find competing investors. It is difficult to raise money but, from the investors' point of view, it is equally difficult to find a good opportunity.
- Have the right psychological mindset. An entrepreneur needs to be determined, resilient, pragmatic and confident, and to work long hours to get it done.
- Make sure that individual roles are clearly spelled out. An entrepreneur should nominate a right-hand man who can focus on driving the business forward while the entrepreneur is engaged in fund raising.
- Conserve the cash – the funding process can take a long time. Focus on the cash position of the company and work on cash-generating initiatives throughout the whole process.
- Unless an entrepreneur already has good contacts and is well known by the investment community, he or she should get external help. Advisers will usually help set the valuation expectations and critique the business plan, but the most significant role they can play is effecting introductions and project managing the whole process to completion.
- Not all money is equal. Funding is not only a matter of money but also of personalities and preferences. A top group of investors brings a lot more than just a cheque to the table and the best way to attract such investors, is being able to show how a spinout will transform an idea into a substantial company.
- The investors and founders should feel that same level of excitement and passion for the startup and the relationship should be solid so that interests are aligned in the short- and long-term.

- The equity component that the founders get and the ratio of ownership is relevant. It is important to remember that founders only get equity once, while management and employees are often given additional incentives at further rounds of financing.
- Most likely, an investor will demand at least one seat on the board of directors, so an entrepreneur should choose a person he or she can work with and learn from. An entrepreneur should take money only from people who have confidence in him or her, and in whom he or she has confidence.
- When funds have been successfully raised, spend wisely and meet the milestones. This is the best way to ensure successive rounds of financing.

---

[1] Thanks to Kim Kamdar for providing this section.

Chapter 12

The process of due diligence for university spinouts

Dr Hermann Hauser and Richard Anton
Amadeus Capital Partners, Cambridge and London, United Kingdom

Introduction

This chapter is written by venture capital experts and based on first-hand experience of the due diligence process. This guide illustrates the due diligence process for university entrepreneurs and shows what to expect when a venture capital firm examines the investment opportunity in great detail. Advice is given to help entrepreneurs better prepare for due diligence and save themselves time, tears and money.

The research that a financier does before making an investment is called due diligence. This covers analysing the technology, examining the market and the defensibility of any intellectual property (IP) and assessing the team and the funding requirement over three to six years. The due diligence process can take as little as six weeks but usually takes several months, particularly in technology spinouts because many prospective customers will be in overseas markets.

Much anxiety surrounds the due diligence process, but it is neither a secret torture chamber nor a house of horrors. Everything is open and everything is up for discussion. Certainly, the results of the process form the basis of the venture capitalist's (VC's) decision on whether to invest or not to invest in a spinout or a business, but it should be viewed as an honest and detailed investigation, by professionals, into the potential for financial return. It is an extension, if you like, of the type of analysis that enthusiastic individual investors in quoted companies undertake.

Venture capital investors raise money from institutional investors, banks and corporate enterprises, usually in the form of 10-year funds. VCs invest those funds in a portfolio of companies from which its investors expect, over the life of the fund, to derive returns commensurate with the risk profile of the fund. Because early stage companies are invariably more risky than established ones, these returns need to be in excess of average public market returns over a similar period.

In the adrenaline rush of seeking and attracting funding for new technologies and product ideas, it is all too easy to lose sight of this. For those accustomed to the non-commercial environment of university research, disappointment and disillusion can follow venture capital funding if the VC's 'bottom line' has not been clearly explained at the outset. VCs have to achieve a good rate of return in order to raise their next fund and thereby continue to back new technologies.

What the VC is looking for

When investing in technology, the VC looks for an idea, a technology, a product that can be taken to market, sold to customers worldwide and that can form the basis of a significant and profitable business. For university spinouts, in practice this means a technology or product that meets a real market need, although that need may be as yet undefined. The end-product may do something that is already being done by other products on the market, but do it much better, faster, cheaper or more simply. The VC needs to assess the customer demand that a new technology might meet and have some indication, if not actual proof, that there is or will be a market.

There may be other academic institutions or the research departments of big corporations developing products or technologies to meet the same market need. Being first helps, but it is seldom enough to attract serious funding. A single-feature company will, in the end, be little more than a blip on the commercial screen. What we are looking for is evidence of continuous creativity – the ability of a team to stay ahead of the competition by constantly refining their product and deploying their technologies to develop a range of other applications.

All the technologies that form the base of such products are innovative. Many are disruptive in that they are designed to bring about a step change rather than an incremental change in the way something is done. For example, the product developed by Cambridge University spinout, Plastic Logic, was the world's first plastic transistor using inkjet printing technology. The technology enables a wide range of end-users to combine inexpensive printing processes with the flexibility of expensive electronics. With such revolutionary technologies, deciding upon the route to market is as important as checking that there might be a market.

The case study on Cambridge Silicon Radio provides a specific example of what VCs look for when deciding whether to invest in a university spinout.

Case study

Identifying and evaluating risks and opportunities

Cambridge Silicon Radio (CSR) is a spinout that developed a disruptive technology based on a new standard called Bluetooth for close-range communications. The team developed a ground-breaking single chip solution that was both a 2.4 GHz radio and a baseboard processor. This met what was, at the time, an unrealised demand from manufacturers of mobile telephones and other wireless electronic equipment, who in the late 1990s were only starting to think about related devices being connected without any wires or cables. Effectively, CSR had to create its own market.

Today, people walk around with wireless headphones for their mobile phones and use wireless desk-top applications. At the time, however, the team not only had to convince large multi-national organisations that the new technology would one day become a standard, but that any big company that could not offer that standard would be at a competitive disadvantage a few years down the road. Having a group of heavyweight investors, who firmly believed the company's products had a future, was influential in bringing in initial sales. Once one large company adopted CSR's technology, the rest realised that they had to follow suit.

Before money was invested in CSR, due diligence demonstrated several vital points:

- CSR had a unique and compelling solution to an important problem; the success of Bluetooth would depend on a highly integrated, low-cost solution and there was, in 1999, no publicly announced single chip complementary metal oxide semiconductors (CMOS) solution anywhere in the market.
- CSR also had some unique IP rights that would allow original equipment manufacturers (OEMs) to work with radio frequency chips in the same way that they were already working with digital chips.
- CSR's technology had applications way beyond Bluetooth, so in the event of our forecasts for the new standard not being met, the CSR technologies could be applied elsewhere.
- It was certainly feasible that CSR could be first to get its product to market.
- CSR's technology would provide sustainable cost advantage in a market where cost would be the most important differentiator.

The main risk lay in the viability of, and size of market for, Bluetooth. Although Bluetooth enjoyed strong momentum, Microsoft, for example, had not at that time joined the Bluetooth industry consortium. All the analyses pointed to industry-wide acceptance, but it was a risk nevertheless.

Due diligence: the steps in the process

How long does it take, who pays and for what?

The due diligence process usually takes a few months and explores in detail the team, the technology, the IP, the potential or actual customers, business models, possible or existing commercial partnerships, the financial forecasts and the legal documentation. Sometimes VCs have the skills and expertise on board to do most of the due diligence themselves. Sometimes, they will outsource parts of the process, especially if there are deep and specific technical or other particular issues, such as health, involved.

The VC initially pays for all due diligence. When a spinout becomes an investment, those aspects of due diligence that have been outsourced – technical, legal, checks on the team – are then charged back to the company. Accounting due diligence is not an issue in a university spinout as there is little or no trading history. VCs will usually use lawyers with whom they work regularly and who therefore understand what is required in the case of a spinout; technical due diligence will be outsourced to specialists known to the VC, although the founders will be invited to agree on the choice of specialist. Costs incurred through the due diligence conducted by the VC's own team are not usually charged.

The resulting analyses, reports of conversations with potential suppliers and customers, team references and financial forecasts are produced in an investment memorandum or deal qualification memorandum (DQM) of some 50–70 pages, and circulated to key members of the VC's own team. Shorter investment memoranda are produced for the team to decide upon funding for each consecutive round of finance.

University spinouts will usually require three or four rounds of finance over two to five years (in a normal economic cycle) before achieving some form of an exit for shareholders. This is done by going to the public equity markets or becoming acquired by a large company that, in the case of spinouts, will often have been a commercial partner. Some aspects of due diligence may be shared between VCs when two or three are investing in the same spinout, although generally VCs perform their own due diligence because the investment criteria and levels of expertise in specific areas will differ.

In our experience, spinout founders and teams should – and well-prepared ones do – give considerable thought to which venture capital firm might best meet their specific needs. This is important, not only because venture capital firms tend to have expertise and contacts in certain technology areas, but more so because shared values will enhance the success of the relationship.

The DQM is a confidential document and reputable VCs treat confidentiality seriously. The document forms the basis of discussion with other members of the venture capital firm's team on whether or not to proceed with funding. Most firms set certain criteria for this. In the case of the authors' firm, in order to gain the support of the team for the investment, the due diligence must reveal a good score for each of the following:

- under-served customer need;
- growth market;
- global potential;
- defensible competitive advantage; and
- strong management.

The next section discusses the specifically important areas of analysis.

Checking the spinout team

Extensive checks are made through confidential discussions with employers past and present, colleagues and collaborators about whether an individual or team have the characteristics sought to build a business. These checks usually go back many years. Professional assessments on leading team members from experienced occupational psychologists may also be obtained. This is not just to test the investor's perceptions of an individual, but to ascertain how others think he or she may cope with the very different strains and insecurities of building a business after years of relatively measured existence. It is also to assure the VC of the probity and integrity of the individuals involved.

The investor is interested in the scale of ambition in the team behind a spinout. In the United Kingdom, Amadeus Capital has proved that it can build billion-dollar businesses on the back of new technologies – witness GlobespanVirata, Cambridge Antibodies and ARM, to name three from Cambridge alone. It is precisely that level of ambition and energy needed: people who want to and believe they can build big, international enterprises.

A good VC will search internationally for people with a good track record of building and running high-growth businesses that have made their mark in their sectors. The very best CEO or chairman can only be attracted if he or she is convinced that there is a world-class team with a mould-breaking technology. So, one of the investor's key roles in the growth of the business is helping to build a team that can harness the creativity and ambition of the founders with the necessity of devising the business model, balancing budgets and taking the product to the world.

This begs other questions: are the founders capable of working in a communal organisation? Are they team players? Do they have leadership qualities or will they be better placed working as part of the team? In the process of checking the technology and its market, the VC often spends a substantial amount of time travelling and visiting companies with the founder or founders. Founders can then be observed in a range of situations to assist in assessing their ability to create a business and work as part of a team. This is a vital requirement.

VCs are sometimes asked if there is anything spinout founders can do to check whether they are the right people to build or lead a business. It is sometimes worth discussing this with head hunters. It is better still to seek out the founder of an established entrepreneurial business or spinout – a Robin Saxby of ARM or a Steve Young of Entropic – and talk to them. Serial entrepreneurs and business leaders have done it and know what it takes.

Verifying the technology

If a VC is backing a world expert in a specific area, it may be difficult to verify his or her expertise and evaluate the proof of concept. Often, a VC will have to seek out and ask rivals about this individual and his research. The academic tradition of sharing IP and publishing information is a world away from that of commerce, in which IP is used to generate profits and research usually has to be protected from competitors. So, approaching rivals and potential business competitors is, while essential in validating the market, high risk. The spinout team that has already achieved proof of concept will be several steps ahead in the process.

The verification process will often begin with visits to a number of exhibitions, conferences and company chief technical officers (CTOs). Much of this will be done with the founder. A recent investment made by the authors' firm in a business developing new technologies for high brightness light emitting diodes (HBLED) involved six months of visiting trade shows in three continents. This enabled the firm to verify the new technologies, and identify and then talk to the handful of bigger companies leading the market in the respective areas of public lighting, outdoor signage and general illumination and longer-term, domestic lighting.

An investor will also go to see big multi-nationals on their own, especially those with whom they have relationships through their own networks, especially corporate investors in their funds, to assess the interest in potential products and the levels of possible cooperation or competition.

In the case of some spinouts backed by VCs, the founding teams have already undertaken preliminary customer trials. This will always impress a VC because it demonstrates engagement with the commercial world and that the team is thinking in terms of customer needs. It does not mean that the investor will not also visit potential customers, especially those whom they are told have indicated an interest in the technology or product, but it certainly shortens the process and makes them more inclined to view the team favourably.

The best thing entrepreneurs can do to prepare themselves for this aspect of the due diligence process is not paperwork, but to get out there and meet prospective customers and partners and prepare to have a business.

Intellectual property rights

Another key area to be considered is whether the idea is defensible. Put simply: if this is so clever, why hasn't anyone else done it? Once the new product is announced, how hard will it be for anyone else to copy it? Finally, do the entrepreneurs actually own what they think they own?

The defensibility problem is particularly acute with software products. It is normally fairly easy to recreate a software product once all the hard work of thinking about what it should do has been done. Copyright only protects the exact code and exact user interface. The only real way of staying ahead of the competition is to keep developing the product so that it is bigger and better all the time. This constant stream of new revisions – 'keep pedalling', as it might be known – keeps the competition at bay, but it is extremely hard work.

It is of course possible to apply for patent protection on your technology, including new software, but the process is extremely time-consuming and normally requires expensive litigation to enforce, as countless entrepreneurs have found to their cost.

Some investors think that checking a company has some patents ensures that it has defensible technology. This is a common misperception. Often the patents refer to work that came to nothing or to a product since discontinued. Just because a company has 20 patents does not mean it has better IP defensibility than a company with three. The issue is to identify the key elements of a company's technology and to determine the way in which the IP has been, or can be, defended. A spinout can prepare for this aspect of due diligence by ensuring that suitable patents are filed and by being aware of other patents in their field.

In the current patent frenzy, it is highly likely that any new company will have inadvertently infringed outstanding patents, but it is vital for potential investors to know of potential infringements in order to assess the risk. The patent owner may come knocking on an entrepreneur's door asking for royalties, sometimes much later down the line when the spinout is big and successful.

Who owns what?

The final issue is that of who owns what. It is common in university spinouts for prior work to have been done by people who are or were, at some point, paid by the university, by government grants or in some research process funded by industry. Every one of these entities will consider that they are due a slice of any profit, even if the input has been minimal. Some universities, for example, having been criticised in the past for letting important inventions go free, now insist on a minimum stake in anything spun out by current employees.

Spinout founders need to ensure that all ownership issues are clear cut. Answering the following questions will go a long way to doing this.

- If a technology or product has been developed with any external funding, is there a licence to use that technology and what is the cost of that licence?
- Is the product only saleable with a licence from one or more existing patent holders? What if they extend and develop the technology?
- Is there a cap on any royalties paid, either over time or by amount?
- Can any of these IP holders stop the use of the licensed intellectual property rights (IPR) and, if so, under what circumstances?
- What other licences and technological paraphernalia are needed – in software, for example, what compiler, development tools and database systems are used?
- Is there a costly licence needed every year to use a vital component?
- Is there a need for customers to purchase licences for these products so that they can use the new product?

146

Serving markets with products and applications of the technology

Who is the best customer for applications of the technology?

Validating the technology will invariably bring a VC into contact with one or two key potential customers. If the response has been positive, they will then wish to gain proof of market and determine the size of that market. Sometimes they will commission market research.

VCs will also travel far and wide visiting potential customers. They can do this with the help of the founders, who may have identified or even approached them, or by going out into the market and finding them themselves. More often than not, it is a combination of the two.

Generally, VCs tend to invest in the technologies that relate to their own networks because that is where their technical and market expertise lie. A glance at the website of any VC should reveal their investors and their advisers. The corporate investors are key. Quite apart from the industrial knowledge and networking capability that they bring, corporate investors may also invest directly in the business, alongside the VC, in the first or future rounds of finance.

What is the route to market and can you access it?

The other issue the VC needs to look at closely and help with is the routes and channels to market of any product: reaching the customers. Setting up a sales force is expensive, if the market is broadly based – in other words, there are a number of companies in different sectors and geographies that might be potential customers, a partnership is often useful.

For example, Clearswift, a software developer, had to consider its routes to market carefully. The market for e-mail content security is broad – large, medium and small enterprises are all potential customers. Selling direct to companies was an option seriously considered but eventually discarded because it would have involved setting up a direct sales force. Instead, a two-tier distribution route through distributors was chosen and, through them, resellers selling direct to companies of all sizes. Research showed that both firewall and anti-virus vendors, with similar market profiles, tend to sell products this way, so it was the cost-effective way to reach the company's customers. Thus far, the route has proved successful.

What business model serves the market best?

Once the investor has agreed that there is a market for the technology under consideration, it then has to decide upon the best business model for that market. The business model is the strategy through which the VC believes the spinout can make money by charging for its technology.

In analysing the correct business model for a possible spinout, a VC will usually look at companies with comparable business models. For example, when the authors' firm was analysing the potential for Cambridge Silicon Radio, it looked closely at ARM, a company that makes money by licensing its IP rather than by selling semiconductors. Constructing and managing a semiconductor plant is horrendously expensive and simply out of the question for a new company, so that was not an option for ARM in its early days or for CSR. ARM chose the route of designing its chips and licensing other companies to produce them. This has been a successful model for ARM because, like Dolby, ARM is one of very few companies to have established a standard that people actually wanted. Customers will buy a product because it has an ARM or a Dolby name on it, in the knowledge that the proprietary instruction set and software is reliable. Manufacturers are prepared to pay for licences to produce ARM's chips for incorporation into end-users' products. CSR, however, was not producing a new standard but opening the way to a range of new applications based on unique technology. CSR designs and sells its chips, but outsources the manufacturing process undertaken on its behalf to specialist semiconductor manufacturers.

Who can help the spinout achieve speed to market?

A key aspect for any spinout is commercial partners, who may be suppliers, customers or strategic partners, who perhaps market the product in return for some access to IP. Most spinouts are developing technologies that will be part of wider solutions to business problems. In order to get the technology to market, they will need to work with another business.

The following are three examples of partnering arrangements.

- Power Paper, an Israeli company developing low-cost, flexible, micro-power sources, can produce power sources for use on novelty gifts and cards as well as in clothing. It has partnerships with companies that produce labels and with companies that can print fuel cells on to those labels. It also partners with cosmetics companies who use the micro-power sources in certain face creams to provide temporary reduction in the signs of ageing.
- Clearswift has partnerships with companies producing anti-virus scanning at the e-mail gateway.
- Cambridge Silicon Radio needed to partner with semiconductor manufacturers in order to get its chips produced.

Once the VC has completed due diligence on prospective customers and partners and agreed upon the business model, it can then review the financial plans.

Financial plans

Business plans for spinouts tend to over-estimate the importance of financial information at this stage. With no trading history, revenues or profits or losses, any accounts are irrelevant. Financial forecasts are invariably wildly optimistic. Although they certainly provide an indication that the founding team are thinking in commercial terms, the forecasts are nearly always discounted and rewritten by VCs. The important thing is to focus on costs and compare revenue forecasts with similar business models in the market.

The authors' firm generally only employs accountants to check the accounts and numbers for existing businesses. In the case of a university spinout, the firm does the checking on costs and forecasts in the light of the other areas of due diligence, especially customers and partners, and mindful of the firm's own requirements as investors. The firm needs to be confident in making an investment that the business it is supporting stands a good chance of making the returns that meet the expectations of its own investors.

The authors' firm also works on the assumption that every spinout will need several rounds of finance, and takes that into account in the due diligence process. The return multiples aimed for will be higher in the seed and first rounds, as the risk of failure is higher. As the enterprise develops, the risk of failure reduces and so, accordingly, will the return multiples that the financiers expect on each successive round. The table in the authors' firm's DQM that summarises thinking and that has to meet their own criteria is called the Return Analysis (see Chapter 13 for further discussion of this subject). It addresses five points:

1. return multiple on the particular round of financing;
2. return on future projected rounds;

3. amount of investment in current round;
4. total likely investment; and
5. gross cash returned.

Legal due diligence

Anyone seeking to spin a company out of a university should engage a lawyer. The company has to be established and registered with proper shareholders. More important, the lawyer must assess whether the company being set up has the appropriate assets and especially has rights to the relevant IP.

The issues involved in spinning out IP can be complex, particularly if the university asserts any right to retain a stake in order to generate royalties.

The majority of VCs prefer to see a clean break, because this is in the long-term interests of the company. The new business should, with the venture capital backers if necessary, negotiate to have current and future IP assigned to it in exchange for the university having some equity in the business.

The legal checking on the business at the time of funding is formulaic. There is, quite simply, a substantial amount of detailed information that the lawyers, on behalf of the investors, need for the investment process to happen. Some of this may not apply to very early stage companies, university spinouts or otherwise, but the checklist is an important facet of due diligence. The list is far, far longer than one might at first imagine. It is set out in the appendix.

Some tips for preparing for the due diligence process

When preparing information for the VC's due diligence, the key thing for an entrepreneur to remember, as with the whole relationship with investors, is openness. If, at any stage, there is suspicion of information being hidden, trust is damaged and once damaged is very hard, if not impossible, to repair. The checklist below outlines what an entrepreneur needs to prepare for the VC's due diligence process.

- Detailed information on the technology and its potential applications.
- Notes on any validation you have undertaken with potential customers and partners.
- How you see the market in terms of sectors, size, geography and so on.
- Business plan.
- Full details of all team members plus referees.
- Financial forecasts.
- The appropriate legal material from the lists above.
- IP details (patents granted or applied for, further IP that might be defensible).
- Details of any potential suppliers or commercial partners.
- Customer and partner referees.
- Details of the laboratory or university department where the IP has been developed.

Appendix

Checklist for legal due diligence

Company information

- Certificate of incorporation
- Memorandum and articles
- Statutory books
- Shareholder consents
- Share or loan capital details
- Other corporate bodies involved in the business
- Issue of share or loan capital
- Purchase of own shares
- Changes in shareholding or officers
- Company name
- Location of business and registration
- Ownership of company

The business

- Principal activities
- Change in nature of business
- Sale of undertakings
- Group reorganisation
- Trust deed or debenture or unsecured loan stock
- Shareholdings in subsidiary undertakings
- Share options
- Partly paid shares
- Distributions
- Material changes since last accounts

Trading matters

- Details required
- Major contracts
- Effect of change of control
- Details of other transactions
- Investigations and proceedings

Assets

- Sale and leaseback
- Good and marketable title
- Intergroup leasing

Finance

- Bank accounts
- Debentures, mortgages and financial arrangements

Borrowings and other liabilities

- Overdraft and borrowings
- Material liabilities

Taxation

- Tax residency
- Tax computations and assessments
- Material matters in dispute
- Book value and tax written down values
- VAT arrangements
- Rates of tax
- Tax liabilities
- Tax losses and allowances
- Material change

Properties

- Properties owned
- Liabilities for properties

Environmental matters

- Pollution and hazards
- Effluents, waste and pollutants
- Consents, approvals and licences
- Complaints, claims and investigations

Employees

- Persons employed
- Wage and salary scales
- Organisation structure
- Bonus and incentive schemes
- Wage claims and bonus awards
- Trade union membership
- Agreements and disputes
- Strike action
- Redundancies and rationalisation
- Golden handshakes
- Material change

Pension schemes

- Pension, retirement and death benefit schemes
- Details of schemes
- Basis of scheme
- Documentation and structure of scheme
- Ex gratia payments

Litigation

- Litigation pending
- Arbitration and dispute resolution
- Disputes and claims
- Potential liability

Health and safety

- Policies and management
- Hazardous substances

Insurance

- Current policies

Intellectual property

- Intellectual property assets

Other matters

- Data protection
- Connected persons
- Business interests of directors

Chapter 13

Structuring the transaction: the key elements

David J. Brophy
University of Michigan Business School, Center for Venture Capital and Private Equity Finance, Ann Arbor, Michigan

Wassim R. Mourtada
CrystalPoint Partners, Ann Arbor, Michigan

Introduction

This chapter and Chapter 14 introduce a framework to help company founders negotiate the structuring of a financing transaction from angels and venture capitalists (VCs). For the sake of simplicity, it treats the structuring of a deal with angels in the same way as VCs, given the increasing sophistication of the angel investment community. While consistent with financial structure theory, this chapter offers the discussion and framework in a way that can be put into practice by company founders in a reasonably straightforward manner.

In the process of starting and building a company, especially one based on high technology that requires external risk capital, there is no single element that is likely to be as contentious or controversial to a founder as the process of structuring the transaction – the subject of this chapter.

This is due to the fact that this process involves issues of critical importance to both founder and investor.

- The economic elements of the deal comprise the questions: what is the venture worth as it stands, or what is the 'pre-money valuation'? How are the gains and losses to be split?
- The control elements of the deal comprise the question: who makes the major strategic and operating decisions?

In fact, both the founder and the financier are interested in maximising their profit and maintaining the maximum amount of control in order to protect their interests. The terms of a transaction, both overt and subtle, exist to make this explicit, and to place a set of incentives and disincentives to enforce the kind of behaviour and decision-making on the part of both the founder and financier that maximise potential profits and minimise total risks.

While the complexity of this may seem to validate many entrepreneurs' fears of dealing with a professional financier, in reality most competent VCs are experienced individuals who have participated in this process many times and behave rationally around their key objective: making a stellar return on their investors' capital invested in the new company. If this is kept in mind, most of a venture capital firms' posture, attitude, approach, incentives and motivations can be clearly understood. Indeed, all control elements of a deal exist to engender the correct economics.

In the most rational vein as well, most professional VCs realise very clearly that their objective can be best achieved by having the incentives of the founder aligned with their own. In plain English, this means that the VCs realise that the founder needs to be in a position to truly maximise his or her profit, in order that he or she properly serves the company such that the VCs profit as well.

While this may seem obvious or trivial, it is often the case that founders impute other motivations to VCs such as economic development, building companies for the future or bringing exciting next generation products to market. At the other extreme, some founders will take issue with a VC's singular focus on investment profitability, because it has little regard to other noble causes such as curing ill people, job creation or building durable companies.

While some of these motivations and others within this vein are exhibited by many of the best firms, this should not be confused with the primary investment objective, especially when it comes to structuring the transaction. In selecting a venture capital firm with which to negotiate, the founder should exercise due diligence to determine the reputation that the investor enjoys in this respect within the entrepreneurial and financial communities.

The venture capital fund

An insight into the structure of venture capital firms shows how and why this set of motivations is enforced. The venture capital firms structure their investment pools as limited partnerships. The fund manager (the general partner or GP) bears the end-risk and investor (limited partner or LP) liability is limited.[1] The investors or 'sponsors' of venture capital firms may include high net worth individuals, strategic corporate investors, and institutional investors such as pension plans, insurance companies and university endowments. Essentially, limited partners capitalise the fund and the venture capital firm manages it. The venture capital firm draws a management fee from the fund to cover overheads and operating expenses such as salaries, rents, consultants, travel and legal fees. These management fees are not expected to be a source of profit for the VCs.

A fund typically has a lifespan of 10 years, often with a discretionary two years' extension available for the purpose of liquidating portfolio companies. Over the first three years of a fund's life, on average, the VCs look for companies in which to invest and make their initial investments. Over the next four years, few new investments are made and most of the effort is directed to supporting and growing existing investments in what are, at this point, called portfolio companies. This may include making follow-on investments in portfolio companies that have already been funded. Starting as early as practicable, usually at the beginning of the fourth or fifth year of the fund, the VCs begin looking for and executing exit strategies for their investments, harvesting value from these deals and distributing net gains to limited partners and to themselves. That means that they look to take their portfolio companies public or to sell them to a strategic buyer in order to recoup their investment at a profit (see Exhibit 13.1).

As the fund's investments are liquidated, the general partner first returns to the limited partners their original investment. Beyond that point, all profit in the fund (capital gains) is distributed, usually on an 80–20 per cent basis in favour of the limited partners. This means that the VCs themselves (the GPs) do not make any substantial profit individually until and unless they make a profit for their investors (the LPs).

Exhibit 13.1

Introduction to the venture capital process

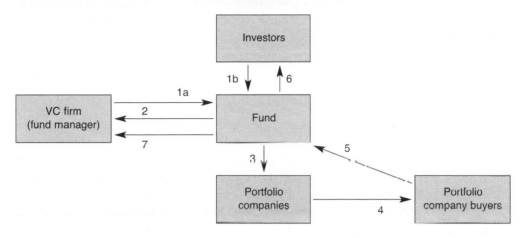

Event	Description
1a	Venture capital firm invests 1–5 per cent of the fund's capital and provides management
1b	Investors contribute 95–99 per cent of fund's capital
2	Fund receives an annual 2 per cent management fee to finance day-to-day operations
3	Fund makes investment in portfolio company
4	Portfolio company shares are sold to the public market or to a strategic buyer
5	Proceeds of sale go to the fund
6	Investors in the fund receive their initial investment and 80 per cent of the profits
7	Venture capital firm receives 20 per cent of the profits

Source: Authors' own.

The same philosophy and discipline that exists between LPs and the GPs is carried over to the contractual relationship between a venture capital fund and its portfolio companies. Founders of the portfolio company can expect to have expenses met (presuming adequate performance) but can reap true profits only when they have been able to make money for their investors.

The venture capital deal process

The other chapters in this book explain the critical elements of business planning and the 'how to' of approaching and presenting to investors. This chapter ties in both these elements as they relate to the actual structuring and negotiation of an investment from a professional venture capital firm.

The first element of structuring: determining the total financing needs over time

When beginning to think about structuring, the first and foremost question that an entrepreneur asks is: what is the valuation? The corollary questions follow. How much does an investor take? How much do I keep? How much are my shares worth? This approach, while common, may lead to deal myopia, where an entrepreneur ends up focusing on the wrong elements (the short-term ones) at the expense of the long-term, value-creating interests of the company.

The authors recommend that a company founder take a much broader and higher level view of financing the company beyond any single financing event. The founders should focus on creating and refining the strategic, operating and resource plan of the company and the financial plan that emanates from it. The financing plan of the company should flow from the financial plan, focusing first upon how much finance to raise and when, and then upon proper capital structure and sources of financing.

Financing events

Individual financing events are sequential, intricately linked together, and should be focused upon matching appropriate sources and uses of capital funds. Valuation, terms and conditions of funding (in other words, essentially the 'marginal cost of capital' of the firm) reflect the accomplishments of the emerging company up to that point, with extent and degree of success influencing the ability to raise subsequent financing on acceptable terms of valuation and structure. This success emanates less from slavish adherence to the linear and unchanging details of a plan and more commonly from the founders' entrepreneurial nimbleness in response to market, competitive, regulatory or technological opportunities.

Each financing event is designed to provide the resources needed to proceed with the development of the firm and is essentially predicated on the completion of building blocks and the achievement of milestones. Many elements that affect structuring of any single transaction are determined far in advance of the actual negotiation and structuring of any specific deal. The key element becomes proper planning and execution.

The founder should think about structuring the financing of the company over its entire development and through the point at which the continued requirements for external equity-based risk capital are eased, which, for the sake of this discussion, we shall call the tipping point.[2] Only within this context can an appropriate structure for any individual financing event be conceived of effectively and evaluated fairly.

Thus, the first question that must be asked is how much money the company needs to raise to get to the tipping point. This chapter and the next take an imaginary case study and carry it through to illustrate these issues.

Case study

University Research Commercialization Inc.

Imagine that a company, University Research Commercialization Inc. (URCI), produces an inert and synthetic nano-material (NanoStain) that can decompose lipids and other elements of stains. The technology was developed by a professor at the National Scientific University. The intended marketing strategy is for the company to market the product directly to industrial cleaners that service commercial properties such as office buildings and hotels. It will also seek to partner with a large consumer goods company to develop a branded consumer product that can be sold through supermarkets and retailers. The professor has been able to synthesise laboratory quantities of this material and to test it on a limited number of types of stains over a short period of time.

In the case of URCI, the financial plan estimates that the company will require about US$20 million in total to run broader tests for effectiveness and safety, to develop a large-scale synthesis process for the material and to market their non-branded product to commercial customers.

The simple fact of the matter is that no single financier will provide all of the money up-front to fund any company through to that point. First and foremost, the risk of the venture is too high up-front to pre-commit all the financing. Secondly, very few financiers have the means to fund a company entirely on their own. Thirdly, if the financiers did have the means, the cost of capital to the entrepreneur in valuation and control would almost certainly be considered too high.

The second element of structuring: the right financing at the right time from the right financier

The estimate of total capital needs brings into focus a second element of venture capital finance structuring: the concept of 'staging'. The capital required for the development of a company over its life cycle is available in smaller parcels from specialised providers.

Funds specialisation

Typically, venture capital firms specialise by technology or markets, by geography and, most relevantly in this case, by stage.

The stage specialisation of venture capital firms is reflected by (a) the amount of money that they are prepared to invest in any one company, as well as (b) the level of personal involvement that they are willing to commit to any single investment.

- Seed stage venture capital firms are willing to invest a few hundred thousand US dollars to around US$3–5 million and are genuinely available to work with their startup companies, even to the point of taking on an interim management role such as CEO or head of business development.
- Early stage venture capital firms are willing to invest US$2–10 million, but require a core management team to be in place and have sufficient commercial and technical validation of the company's market and products. They are willing to work as active board members in guiding the company's development, introducing it to appropriate customers and strategic partners and aiding in critical negotiations.
- Later stage VCs are willing to invest anywhere between US$10 million and US$50 million, but tend to be financially oriented and will typically invest only once the financial picture of the company is clear. They will add value by working with the management to achieve appropriate liquidity for the investors and founders.

Strategic corporate partner

Another class of financier is the strategic corporate partner. While the perception is that they only invest in later stages, they tend to be open to involvement at the earlier stages, depending on the strategic relevance of the startup to their future direction. Founders should be aware that VCs generally prefer to invest ahead of strategic investors due to what is often called the 'strategic pricing premium'. In general, strategic corporate investors can profit from an investment in a young company in several ways.

- As a minority investor with an eye toward eventually buying the company and its technology, the strategic investor can 'try it before they buy it' to test the effectiveness of the technology on its cost improvement, efficiency or product efficacy before involving the company and its technology directly in their primary business through acquisition.
- Should the company prove not to be a strategic fit, but to have value in other market applications, the strategic investor may pursue and participate in an exit from their investment through trade sale of the company or in initial public offering (IPO).

Strategic buyer versus financial buyer

Because of this flexibility, strategic investors are often willing to pay a premium price at an early stage of the company's life. Because VCs are 'financial' buyers, they often find the strategic valuation too high for their return expectations and decline to invest at that price at that stage. VCs prefer to invest before strategic investors, thus sharing the strategic premium with the founding investors and achieving a step-up in valuation at the strategic round. Founders should be aware of this condition, the reason for which is not always intuitively obvious to a first-time founder. A founder of a company must match the phase of the company development to the amount of money needed for that phase and match both to the source of money that is oriented to finance that amount of capital investment for that development phase.

In the process of staging investment, most of the investment triggers and hurdles revolve around the achievement of 'milestones', which may be classified according to the headings below.

Internally significant milestones (ISMs)

ISMs are the kind of milestones that are important to track progress over short periods of times such as weeks or months.

An example of an ISM for URCI is reaching an agreement with a carpet and furniture manufacturer to supply the company with 2,000 samples of fabrics that are used in the vast majority of households and commercial buildings. While this is critical to the company, it does not in itself validate any of the prospects of the company or clearly eliminate any perceived or actual risks.

Externally significant milestones (ESMs)

ESMs are the kind of milestones that conclusively resolve the kinds of questions that a rational risk-reducing external party looks for as genuine and robust validation of the company's prospects.

An example of an ESM for URCI is the successful testing of the material against the variety of fabric types with the large variety of stains to demonstrate that it clears the stains without harming the fabric.

The most important feature of ESMs is that their achievement is a strong trigger for new third parties to become involved in the financing because the new investors' 'expectation hurdle' has been met. New third parties, such as venture capital firms or corporate partners, are willing to become involved at different stages, given improvement in the risk profile at successive stages. It is important for the entrepreneurial management team to be aware of what 'triggers' or 'hurdles' are important for the different parties that the company needs to have involved. This will enable the team to plan the company's development rationally to meet these triggers and hurdles.

Plan financing around ESMs

Many company founders make the mistake of planning involvement of new parties, especially financiers or strategic partners, around ISMs, and are disappointed by a response that translates roughly into: 'So what?'

Most ESMs revolve around answering some of the 'critical open questions' regarding the viability of the company's technology, market and management's ability to execute. Some of the early stage 'open questions' that revolve around NanoStain are:

- does the material work on a large variety of fabrics combined with a large variety of stains?
- is it economically feasible to synthesise the material in a large-scale fashion?
- will the market actually support the product?

Structuring milestones and stages around answering these critical open questions, and achieving ESMs, are the entrepreneur's best bet for continued support from the professional investment community and from corporate partners.

A possible staging scenario for URCI is as follows.

- *Round 1:* US$2 million
  The financing from this round will be invested in the testing of the NanoStain compound against a very large variety of fabrics and stains. The success of this will validate the technical viability of the product from a commercial perspective.

  Financiers of this round are likely to be either private individuals or a seed/early stage venture capital firm.
- *Round 2:* US$6 million
  The financing from this round will be invested in developing a process for the large-scale manufacture of the NanoStain compound, which has so far only been synthesised in a laboratory setting. This is critical because this class of nano-material has not been synthesised in commercial quantities before.

  Simultaneously, and building on the success of the testing undertaken in Round 1, URCI will seek a commercial partner to co-develop and market a branded consumer version of the product.

  This round is likely to be financed by an early/mid-stage venture capital firm.
- *Round 3:* US$12 million
  Based on the successful design of a large-scale synthesis process in the previous phase, as well as the successful acquisition of a product development partner for the branded consumer product, the company will build a small plant to produce the material. In parallel, the company will build up a small sales force to market the non-branded product directly to commercial building cleaning firms.

  This round is likely to be financed by a later stage venture capital firm, as well as the strategic partner that is working on the branded product.

This makes for a tricky balancing act because, in practice, things rarely turn out as predicted: it almost always takes more money and time to reach the appropriate milestones and the providers of capital are rarely prepared to inject it at the time that it is needed.

The third element of structuring: the right valuation

Perhaps the most important concept for the company founder group to understand in negotiating deal structure is 'the pre-money valuation of the firm'. This refers to the value of the company mutually agreed upon by entrepreneur and financier as a basis on which the outside investment will be made. It is the value of what the founder 'brings to the table'. This estimate of value reflects:

- the assets and characteristics of the company, which may include proprietary technology protected by a family of defensible patents;
- a solid management team with a proven track record of success in relevant businesses; and
- a business plan built on a winning business model that maps the way to business success and a 'harvest value' within four or five years by IPO, merger or acquisition that will achieve or exceed the investor's target rate of return.

Pre-money value is a major point of negotiation in venture capital financings. When combined with the amount to be invested, pre-money value determines the percentage of the firm's equity that will be exchanged for the new capital raised. The most important activity of the founder seeking to raise new external capital is to take steps specific to his or her company and its market to maximise its pre-money value. This will involve maximising the quality of its technology, its management team and its business plan. The criteria set forth in Exhibit 13.2 serves as an example of standards to which the entrepreneur might aim in order to maximise the firm's pre-money value.

The importance of pre-money value raises the question of its proper calculation so as to produce a mutually acceptable value upon which a deal may be based.

Methods of valuing startups

Valuation is considerably more difficult in the case of early stage companies than mature companies, given the lack of a proven track record. Wide variance in estimates will typically exist and provide a major challenge to parties who otherwise may wish to proceed with structuring a deal. Certain understandable biases become evident. The founder may have a lofty impression of the value of the resources that he or she has assembled. Meanwhile, the investor – based upon personal investment experience – may apply a healthy discount rate to reflect an expectations 'gap' as well as the risk of startup companies in general and the dilutive effect of the future rounds of financing that the investor knows will be required.

Unfortunately, and often unsatisfactorily for the technically minded individuals who are typically responsible for university-based spinouts, the valuation of startups is not a rigorous science. It is more of an approximated approach. This approximation is (usually) firmly grounded in the realities of financing the early stage companies. VCs know from experience that there are far more outright failures of startup companies than most entrepreneurs would like to believe. Also, every early stage company needs to raise substantial follow-on financing that is dilutive to early investors. Furthermore, exit valuations, except in rare cases (which also happened to be the ones that are most publicised), rarely meet expectations.

While analysis of comparable companies and deals appears to provide a ring of authenticity to valuation estimates, it may carry a 'survivorship bias' that must be recognised. Ideally, all current and past deals comparable to the instant deal should be analysed. The analysis should include the successful companies, the outright failures (in other words, the

Exhibit 13.2

Four components of a 'super-deal'

Team A core team that has worked together previously and has had success in building a company in the relevant industry. In the case of a spinout, a scientific 'star' leading the company's development effort.	**Financing** Low to moderate needs for contined venture capital-based financing. A large appetite by potential follow-on investors and public market to invest in the company's later stages
Technology/product Highly differentiated product serving explicit needs of customers that other products do not. Product and technology is protected by a set of issued robust patents, as well as trade secrets.	**Market** Growing multi billion dollar market served by a very small set of players. Company has an unrestricted access to market channels.

Result in a highly profitable company that can be sold to a strategic buyer or taken public at a very large valuation premium.

Source: Authors' own.

writeoffs) and the 'living dead' (the firms barely hanging on to life with little promise of an investors' harvest). Because data on the second two categories is usually scarce, there is a bias toward using only the successful firms in the analysis. An adjustment in value is usually made to account for the 'likelihood that the instant deal will achieve a degree of success similar to that of the comparable'.

A good 'certification' of the value of the deal is the ease with which the founders can assemble a set of investment offers from among the market set of VCs. As attractive as this process may seem to the founder, it has its unique costs as well. The process of fund raising is very time intensive and travelling can also become expensive. On the very negative side in distributing the 'pitch book' to prospective investors, the company runs the risk of giving away competitive information to rivals who may use this information against the firm. VCs are reluctant to sign non-disclosure agreements (NDAs) unless they are thoroughly convinced that they have an inside track on getting an exclusive position in the deal. In any event, NDAs are only as good as the ability of the company to pay for legal pursuit of remedies.

Basis of a VC's valuation

In practice, the basis of a VC's valuation estimate starts at the very 'end' of the investment cycle with an estimate of what the most realistic exit value in four to five years is likely to be. This is largely an experiential number, based on the collective experience of the venture capital industry under similar or projected circumstances. From that point, VCs will calculate how much additional external equity capital investment they believe this venture will require. They will match up future financing amounts ('financing rounds') to where they believe appropriate milestones exist.

Venture capital firms investing in the different stages of a company's development have different return expectations. The later stage investors have lower expectations than the early stage investors, due to the comparatively reduced risk that they are underwriting. Exhibit 13.3 sets out some rules of thumb regarding investor expectations.

While this is a very simplified schema of return expectations, there is a significant amount of information 'baked' into that number that allows for relative risk, stage of development of the company and the state of capital markets.

Following industry practice, the returns above are expressed in terms of multiples of amount invested (also known as cash-on-cash) rather than internal rate of return (IRR). IRR can be thought of as the rate of growth of the value of an investment over a specified period of time. While both should, arguably, be calculated and used, investors seem more comfortable with the 'cash-on-cash' approach than with the IRR approach. The differentiating element between the two measures is the time dimension: how much time is assumed to elapse between rounds and until 'harvest'? Despite the widened adoption of more complex valuation and discounting methodologies in other areas of finance, VCs are still most comfortable with 'cash-on-cash' returns coupled with simplified assumptions of assumed time requirements between financing rounds and exit opportunities.

Demonstrated example

To demonstrate how a VC might think of the financing plan of a firm from startup through several rounds and on to exit, assume that the projected 'reasonable' exit value of URCI is estimated to be US$100 million. This exit valuation is a 'comparable' based on the historical record of acquisitions by the cleaning chemicals industry of companies in 'new product' categories with proprietary technology, market leading position and robust, growing revenues.

Exhibit 13.4 represents a simplified[3] backwards valuation calculation, which is typical for investments structured by VCs.

The 'Total return expected (US$ basis)' is calculated by multiplying the 'Amount invested' by the 'Return expectation (multiple basis)' from Exhibit 13.3. The 'Required ownership at exit (ROAE)' is calculated by dividing the 'Exit value' by the 'Total return expected'.

Exhibit 13.3

Return expectations

Round of investment	Return expectation (multiple basis)
First VC round	10–15x
Second VC round	5–10x
Mezzanine round	2–5x

Source: Authors' own.

Exhibit 13.4

Hypothetical valuation and equity requirement calculations (US$ million)

Exit value: 100

Investment round	Amount invested	Return expectation (multiple basis)	Total return expected (US$ basis)	Required ownership at exit (%)	Required ownership at investment (%)	Implied post-money valuation at investment	Implied pre-money valuation at investment
Series C	12	2	24	24	24.0	76	64
Series B	6	5	30	30	39.5	15.2	9.2
Series A	2	10	20	20	43.5	4.6	2.6

Source: Authors' own.

This is a critical number and determines the final ownership of the company that a venture capital firm needs to have at the time of exit to realise the return requirements for their investment.

From there, the VCs will calculate what their 'Required ownership at the time of investment (ROAI)' is to account for subsequent dilution by follow-on investments. In this case, Series C investors are involved in the last investment round and as such they do not get diluted by follow-on investments and therefore their ROAI is the same as their ROAE.

The calculation for the ROAI is calculated by dividing the ROAE by the 'Dilution factor (DF)'. DF is in turn calculated as:

$$DF = \prod (1-ROAE)$$
Using the ROAE of all subsequent financing rounds

This is the cumulative product of (1–ROAI) for each subsequent investment round. For example, the calculation of DF for the Series A investment, would be:

$$DF_{\text{Series A}} = (1-ROAI_{\text{Series B}}) \times (1-ROAI_{\text{Series C}})$$
$$DF_{\text{Series A}} = (1-39.5\%) \times (1-24.0\%)$$
$$DF_{\text{Series A}} = 45.98\%$$

Therefore:

$$ROAI_{\text{Series A}} = ROAE_{\text{Series A}}/DF_{\text{Series A}}$$
$$ROAI_{\text{Series A}} = 20\%/45.98\%$$
$$ROAI_{\text{Series A}} = 43.5\%$$

The 'Implied post-money valuation at investment' is calculated by dividing the 'Amount invested' by the ROAI. 'Pre-money valuation' is arrived at by subtracting 'Amount invested' from 'Post-money valuation'.

Founder's perspective

This process mirrors the steps that were prescribed in the previous section for the company founder to go through in planning financing. Being judicious and realistic in this process and its necessary estimates pays genuine dividends in reaching a most reasonable deal with the financiers, by matching expectations, seeing eye-to-eye and building trust. By doing so, the founder will have progressed a long way toward structuring a deal that is favourable to his or her company.

From a founder's perspective, it is often the case that the percentages they are being asked to give up in these circumstances are greater than their initial expectation. This is especially so for the first investment, which includes an allocation for an employee pool.

Again, it is important to look at this from the total perspective. That is to say, that when all is said and done, what is the actual monetary value of the founder's shares at exit? Exhibit 13.5 carries forward the example shown above, but from a founder's perspective.

At the end of the day, that founder needs to ask himself or herself whether or not the whole experience is worthwhile in order to understand the value of risk capital in enabling the startup and operation of the company.

As for the remainder of the equity that is not shared between the founder and subsequent groups of investors, it is reserved for and distributed to managers, employees and directors of the company. See the section 'Shares reserved for employee compensation' in Chapter 14 for a more detailed discussion.

Exhibit 13.5

Founder's equity

	Percentage of ownership (%)	Value of company (US$ million)	Implied founder's equity value (US$ million)
At founding	100	0	0
After Series A	37	4.60	1.68
After Series B	22	15.20	3.36
After Series C	17	76.00	12.77
At exit	17	100.00	16.80

Source: Authors' own.

Conclusion

Founders may draw several important conclusions concerning deal structuring from the material presented and discussed in this chapter. The authors suggest that the most important of these are presented below.

- *Plan ahead*
  Determine the need for a financing partner. If the company's ability to accumulate earnings lags behind its growth rate, an equity-financing partner is needed to achieve fast growth. If this is the situation, the founder must learn to live with the terms, conditions and responsibilities involved in a financial partnership.

  The founder must understand the total capital needs and the overall sources and uses of the capital.

  The founder should make sure that the business breaks up its capital requirements into stages that will match its properly defined ESMs and will accommodate the needs of the company, as well as the availability of capital from appropriate classes of investors.
- *Negotiating strength and leverage come from only two sources*
  Execution. Good execution on all fronts will increase the credibility of claims made by the company and reduce actual and perceived risk. This in turn will allow any single investor looking at the company to give the company some benefit of the doubt, which can be reflected in an improved valuation or improved terms.
  Competition for the deal. The more recognised and relevant investors there are genuinely interested in making the investment, the fairer the pricing of the investment will be. At the same time, it is rare for investors to overbid pricing in such scenarios.

  Further, investors are interested in companies that execute well: the two points mentioned above are tied together.
- *Focus on the end goal*
  The goal should be to build a robust and viable company that can deliver on its initial promise of bringing a relevant product to satisfy a real market demand and to create wealth for the founders, employees and investors of the company.

Despite the dilutive aspect to founders' equity of raising external capital, and the rigour and discipline to be expected from professional venture capital investors, the opportunity does exist for the founders to reach that goal.

---

[1] While an increasing number of funds are formed as limited liability corporations (LLCs), this chapter and the next focus on the more common limited partnership structure.

[2] Often, this is judged to be the point of profitability or cash-flow breakeven. The fact of the matter is that most high-growth companies continue to require external capital to fund growth beyond profitability or cash-flow breakeven. However, at such a point, the relative abundance of capital and the diversity of its sources (growth capital funds, public markets, corporations) allow for some simplification.

[3] The key simplification is that the exclusion of terms such as Liquidation Preferences and Dividends (explained later) are excluded from the structure of the investments.

Chapter 14

Structuring the transaction: term sheet and deal structure

David J. Brophy
University of Michigan Business School, Center for Venture Capital and Private Equity Finance, Ann Arbor, Michigan

Wassim R. Mourtada
CrystalPoint Partners, Ann Arbor, Michigan

Introduction

Following on from Chapter 13, in this chapter the authors look at the term sheet and discuss its key features.

The term sheet: summarising the deal structure

This chapter continues to use the hypothetical example discussed in the previous chapter, University Research Commercialization, Inc (URCI).

URCI has now reached the stage where it is satisfied with the multi-stage financing plan and the implied valuation estimates by stages set out in the previous chapter. How might the first round of venture capitalisation be structured? The terms that reflect the structure of a deal are set forth in detailed and legalistic language in later documents, principally the stock purchase agreement, the shareholder's agreement (sometimes referred to as the information and registration rights agreement) and articles of incorporation.

A concise summary of the above investment agreements is provided by the term sheet, which has far fewer pages and is a useful form in which deal structure may be presented, analysed and perhaps renegotiated. The key here is to recognise that the term sheet is only a summary of a whole lot of details that will be memorialised in later documents.

The term sheet and the documents that it summarises spell out the mutual rights and responsibilities of the parties contracting for the exchange of capital in return for securities at each financing event over the lifetime of URCI. The capital to be raised by URCI in this financing event will take the form of a private equity investment by Big Venture Fund, LP. Big Venture Fund is a limited partnership that specialises in making investments in companies like URCI that have not yet achieved cash-flow breakeven, or the 'tipping point' in the life cycle referred to in the previous chapter.

Unlike the shares in a public offering sanctioned by the Securities and Exchange Commission (SEC) for trading in the public capital market, the securities exchanged for cash in such a deal have transfer restrictions that prohibit them from being freely bought and sold. The stock purchase agreement will contain, among other things, appropriate representations and warranties of the company, and covenants of the company reflecting the provisions set forth in the documents. An opinion of counsel to the company as to the validity of the shares being issued and other customary matters will be delivered at the investment closing, along with the documents for signing. The company will pay at closing reasonable legal fees and expenses.

The URCI example is helpful in understanding the contents of the term sheet and in demonstrating the purpose of the various terms both singly and relative to each other in the deal structure. By analysing the term sheet, the meaning of certain terminology can be clarified and it is possible to understand how certain provisions (covenants or agreements) in the term sheet achieve the economic and control objectives referred to in the previous chapter.

By modifying some of the terms, it is then possible to analyse how one combination of terms may be more or less favourable to the founder under different outcomes of the company's performance. This provides a framework for understanding deal structures by comparative analysis of term sheets, and deriving a sense of how the covenants define the sharing of economic benefits and control between founder and investor. It will be useful for the reader at this point to become familiar with the contents of the URCI term sheet in Appendix A so as to follow better the discussion that follows.

The description of the financing

As stated in the opening sentence of the term sheet at Appendix A, at this point the term sheet is not a firm offer. In practice, the founder should consider it as the venture capitalist's (VC's) 'first volley' in the negotiation of the financing. The 'description of financing' section spells out the basic elements of the offer: amount to be invested, the type of security to be exchanged for the investment, the number of shares of stock to be purchased, the price per share, the closing date and ownership of the company in common stock terms post-investment. The ultimate binding offer of final negotiated terms is contingent upon the investor completing a satisfactory 'due diligence' examination of the company and the deal.

Term sheet description of financing

Exhibit 14.1 summarises the principal terms of venture capital financing for University Research Commercialization, Inc. (the 'Company') as offered by Big Venture Fund, LP.

The description of financing shows that Big Venture Fund is offering terms under which it will consider investing US$2 million in URCI in exchange for 4,050,000 shares of Series A convertible preferred stock of URCI at a price per share of US$0.50. The capitalisation statement shows the distribution of common shares post financing, reflecting the 1:1 conversion ratio of preferred into common stock. This shows the company's post money value to be US$4.5 million at the Series A financing round. 'Post money' valuation refers to the value of URCI immediately after the financing, and is calculated by adding the amount of the new investment (US$2 million) to the pre-money valuation (US$2.5 million).

Because the Series A holders will vote on an 'as if converted' basis, they hold voting control until all the common shares held in reserve for founders, managers and employees are fully vested.

If the URCI management accepts these terms by signing the term sheet, Big Venture Fund will issue a letter of intent to invest, conditional upon its due diligence investigation,

Exhibit 14.1

Principal terms for URCI

Description of financing

Amount	US$2,000,000
Type security	Series A preferred stock
Number of shares (as if converted at 1.01)	4,050,000
Price per share	US$0.50
Closing	15 June 2004

*Post financing capitalisation**	*No. of shares*	*Percentage*
Shares of common held by founder	3,150,000	35.00
Shares reserved for employees	1,800,000	20.00
Series A preferred stock	4,050,000	45.00
Total	**9,000,000**	**100.00**

* The percentages used in this term sheet are approximated from the initial valuation calculation. This both reflects the practice within the industry as well as the fact that the real influence on the final economic outcome to the founders and investors are not over-precise initial valuations but more a result of successful execution of the company buildup. *Source:* Authors' own.

and will start its due diligence investigation. This will usually take five to seven weeks and will involve detailed examination of all aspects of the company and intense personal and professional scrutiny of the founder/managers.

While virtually any 'change of heart' may cause a fund to withdraw from a financing at this stage, discovery of negative items previously undisclosed by the founders or managers (in other words, bad surprises) – especially falsehoods, exaggerations or duplicitous representations – are sufficient cause for a venture fund to withdraw from the deal. Adverse market changes (such as the sharp decline in equity markets in 2000) during the examination period may also cause investors to withdraw.

Upon completion of the due diligence examination, the fund will prepare the final documents for the closing of the investment, at which point final signatures will be affixed. While the due diligence may cause the initial conditional offer to be withdrawn, or to be recast in ways more favourable to protect the investor after the discovery of certain information, it is rarely the case that the terms improve for the founders and managers because of previously undisclosed material.

The final act in this melodrama is the transfer of the money involved as per agreement. It is only at this point that the founders and managers should consider the deal 'done'. Clearly, URCI management should analyse the terms of the deal, as well as the implications of the terms and the due diligence investigation, before signing and accepting the term sheet and letter of intent (LOI) in which they are contained and transmitted.

The choice of securities used: why convertible preferred shares instead of common stock?

At the start of the negotiations that led to this term sheet, the outstanding shares were all common shares and were held by the founders and some individual investors. The term sheet offered by Big Venture Fund implies that, post financing, the VCs would hold Series A convertible preferred stock (later rounds would be referred to as Series B, C, D and so on), the founders and employees would hold common shares, and newly issued common shares would be held in reserve for the management and employees' option pool. How and why this transformation occurs in the amount and form of the equity holdings is the first question to address.

A simple example demonstrates the problem solved by this transformation and the rationale for this. If investor and founder agree through negotiation that the founder should receive more than 50.1 per cent of the 'economics' in the deal but that the investor should have control over some or all of the decisions to be made in the company, a problem exists if common stock is used. If allocation of economic value is to be brought about by distribution of equity shares, the use of common shares bestows not only 50.1 per cent of the economics, but also 50.1 per cent of the control of all aspects of the firm's management. With this voting majority, the founder 'wins all the votes' and effectively controls the company. Both parties, however, may agree that some or all of the control should rest with the investor in order to mitigate the management risk. Usually, failure to accommodate this demand by the investor would be a 'deal breaker'.

In the United States and in some, but not all, other countries, convertible preferred stock provides the answer to this problem and is the security type of choice for practically all venture capital firms and their deals. In other jurisdictions, the same distribution of economics and control may be achieved with different securities, depending upon local laws and regulations. This 'complex security' enables the differential distribution of voting and control rights and cash-flow rights between investor and founder.

This complex security is best understood by further comparison to another type of security that sits on the opposite end of the equity spectrum to common stock: 'straight' preferred stock. 'Straight' (in other words, non convertible) preferred shares enjoy superior contractual rights relative to common shares, such as preferred rights to dividends and preferential treatment upon liquidation or sale of the business. In exchange for these rights, preferred shareholders accept a fixed promised dividend return and, unlike common shareholders, have no vote in the affairs of the company. Preferred shareholders are specifically established as a class of stock separate from common stock in the company's articles of incorporation.

These characteristics give the investor protection (but no guarantee) against failure or 'living dead' performance (in other words, the firm is barely hanging on to life with little prospect of being sold or making an initial public offering, or IPO) by the company. Upon wind-up, preferred stockholders get their money back before common stock holders, assuming there is cash available following settlement of debts. By declaring cash dividends, the preferred class can retrieve its investment and a certain amount of profit should the company turn out to be a cash-generating but low-growth performer. Most importantly, straight preferred stock does not share the 'upside' with common.

Thus, the conversion-to-common stock aspect of convertible preferred stock is vital to the acceptability of this investment form by investors. Combining the right to convert to common in a fixed or variable ratio with the advantages of preferred stock creates a powerful complex financial instrument with control features and downside protection (relative to common) and an option to participate in the upside through conversion to common stock. Conversion to common stock is optimal at the time of a liquidity event (company merger, sale, IPO or wind-up). By using a complex security, the voting rights and cash-flow rights in the company may be distributed through negotiation.

169

Along with providing the investor with general voting rights on an 'as if converted' basis, specific affirmative ('thou shalt do this') and negative ('thou shalt not do this') covenants may be included in the preferred stock investment agreement to address specific risk concerns of the investor. In this example, the result may well be that the founder can retain the majority of the 'economic interest' while the (minority) venture capital investor is provided with protection against risks inherent in specific outcomes.

The balance of this chapter examines each of the remaining provisions of the Big Venture Fund term sheet and relates each one to the grand design of negotiating the distribution of control and cash-flow rights between the parties, thereby aligning their interests in the pursuit of success in the venture.

Why does the convertible preferred stock have cumulative dividends?

The payment of dividends as declared periodically may seem counterproductive in the early stages of company life when the firm is incapable of sustaining a positive cash-flow other than from capital financing. However, there is compelling logic (from the VC's perspective) to declaring and accruing dividends on the preferred stock. When Series A investors convert their preferred stock into common stock, typically at the time of acquisition of the venture-backed company or an IPO, some agreements allow them to collect declared but unpaid dividends in the form of cash or additional shares of common stock. These provisions effectively enable investors to count on a specified minimum level of return on their investment, especially if original expectations of harvest value (the value raised when the company is sold or subject to an IPO) through other means are not met.

In this term sheet, Big Venture Fund has, in effect, set its minimum return at 7 per cent compounded annually, with the cash payment due at time of liquidation. The dividend preference section of the term sheet spells out details about dividends that will be paid or accrued on the Series A preferred shares. It also establishes that the newer investors (Series A) have priority over holders of common stock (founders, earlier investors or employees) for the payment of dividends.

This provision is effective only if cash exists to pay it at liquidation and its payment would be subordinate to the return of capital to all preferred investors; if the firm is illiquid, the dividend claim has no value. If the liquidation event is a trade sale, and the proceeds are sufficient, the cumulative dividends will be paid along with the capital value of the preferred stock. If the firm achieves a qualified IPO, in other words, one at a price and total value negotiated at closing that is acceptable to all investors, the preferred shares and their accrued dividends will automatically convert to common.

While this does not protect the investor from a 'downside collapse' or total failure, it does protect against a 'living dead' situation, in which the venture creates only modest value, sufficient to pay the 7 per cent return but not enough to justify an IPO. Use of cumulative dividends and liquidation preference provides the VC with protection against the firm's inability to achieve an IPO, either due to inadequate performance or a decline in the IPO market.

Liquidation preference: the surprising 'participating preferred'

The second preference right in preferred stock is preference in liquidation. Most founders intuitively believe that this means that in the event of a 'wind-up' liquidation of the company, preferred and common stock will share the proceeds, net of debt repayment, on a pro rata basis determined by their 'as if converted' percentage of common stock ownership.

In venture capital deals, liquidation events are often specifically defined to include sale or merger of the company, sale of its assets, or a transaction of any of these types in which 'change of control' occurs. In the Big Venture Fund term sheet, preferred holders are entitled to an amount equal to the purchase price of the Series A preferred per share plus declared but unpaid dividends. In some deals, this amount may be negotiated to be a multiple of the initial purchase price ranging from 1x to levels as high as 5x or 6x. In deals in which the return falls short of the expected return from IPO and in which the company is sold or merged, this multiple serves to compensate the investor for the company's failure to achieve the return expected from the intended IPO route.

The liquidation preference section gives investors the right to recoup their investment if the company ceases to operate, is liquidated or sold. For example, if URCI is liquidated sometime after the A round for US$3 million value of total equity, preferred stock investors, with liquidation preference, would receive the first US$2 million of proceeds to repay their investment (plus more if they have accrued the right to additional common shares through the dividend provisions), plus 45 per cent (their percentage ownership) of the remaining US$1 million.

The structure of the liquidation preference determines the allocation of the proceeds between the common stock and the various classes of preferred stock (just the A class in this example) when the company undergoes a liquidation procedure. That is, investors may have the opportunity to participate in the amount of proceeds in excess of their investment on a pro rata basis up to some predefined cap, or not at all. If there is no right of participation in proceeds in excess of the amount invested, and if preferred shareholders choose, they will convert their shares of Series A preferred stock into common stock, and receive a pro rata distribution. In the URCI example, and in the absence of a liquidation preference, the preferred shareholders would convert to common and would receive their 45 per cent of US$3 million, or US$1.135 million instead of the US$2.45 million described above. While this is a significant differential wealth transfer in favour of the VC, as an investment term it is considered to be 'fair compensation' for the failure of the company to provide the expected returns that formed the initial basis for the deal. As such, this is considered a deterrent to the problem of adverse selection of deals, in other words, companies that look good but have flaws that defy discovery by even the best due diligence by venture capital investors.

Finally, this section of the term sheet spells out rights in later rounds of investments with respect to the priority of specific series of shareholders. It is not uncommon for the rights of shareholders of Series B and the following Series to suppress those of Series A. Thus, after all the covenants of the Series B shareholders are met, the Series A shareholders receive their distribution. This would be especially true in a 'down round', that is, a round in which the value of the firm is lower than it was in the prior round.

Shares reserved for employee compensation

Because the firm must hire and compensate skilled employees to enable its development and growth, shares to be used in plans for incentive stock options or the sale of restricted stock to employees must be set aside in reserve and must be acknowledged in the capital structure.

The first consideration for the founder is: how many shares are to be reserved and where do they come from? Founders are usually surprised to learn that investors often require the

Exhibit 14.2

Employee equity pool

	Relative size of employee pool (%)	Value of company (US$ million)	Implied value of employee pool (US$ million)
After Series A	20	4.60	0.92
After Series B	12	15.20	1.84
After Series C	9	76.00	6.99
At exit	9	100.00	9.20

Source: Authors' own.

shares to come from the founder's initial ownership. This reduces the effective pre-money value of the founder's personal share of the company. This runs counter to a founder's intuitive assumption that the pool would be fed with newly issued shares post financing, an arrangement that would share the dilutive burden of providing stock for employees between founders and investors.

Providing such a specified and capped number of shares makes sense, in that it is a known quantity from the beginning rather than subject to negotiation at a later time. The shares will also be subject to vesting or repurchase rights in favour of the company. Typically, vesting occurs over four years, with the first 25 per cent of the shares vesting at the end of one year of employment ('cliff' vesting), and the remaining vesting in equal monthly increments over the next three years.

Another surprise to founders in term negotiations is the requirement in some cases that the founder's initial shares held in the company be returned to the company and reissued, subject to vesting. It is not unusual for 25 per cent of original shareholdings to vest immediately with the balance 'earned back' in the future by performance or by an arranged time schedule. This is sometimes viewed by founders as reducing the pre-money value of the founder's personal contribution to the company and can be a negative factor in negotiations. Clearly, the negotiating strength of the founding group (that is, the extent to which they have maximised the pre-money value of the company) will determine the extent to which founders can negotiate more favourable terms in their deal. As shown in the term sheet, the URCI founders face share vesting, which lowers their personal pre-money value as a result.

Exhibit 14.2 tracks the size of the URCI employee pool and its value through successive investment rounds and through exit, from a value and size perspective.

Anti-dilution provisions

If future financings occur at a price lower than that paid by preferred Series A investors (referred to as a 'down round'), the Series A shares, as well as all the common shares, will be devalued and their proportional ownership will be diluted on a value basis (not a percentage of shares basis). To protect their investment's dollar value, Series A investors usually require dilution protection as a condition to investing in a company. This protection, of course, comes out of the share ownership of the founders and employees, whose ownership percentage has already been diminished by the down round.

The most severe form of anti-dilution protection from the founders' viewpoint is the full ratchet adjustment of Series A shares or conversion ratio. To see its effects, assume in the URCI example that in a subsequent preferred Series B round the company sold investors 10 million shares at US$0.25 per share to raise US$2.5 million and that the A round investors had full ratchet protection. Under this contractual agreement, the A round investors would be granted 4.05 million new shares to go with their existing 4.05 million shares. This will reduce their average price to US$0.25 per share and keep the dollar value of their investment at US$2 million, even though the value of the company has declined essentially by half. The new financing would be done on the basis of the adjusted ownership and the US$0.25 price per share. This would lower the percentage of total common stock, post conversion, that the founders and employees would own, as well as reducing the percentage of ownership that the new Series B investors would acquire for the dollar investment made.

In the URCI term sheet, however, weighted average formula dilution protection is used. The effect of this adjustment on the founders and employees is less extreme than that of the full ratchet, because the A round investors share with the common stockholders the impact of the value decline. With respect to the B round financing of US$2.5 million at US$0.25 per share, the anti-dilution adjustment to the conversion price of the Series A shares would be calculated using the following formula:

$$NCP = CCP \times ((CSO + DS) \div (CSO + NS))$$

Where
NCP = new conversion price to be determined
CCP = current conversion price (US$0.50)
CSO = number of shares of common stock outstanding prior to the dilutive Series B financing, including all Series A preferred (as if converted), all common shares and all common shares reserved for employee stock option plans, a total of 9 million shares in this example
DS = number of shares 'deemed' to be issued in the dilutive financing, that is, the number of shares that would have been issued had the offering been priced at the per share price paid in the A round (US$2.5 million/US$0.50 per share = 5 million shares)
NS = number of new shares actually issued in the dilutive financing (US$2.5 million/US$0.25 per share = 10 million shares)

$$NCP = CCP \times ((CSO + DS) \div (CSO + NS))$$
$$= US\$0.50 \times ((9 \text{ million} + 5 \text{ million}) \div (9 \text{ million} + 10 \text{ million}))$$
$$= US\$0.50 \times (14 \text{ million} \div 19 \text{ million})$$
$$= US\$0.50 \times 0.74$$
$$= US\$0.37 \text{ new conversion price of preferred Series A}$$

Thus, instead of an adjustment from US$0.50 to US$0.25 per share in the value of their equity, the A round investors experience a decline in conversion price from US$0.50 to US$0.37, thus sharing the decline with the common shareholders such as the founders and employees. The 'free shares' awarded contractually to Series A holders amount to 1,355,405 as opposed to 4,025,000 under the full ratchet approach. A concise comparison of the two methods is shown in Exhibit 14.3.

Because of the differential impact noted above, founders of companies with strong pre-money characteristics will negotiate with VCs for terms without an anti-dilution clause or

Exhibit 14.3

Comparison of anti-dilution methods

	Full ratchet	Weighted average ratchet
Founders and employees common	4,950,000	4,950,000
Shares bought by A round investor	4,050,000	4,050,000
Free shares to A round investor	4,050,000	1,355,405
Total B round investor shares	10,000,000	10,000,000
Total outstanding shares	23,050,000	20,355,000
Average investor share price (US$)	0.25	0.29
Percentage owned by A round investor	35	27
Percentage owned by founders and employees	21	24
Percentage owned by B round investor	43	49

Source: Authors' own.

with, at most, a weighted average clause. VCs will acquiesce in negotiations if they have great confidence in the company's management and future. As with other 'tough' terms, however, VCs feel better with contractual rights that give them comfort against adverse selection of deals. Sometimes, investors will rely partly on the protection afforded by their right of participation in future financings. Usually, however, investors will also seek 'ratchet' or 'weighted-average' formula dilution protection.

Unless specifically agreed to the contrary, dilution benefits apply equally to all Series A investors, whether or not they continue to support the company by participating in a down round financing. Commonly, investors require co-investors to participate in future financings in order to receive the dilution protection. This requirement is referred to as 'pay to play' and it is appearing in deal terms at an increasing rate, especially given recent market conditions.

Pre-emptive rights

As shown in the URCI term sheet, pre-emptive rights apply to specific types of new share issues and not to others. These rights complement staged financing by providing investors with the option to maintain proportional ownership in the next round of financing, assuming the investors do not exercise the option to abandon by declining to participate in the next round. Early round investors often prefer the right of continued participation over ratchet or weighted-average formula protection. This is because it protects only those investors who continue to support the company by participating in a down financing and because the principal beneficiaries of the other forms of dilution protection are usually the later investors.

Often, the price paid in a down financing is low enough to trigger ratchet formula dilution protection for later investors who bought at a higher price, but still exceeds the price paid by the early investors. Accordingly, the early investors are entitled to no adjustment. Even when a down financing is at a price less than that paid by early investors, later investors will be the principal beneficiaries of ratchet and formula dilution protection if they bought at a higher price than earlier investors, as is usually the case. In such a scenario, later investors will receive a greater equity adjustment than early round investors. Thus, the stake of the founders and early investors will be reduced.

Investment liquidity and co-sale rights

Both investors and founders negotiate rights that address the attainment of liquidity for their investments. As another defence against 'adverse selection', investors negotiate for rights to ensure they have the opportunity to realise liquidity for their investment at a time of their choice. To ensure that an IPO will not be delayed or denied by majority owners, investors negotiate for the right to force SEC registration of shares for public sale rights. These registration rights and the subsequent public offering are among the most important issues in a financing. If the investor holds a minority position in a non-public company, the exit possibilities depend on the decisions made by others who control the board and have the majority of the votes. If the founder group is happy for the business to remain a private company, and so long as additional funds are not needed, the investor group cannot force a public offering except by exercising a contractual registration right.

Investors typically look for two kinds of rights regarding a public offering of the company's shares: demand registration rights, and piggyback rights.

Demand registration rights, as the name implies, allow investors to require the company to file a public offering. This can be important in cases in which the majority prefers to have the company stay private because of their ability to generate private benefits for themselves, rather than for investors (for example, sales bonuses rather than dividends) or to avoid transparency and regulation that may accompany being a public company (such as SEC reporting).

Piggyback registration rights allow investors to add their shares to other shares (usually being sold by the company itself or opportunistically by majority holders) to be sold in a public offering, with offering expenses being paid by the company.

Investors also negotiate redemption rights that require the company to redeem (that is, repurchase with company funds) investors' stock at a premium after expiration of a certain time period. The time period is negotiated as that during which the harvest event implicit in the investment should reasonably have occurred. If the event does not occur in this time frame, the company must return the original investment and a premium (usually a multiple of the amount originally invested) to compensate the investor in lieu of the expected return on which the investment as based. While founders often try to negotiate call option rights, VCs are loath to agree, being unwilling to 'cap the upside' of a deal. Essentially, they want the put option of redemption but do not want to give up a matching call option. This is one of the instances in which the 'golden rule' often seems to apply, in other words: 'The one who has the gold, rules.'

Both of these rights provide investors with the opportunity to realise a return on their money in the case that there is no clear exit potential pending or in the future. For example, if the company chooses not to go public or have a liquidation event of any kind, yet becomes a sustainably profitable operating organisation, the investors will have the right to extract their invested amount with a profit to return to their limited partners. This is a particularly vital covenant for VCs because it captures for them a return on a prosperous company if there is a lack of majority will or a market opportunity for the company to exit.

Company founders will negotiate for automatic conversion requirements as well as for 'tag along, drag along rights'. While Series A investors may convert to common stock at any time, under automatic conversion they must convert if a public offering will bring them their required return. As shown in the URCI term sheet, automatic conversion of the investors' convertible preferred stock may be triggered by actions of the founder/management group or the investment group. In URCI, if a majority of the Series A investors vote to do so, the Series A investors as a class must convert. From the founder/management group's viewpoint, automatic conversion is triggered by registration of a 'qualifying initial public offering' of a certain size at a certain price per share. In other words, it is designed to achieve a return for the investors within their range of expectations and avoiding, say, 'penny stock' status due to a low share price.

To address the issue of 'willingness and ability to sell' in a merger or acquisition harvest, the tag along right gives each party the right to join in a transaction initiated by the other. Likewise, the drag along right requires each party to join in such a transaction instead of, say, being the 'spoiler' of the deal.

General control

While preferred stock usually does not confer the right to vote, its use in venture capital deals is typically accompanied by voting power. The voting rights section of the term sheet gives the Series A investors voting rights as though they owned an equivalent number of common shares. By having the right to choose one or more board members, the new investors can participate in the governance of the company.

Some investors, to avoid liability, may choose 'board observation rights' over a board seat. Some investment agreements will include a provision to 'flip' control to the investor if certain benchmarks are not met. Others will include a voting agreement where founders and investors agree to vote their shares to elect certain persons or designees to the board, notwithstanding their relative shareholdings. As a company matures, management and investors often seek to add outside board members, people with relevant industry or other experience and stature who can assist the company in anticipating and meeting the challenges of growth.

In cases where the VC is a Series A minority shareholder and has a minority board position in which unanimity on board decisions is not required, specific protective covenants become important. In such cases, the inability to negotiate them would be a 'deal breaker'. Protective covenants set forth certain events that will require consent of the investors. Investors' consent might be required for financing, pledging of assets, any material change in the company's business, transactions with related parties, payment of dividends and executive compensation.

Consent of the holders of a majority of preferred stock will be required for the creation of any new class or series of shares having preference over or being on parity with the Series A preferred. Similar consent would be required for any increase in the authorised number of shares of preferred stock, any amendment to the articles of incorporation, any change in the authorised number of directors, or any transaction in which control of the company is transferred or the company is acquired.

Conclusion

Founders may draw several important conclusions concerning deal structuring from the material presented and discussed in this and the previous chapter. The authors suggest that the most important of these are as set out below.

- *Caveat emptor*
  It is extremely important that founders spend time and effort learning the practical meaning and implications of structural aspects of the deal presented in the venture capital term sheet. While VCs review thousands of business plans per year, and are very familiar with the legal terms and jargon contained in term sheets, company founders usually have limited experience and are likely to be doing their deal for the one and only time in their lives. Clearly, education on deal structuring is extremely important and valuable to them.

- *Focus on the correct elements of structure*

  Most venture capital firms have fairly standardised deal structures that they have grown comfortable using. This comfort comes from the fact that these structures have served to protect the investor in those cases where the company has not performed according to expectations.

  It is an unwise use of time and goodwill to spend too much effort trying to alter the actual structure of deals. It may send the wrong signal to investors when an entrepreneur is negotiating for terms that favour them if their company is not performing according to their expectations and promises. The best approach for a founder is to perform a due diligence investigation on alternative venture capital funds to learn their preferences. Part of the matching process from the founder's viewpoint is determining what venture capital characteristics best suit the founder and company.

- *Have appropriate representation*

  It is also important to have a lawyer representing the founder who is experienced in venture capital financings in that particular business area. They understand the actual terms and deal structures and can help the founder to navigate it efficiently. On the other hand, an inexperienced lawyer can result in either a bad deal due to misunderstood terms, or no deal at all by driving away potential investors because of focusing on the wrong elements of a negotiation.

- *Focus on the end-goal*

  The goal should be to build a robust and viable company that can deliver on its initial promise of bringing a relevant product to satisfy a real market demand and to create wealth for the founders, employees and investors of the company.

  Despite the dilutive aspect to founders of raising external capital, and the rigour and discipline to be expected from professional venture capital investors, the opportunity does exist for the founders to reach that goal.

  Exhibits 14.4 and 14.5 illustrate a 'bottom-line' for the URCI company tracking relative value from its initial capitalisation at the Series A financing through to exit.

Exhibit 14.4

Initial Series A capitalisation

Employees US$0.90 (20%)

Series A US$2.03 (45%)

Founder(s) US$1.58 (35%)

Source: Authors' own.

Exhibit 14.5

Capitalisation and valuation at exit

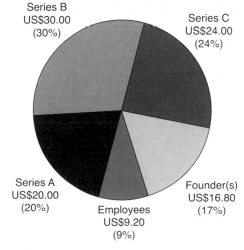

Series B US$30.00 (30%)

Series C US$24.00 (24%)

Series A US$20.00 (20%)

Employees US$9.20 (9%)

Founder(s) US$16.80 (17%)

Source: Authors' own.

177

Appendix

Summary of proposed terms and conditions for University Research Commercialization, Inc. 30 June 2004

Note: These terms do not constitute any form of definitive offer or binding contract but rather are solely for the purpose of outlining those terms pursuant to which definitive agreements ultimately may be entered into. Any investment by the investors is contingent upon, among other things, the negotiation and execution of a satisfactory investment agreement (containing customary closing conditions, covenants, representations, warranties, indemnification provisions, etc.) and other appropriate documents.

Definitions

Issuer:	University Research Commercialization, Inc, (The Company)
Investors:	Big Venture Firm, LP
	Other Investors (collectively, the 'Investors')
Founder:	Dr Jane Smith, chief science officer

Description of financing

Amount	US$2,000,000
Type of security	Series A preferred stock
Number of shares	4,050,000
Price per share	US$0.500
Closing	15 June 2004

Post financing capitalisation

	No. of shares	*Percentage*
Shares of common held by founder	3,150,000	35.00
Shares reserved for employees	1,800,000	20.00
Series A preferred stock	4,050,000	45.00
Total	9,000,000	100.00

Terms of Series A preferred stock

- *Dividend:* The Series A preferred stock will earn cumulative dividends in preference to any dividend on the common stock or Series A preferred stock, at the rate of 7 per cent of the purchase price per annum, compounded annually. Dividends will accrue and be payable upon certain events, including a sale or redemption of the Series A preferred, a sale of all or substantially all of the assets of the Company or conversion or liquidation of the Company. The holders of Series A will also be entitled to participate pro rata in any dividends paid on the common stock on an 'as if converted' basis.
- *Liquidation preference:* In the event of any liquidation or winding-up of the Company, the holders of Series A preferred will be entitled to receive in preference to holders of

common in an amount equal to four times the purchase price of the Series A preferred per share plus declared but unpaid dividends. All remaining proceeds shall be shared pro rata by all the holders of common and Series A preferred. A consolidation or merger of the company or sales of substantially all of its assets shall be deemed a liquidation or winding-up for the purposes of the liquidation preference.

- *Automatic conversion:* The Series A preferred will automatically convert into common stock upon (i) the closing of an underwritten public offering with aggregate proceeds to the Company of at least US$20 million and a pre-money valuation of at least four times the purchase price of the Series A preferred on an 'as if converted' basis, (ii) the vote of a majority of the outstanding Series A preferred, or (iii) a sale, merger, redemption, dissolution, liquidation or winding-up of the Company if the holders of the Series A preferred are entitled to receive at least four times the purchase price of the Series A preferred (exclusive of accrued dividends payable with respect to the Series A preferred).

- *Redemption:* Upon the written request of holders of at least 25 per cent of the outstanding Series A preferred, at any time after the fourth anniversary of the closing, the Company will be obligated to redeem the shares of Series A preferred covered by such written request, at the higher of (i) four times the purchase price of the Series A preferred plus any accrued but unpaid dividends, or (ii) the fair market value (without any private market, minority position, control premium or liquidity discount). The fair market value would be determined by an independent third party if the parties cannot agree.

- *Anti-dilution:* The Series A preferred will initially be convertible into common stock at a ratio of 1:1. The conversion ratio will be adjusted proportionally for stock splits, stock dividends, stock combinations and the like. The conversion ratio will also be subject to a standard weighted average adjustment for dilutive issuances. Issuances of stock, options or warrants to employees, consultants or directors pursuant to plans or arrangements approved by the Compensation Committee would not be deemed to be dilutive issuances. Securities issued in connection with (i) the acquisition of another corporation or (ii) technology licensing and/or corporate partnering transactions would not be deemed dilutive if the issuances are approved by the director elected by the holders of the Series A preferred.

- *Pre-emptive rights:* Each holder of Series A preferred will have the right to purchase its pro rata share of all new issuances of securities of the Company on the same terms as they are offered to any person. Such pre-emptive rights will not apply to (i) registered public offerings, (ii) securities issued in connection with the acquisition of another corporation, (iii) securities issued or issuable to employees, consultants or directors pursuant to plans or arrangements approved by the Compensation Committee, or (iv) securities issued in connection with technology licensing and/or corporate partnering transactions, which issuances are approved by the director elected by the holders of the Series A preferred.

- *Non-compete, proprietary information and inventions agreement:* Each officer and key employee of the Company designated by the Investors will enter into a non-competition, proprietary information and inventions/technology preservation agreement satisfactory to the Investors. Founders would assign to the Company all pertinent past and present technology rights.

- *Voting rights:* A holder of Series A preferred will have the right to that number of votes equal to the number of shares of common issuable upon conversion of the Series A preferred. Holders of Series A preferred shall have the right to elect one director. On all other matters, the preferred and the common shall vote together, except as provided by law.

- *Board representation/Compensation Committee:* The board will consist of five members. The Investors will have the right to designate and elect two directors. The three remaining directors will be designated by the holders of common stock. There will be a Compensation Committee with three members, two of whom will be directors designated by the Investors. The Company will reimburse board and committee members' reimbursable expenses associated with attendance at board meetings.
- *Reserved employee shares:* The founders shall immediately receive 1,150,000 shares of voting common stock, with ownership of 2,000,000 shares of common stock reserved for vesting to their ownership on the anniversary of this financing in equal instalments over the next two years. Also the Company has reserved 1,800,000 shares of common for issuance to employees (the 'Reserved Employee Shares'). The Reserved Employee Shares will be issued from time to time under such arrangements, contracts or plans as are recommended by management and approved by the board. All such shares will be issued subject to vesting restrictions.

Part IV

Running the spinout

Chapter 15

Strategic design and risks mitigation in emerging technology

Ellie Runcie[1]
Design Council, London

Introduction

A vibrant and sustainable economic future cannot be brought about by technology alone; design will also be an important factor. As a strategic discipline, design connects businesses more deeply with market opportunities, helps them create inspiring and revolutionary products and services, and allows them to better engage with international best practices.

There are two fundamental ways in which design, used strategically, can have an impact on the economy:

- by strongly connecting products and services to market need; and
- by understanding and mitigating internal and external risks.

To illustrate these points, this chapter focuses on two early stage companies in the emerging-technology sector that have taken a range of design approaches in the earliest stages of their growth: Ceres Power and Oxford Biosensors.

Strategic design – humanising technology

It is a stark fact that in the United Kingdom too few emerging-technology ventures survive beyond the second round of funding. Rather than being market driven, there is a tendency among most science-based ventures to take a narrow focus during the development process. They concentrate too heavily on the technology at the expense of wider factors that can influence market success.

Recent history has shown that when companies rely purely on new technology to attract consumers they often trip up. Functions and features do not in themselves mean better products or services. For example, the first personal digital assistant (PDA), the Apple Newton, performed many different functions – none of them all that well. In reality, people wanted simplicity, but it would be 10 years before Palm offered it to them in the form of a design-driven solution.

Startups and early stage ventures under-utilise design skills and methodologies in the process of commercialising technology. Design is not valued as a key strategic discipline that can be used to unlock market opportunities by understanding customer and end-user needs.

Exhibit 15.1

Design is a strategic discipline

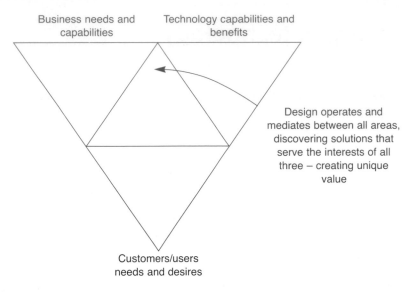

Business needs and   Technology capabilities and
capabilities   benefits

Design operates and
mediates between all areas,
discovering solutions that
serve the interests of all
three – creating unique
value

Customers/users
needs and desires

Source: Design Council.

According to Design Council research, businesses that see design as integral to their strategy are rapidly growing and increasing their competitiveness. Some 40 per cent of the fast-growing companies use design in the idea generation, and the research and development (R&D) stage of new product development, compared with only 9 per cent of businesses overall.[2]

Design is often seen to relate only to aesthetics, usability and styling of products, or perhaps a company's logo. While it is true that these are tangible examples of what design can contribute, they are by no means the full story. Design approaches, skills and methodologies can be used not only to determine what product or service a company should create, but more critically to guide the business through an extensive range of business, technology and market issues, helping companies to make decisions and not just implement them.

Even in its narrowest form, designing a new technology-based product means first understanding and responding to a variety of needs, values, lifestyles, states and contexts of use, as well as making the product stand out at point of purchase and also communicate its functionality. This is challenging when you are developing a novel technology that must not only address needs in new and emerging markets, but could actually create those markets.

Emerging-technology companies deal with the future – so does design. The problem is that many emerging-technology startups are driven by a technological mindset that is often not effective in addressing and tackling the myriad complexities of a marketplace and the steps required to reach it. Managed well, the outcomes of a strategic design process can positively influence what the company creates, while helping it to identify future target consumers and establish strong 'first mover advantage' (see Exhibit 15.1).

Case studies

Ceres Power and Oxford Biosensors

Ceres Power is a spinout from Imperial College, London. It develops fuel cells – stand-alone energy sources that create heat and electricity when oxygen and fuel gas (such as natural gas, LPG or hydrogen) react with each other as they pass through the cell. This process is highly efficient and, if the fuel gas is hydrogen, the by-product of this reaction is pure water, making fuel cells a very environmentally friendly power source. Ceres fuel cells are small, about the size of a coaster or beer mat, so for most applications they need to be combined together in 'stacks'. Ceres's baseline aim is that a product containing a Ceres stack large enough to heat a house should be no larger than a gas boiler of equivalent heat capacity and no more expensive to run.

Oxford Biosensors is a spinout from Oxford University. It is developing medical devices for measuring multiple parameters in a blood sample quickly and accurately. Its technical expertise is in electrochemistry and it develops strips that can be used to detect chemicals in the blood. The strips are then read by a machine — in this case a hand-held device. The first device is intended for hospital as well as GP use. One of the first tests will be utilised to determine whether someone has had a heart attack. Another test will be utilised to assess a patient's risk of developing cardio-vascular disease (CVD), the leading cause of death in the Europe and North America. Developing a product that gets approval from the United States' Food and Drug Administration is central to the company's success.

Both companies were at very early stages and had received little or no design input when they became involved in the Design Council's Humanising Technology programme. The initiative brought inter-disciplinary design teams into both companies to understand their strategic business priorities and identify where design might help to meet them. Each business then made practical design roadmaps for one to three years ahead, depending on when they expected to deliver a product to market, and received regular visits by a design mentor to support them in making progress with their plans. Each step of the way, design approaches and methods were used to help the companies to:

- identify the right application for the right market – and new markets;
- define the key benefits to those markets and create a more compelling business case;
- establish a strong market position;
- understand and create good product and service development processes allied to an interdisciplinary, collaborative culture; and
- inject creative vision into science-based teams.

Critical success factor 1: strongly connecting to new and emerging market need

'Scientists and engineers need to be trained to realise that people will not buy their skills because they are good, but because they fit a need in the market.'[3] One of the key reasons why technology startup companies fail is that they do not identify appropriate market need for a new technology. Many businesses make assumptions about what the target market should be and base their entire strategy on the basis of market research that, while important, only gives statistical information in generalised and aggregated terms. It does not give the full picture of what customers and end-users in those markets actually need and value from a product or service, nor does it identify other possible market opportunities. User research provides in-depth insights into what motivates and delights end-users, by observing behaviours and revealing their explicit and latent needs and desires. A compelling offer can then be created that is attractive to potential customers, investors and most importantly end-users.

Priming the market is particularly important for companies dealing with emerging technologies. It may take them several years to get their technology to a stage where it can be sold, so in the meantime it is vital that the company understands and continually explores what the market will be, has a vision of it that will inspire and guide its own team and will keep alive the confidence and interest of investors and partners.

Design plays a critical role here ensuring the business explores more than one market, and brings the company's technology to life by communicating its benefits – whether through visual concepts, working prototypes of compelling applications, brand stories or scenario-based futures.

Create compelling applications

A design technique that can be particularly beneficial in priming the market is 'scenario creation'. This is a method used to visualise both how a product might be used in a particular context and the benefits that it can bring to the end-user, which includes visual methods, scenario building and stories to bring to life new concepts. By creating stories based on benefits to illustrate the potential uses of the emerging technology, the company can make the benefits concrete even if a final product is a number of years away.

Case studies
Ceres Power and Oxford Biosensors

Ceres Power is developing fuel cell technology that it plans to present as a cleaner and more cost-effective alternative to oil- or gas-fired domestic boilers. Most of us have boilers in our homes — the question is: can consumers, and those who supply the existing forms of energy as a service, be persuaded to use fuel cells? This would require fundamental changes of behaviour and business models on the part of the end-user and customer, presumably at a significant cost. Through being more aware of design thinking and methods, Ceres's mission is to communicate the benefits not just of their own technology, but of fuel cells in general. They have used the trade press and the national media to present the case for fuel cell technology, in particular its positive environmental characteristics.

Ceres took a particularly positive step in entering the 'Carbon Trust Award for Innovation' in 2003, which it won for demonstrating innovation, environmental responsibility and clear potential for commercial success. For this award, co-sponsored by the Carbon Trust and *The Daily Telegraph*, Ceres Power were required to submit considerable technical documentation with its entry, but felt its chances were boosted most by having developed a compelling story from an end-user perspective about how its products would fit into people's future lives and what advantages they would bring. This has given Ceres a great platform to raise more informed awareness about the potential of fuel cells to both a commercial and public audience.

Oxford Biosensors has a product that brings accuracy, speed and simplicity to important diagnostic procedures. The company has actively promoted the benefits to users – not just the technology – by describing and highlighting the value of the product in different user scenarios. Raising awareness of the benefits among end-users has been a key component of the Oxford Biosensor communications strategy. Articles about the product have been featured in professional journals such as *Medical Device Technology*, which is read by those likely to be involved in the use and procurement of medical technologies. This approach has been successful in attracting great interest in the company as well as raising awareness of point-of-care testing among end-users as a result.

Involve end-users as early as possible

User research can give a technology startup business more reliable insights into what end-users and customers will need and this should be carried out in parallel with traditional market research. Even if a venture only plans to license its technology via larger customers, it stands more chance of success if it can anticipate changes in behaviour and needs at the ground level, and then feed the insights back into the laboratory and pre-development stages.

Case study
Oxford Biosensors

Oxford Biosensors conducted user research through the use of design very early in its development. Rather than simply running conventional focus groups, Oxford Biosensors started doing much more in-depth user research directly with potential end-users – in this case medical professionals. The business began by understanding the real-life context in which its product was likely to be used – whether in pressurised hospital situations or busy GP surgeries. It then created prototype designs that it could show to medical professionals, engaging them in this new concept to get their feedback at the earliest stage. This was not just to inform the ergonomics, but to capture their ideas and feelings about what the product could be, the experience of using it and therefore what value could be added. This feedback helped Oxford Biosensors to identify other possible ways that it could add value for its customers.

Check the business's reputation

Another important factor both in priming a new market and creating a compelling offer, is to build an impression that creates confidence in the minds of investors, partners, and ultimately

187

customers and end-users. Again, the long lead times to market faced by many emerging-technology ventures mean that it is important to start building the brand story right from the start of a company's development, irrespective of whether its focus is consumer or business to business. A company's brand goes much further than the corporate brochure or logo – it reflects the essence of a company's culture and should strongly differentiate a business from its competitors, touching its customers and end-users, investors and shareholders, suppliers, and partners and employees. In its most tangible form, brand is also about the way the company presents and conducts itself.

Case study
Ceres Power

Being design-led from the beginning, Ceres Power has taken its reputation very seriously. The company is meticulous in creating an authoritative feel that is reflected in everything it does, from the quality of its communication materials, to the design and layout of labs and workspace, to the necessary and strictly enforced dress code. The company believes this has helped to create an authoritative position that will not only help it to establish its reputation quickly when it comes to market, but which also makes it attractive to the partners and investors that will support its growth.

For a young business with no previous track record in a market, an authoritative brand is critical in creating effective routes to that market and attracting strategic partners that can help to form the best distribution networks. Attempting to do this alone can be time-consuming and costly to new ventures, while established competitors in the target market can make life difficult by signing exclusive deals at competitive rates with retailers and distributors.

Case studies
Ceres Power and Oxford Biosensors

Ceres Power formed an alliance with a company in an adjacent market, namely gas distribution. Because the Ceres Power fuel cell works by generating heat and energy through the combination of gases, it is clearly to the advantage of gas distribution companies if people heat their homes using Ceres Power's fuel-cell boiler rather than the gas or oil boiler currently found in most homes.

Partnership means giving Ceres Power the support of a large company in helping its product to succeed. Although Ceres's partner is not in the boiler industry, it transports gas cylinders to and from people's homes and therefore has the infrastructure in place to supply the product. In terms of their brand position in such a relationship, the fuel-cell boilers will be co-branded as a Ceres product in a similar way to the 'Intel Inside' approach to PCs.

Oxford Biosensors has driven design thinking through the core of their brand strategy which has had an impact on the name of the product; the strategic partnerships the company needed to form; and the tone, content and placements of the publicity material it needed to produce.

It established a partnership with a leading company within the biomedical field. It has agreed that the product will carry the partner's brand rather than its own. In effect, Oxford Biosensors' innovative product will be used to give its partners an advantage over their competitors. The benefits of this for Oxford Biosensors are that it now has access to an established distribution network. Its product will be branded under a name that is well known and trusted in the field, and it will have the sales and marketing departments of the partner company promoting its product.

Explore more than one market

A key design factor in helping an emerging-technology business get the route to market right is to really understand what the market is, or will be. As obvious as it sounds, this issue can trip up companies that take it lightly unless, with design thinking, they explore what other market opportunities there could be.

Case studies
Ceres Power and Oxford Biosensors

In the case of Ceres Power, the market for its product is likely to change rapidly over time but brainstorming and scenario building has helped the company move to market quicker by coming up with several new possibilities for applications that require less technological development than their primary longer-term target market. The chances are that the first people to choose a fuel-cell power unit for their home will be people motivated by environmental concerns or an interest in the technology. Such implementation can be carried out via established utility companies wanting to offer added value services to their existing customer base. Ceres will need to target those likely early adopters to get the product off the ground. As and when the product starts to prove itself in the market, the company will concentrate on more traditional markets for boilers, such as home-builders, energy companies and the general public.

For Oxford Biosensors, this issue is complicated because medical procurement procedures can vary significantly from market to market. In the United Kingdom, for example, most health care is provided by a nationalised service with a complex procurement process. This means that individual doctors may have little say over the equipment the health service buys, making it a comparatively difficult market to break into.

In the United States, however, where the majority of health care is provided privately and health care procurement is less centrally regulated, individual doctors have a far greater say over what equipment GP practices, hospitals and health centres should buy. Because of this, Oxford Biosensors is concentrating its efforts on the United States and working with medical practitioners there to understand their needs and develop a device tailored to that market. However, with continual exploration they have other plans for the product later for which, through further design input, they will be able to define the requirements.

Tips for entrepreneurs

Use design to:

- *Explore more than one market*. Run a brainstorm to identify what is obvious, what is possible and what is impossible. The resulting ideas can take the business in new, innovative directions.
- *Spot the unexpected*. Explore what the technology enables, not what it can do. Is there a range of problems from other market sectors to which the technology, if appropriately applied, could provide a unique solution?
- *Create compelling applications*. Use visual methods, scenario building and stories to describe the benefits of the technology as a means of bringing it to life through new concepts. This can help to demonstrate to potential investors, customers and end-users what it would be like to use the product or service, creating more interest and demand.
- *Involve end-users as early as possible*. What customers say they want is not always what they need. Strategic market research and focus groups will only tell the business about what exists today, and will not reveal insight into tomorrow's needs. Engage user research early to understand customers' behaviours, values, latent needs and the real-life contexts in which the future product will be used.
- *Check the business's reputation*. A positive brand image will impress and reassure others. Understand that brand is more than a logo or brochure – it is everyone and everything the company touches and it is important to understand how that interaction happens. Ensure that the brand means to others what it is intended to mean. Review encounters with customers to make sure the impression the business gives is the right one, and differentiates it in the right way. Be certain that everyone in the company takes responsibility for delivering their part of the brand.

Critical success factor 2: understanding and mitigating risk

Design is an effective risk management tool – and a potential time and cost saver – because it helps identify and anticipate what customers will respond to well into the future. It can, for example, give marketing and engineering specialists a firm base for strategic decision making. This is because design techniques can usually give a startup business insights into what end-users will need that are more reliable than the often generalised conclusions derived from market research alone. What this adds up to is the ability to make mistakes and kill potentially damaging ideas early, before too great an investment has been committed. By placing investment closer to the customer, or end-user, businesses can limit the risk of suffering the much costlier scenario of launching a new technology-based product that fails in its first generation.

However, technology entrepreneurs often have a passionate and single-minded belief in the technology. The risk is that its qualities, however unique, can also make them blind to the obstacles to getting product to market, be they potential problems with the technology, the lack of a compelling application or fierce competition. Successful technology teams ask the right questions at the right time during the design process to give them an understanding of the risks they face, and to help them to develop contingencies and effective strategies for dealing with them.

Iteration includes your business plan

A business plan should attract investors to the vision of the startup. It involves design thinking to reflect realistic and deliverable futures rather than over-promised scenarios of market share. In the case of many emerging-technology startups, the business plan is reliant on developing the technology to a certain level of performance. The risk is that if the company does not manage this, it will not be able to bring a product to market in the projected timescale.

It is important that startups do not see their business plans as being set in stone. Rather, the business plan should incorporate design thinking in the process that then opens up new options, producing an iterative, live planning tool that requires constant review and design thinking. As new external threats or opportunities arise, the business plan should be adapted to take these into account. By treating the business plan in this way, it helps to avoid taking too narrow a focus and gives the company flexibility in its approach to market that it might not otherwise have taken into account.

Case studies
Ceres Power and Oxford Biosensors

For Ceres Power, the plan is to develop a fuel cell that is powerful and efficient enough to be used in place of a domestic boiler – a domestic power unit producing hot water, heating and electricity. Although mainstream adoption is still some years away, Ceres's focus is on the technology performing at the optimum level by the time it reaches the market. However, as with the case of many emerging technology companies, what if by that time a major and unforeseen problem occurs with the target market? Or the performance targets of the technology are not met?

Ceres has guarded against this problem by evolving a series of other potential market opportunities for their technology as a result of strategic design input. One of the most compelling ideas is the use of fuel cells to power mobile refrigeration systems, for example those that are used in the transportation of food. Because Ceres fuel cells are silent and portable, another line of opportunity is military applications where the product could be used to power devices in the field. There is also huge potential within the developing economies for small-scale power generating units that can be put in place very quickly at the point of power use, thus removing the need for the huge infrastructure relating to centralised power production and associated grid transmission networks. The Ceres units can run on existing field proven fuels – such as Calor gas (LPG) or natural gas. However, if running on pure hydrogen, then the pure water by-product of the cell can also have great benefits in these contexts.

Because these applications would not require as much complexity in control and certification as, say, a domestic power unit, they would enable Ceres Power to come to market with a product even if it does not reach its technology performance goals. While there is a potential danger that too much diversity could lead to a lack of focus, it is sensible and appropriate to develop some feasible and attractive alternatives to the main product so that it need not necessarily be a disaster if the original performance goals are not met (see Exhibit 15.2).

Exhibit 15.2

Identify unforeseen market opportunities

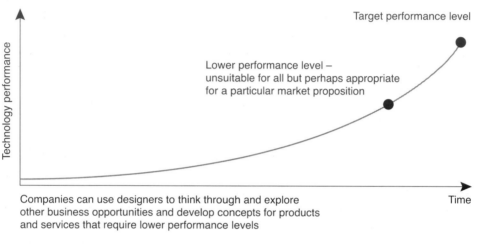

Target performance level

Lower performance level – unsuitable for all but perhaps appropriate for a particular market proposition

Technology performance

Companies can use designers to think through and explore other business opportunities and develop concepts for products and services that require lower performance levels

Time

Source: Design Council.

Fail often

Another potential problem is that, even if everything goes to plan in the technical and product development phases, the product may not succeed when it comes to market. Again, the key to mitigating this risk is to be prepared to enter more than one market.

Case study
Oxford Biosensors

Oxford Biosensors has essentially one platform technology that is utilised to detect specific analytes in human blood for the professional medical market. This platform technology will enable the company to develop a range or 'menu' of different human diagnostic tests. With design thinking, the company has continued to explore other opportunities for areas that the technology could be further exploited such as personal health care, animal health, food diagnostics and environmental diagnostics. The company has now built up these concepts into tangible prototypes that can be developed further in-house or out-licensed. In this way, the company maximises its existing technology opportunities while also building contingency plans that help to diversify the product portfolio and spread market risk. That way, if the business should prove unsuccessful in one market area, it can always have others to fall back on.

Seek perspective

Sometimes it can be emotionally difficult to let an idea go or entertain the prospect of things not going to plan, and run counter to the driven, focused nature of the people involved in the business. This is something that needs to be addressed in the company culture. Strategic design involves team collaboration, encouraging a range of internal and external disciplines and perspectives to create a base of wider expertise and a truly innovative culture.

Both Ceres Power and Oxford Biosensors have fostered cultures of innovation, encouraging employees to come up with new and exciting ideas and to look at the bigger market picture rather than just at the technology.

While attitude to risk is influenced by company culture, it is also influenced by the way in which the company is structured and by how knowledge is managed internally. By their very nature, technology startups tend to be staffed by technical people. While these people may have a great understanding of the technology they are developing, they may have far less of an idea about how to bring it to market effectively and how to create applications that are compelling and useful for those they aim to sell to.

It is important that, from an early stage, startups bring in people who can offer the company guidance and support across all the disciplines of the business, or that they receive such advice from outside in the form of strategic design mentoring. This not only ensures that the companies are steered by technological considerations, but that these are benefits driven and take into account wider market-based issues in the forefront of their strategies.

Shared vision

A common danger in startups is having structures that revolve entirely around the founder or owner. This person may insist in getting involved in every decision that the company makes and may be reluctant to let others take responsibility for their own areas of expertise. This can close off important avenues of development and cause resentment even at an early stage of a company's development (especially if this person is someone who is inclined to being impulsive or constantly changing their minds). However, as a company starts to grow, this problem becomes exacerbated as the individual frantically tries to deal with a vast range of complex issues, many of which he or she may be ill-equipped to understand. It is vital, then, that those at the senior level of startups develop a mindset of being comfortable to delegate both decision-making and responsibility to employees with the appropriate skills and expertise.

Failure to mitigate risk is often a result of the culture that pervades in many new firms, particularly technology startups. Often they are founded by an individual or small group of people who have a very clear vision about what the company will do and how it will succeed. They are often very sharply focused on this vision and this is, of course, very important. However, a potential drawback is that those running and involved in startups can become rather too narrowly focused on a single plan, missing other potential opportunities and failing to make contingencies in case things do not work out. Creating a shared vision of the company and allowing the whole team to participate is an approach that design-led companies take.

Case studies
Ceres Power and Oxford Biosensors

Ceres Power and Oxford Biosensors have been meticulous in terms of sharing vision and communication. Although they are still in the early stages of their development, these companies adopted a 'big company' mentality to their operations, in both infrastructure development and lines of communication. During their expansion, both companies have striven to keep vision, knowledge and expertise available and usable, which has allowed them to maintain a consistent but responsive company culture.

Tips for entrepreneurs
Use design to:

- *Fail earlier.* A design-driven approach is one that from the start uses primary research – end-user research – to identify problems and issues in the pre-development stages. At this stage they can make changes at little or no cost, develop a range of alternative ideas of how to meet their needs, fully explore possible assumptions and kill the poor ideas early.
- *Fail faster.* Use rapid prototyping techniques and scenarios to evaluate the strength of a new idea quickly. If there seem to be too many difficulties with it then it may be best to accept this up-front and let the idea go.
- *Fail often.* Do not become too attached to one idea, market or product. Make a continuous range of alternative and increasingly sophisticated prototypes during the development of the product/service. These can start as paper-based, moving through to rapid prototypes, allowing the development team to explore and design out problems along the way.
- *Seek perspective.* Design involves a range of disciplines and perspectives. Build a team that is interdisciplinary and encourage flexible and innovative thinking. Create an environment where failing faster and earlier is encouraged rather than criticised, as your team are more likely to expose concerns and problematic areas, ensuring the ideas that are developed are robust and appropriate for the marketplace.

---

[1] The author would like to acknowledge Gill Wildman, Design Strategist on the Design Council's technology campaign, for contributing thinking and illustrations. Gill develops approaches that bring strategic design thinking and methods into early stage emerging-technology companies.

[2] *Design Council National Survey of Firms 2003* (PACEC).

[3] Quote: Professor Gordon Edge, Chairman, The Generics Group.

Chapter 16

Organising to sell: pipelines versus pipedreams

Giffin Lorimer and Colin Spiller
G4h, London

Introduction

To make progress with a new university spinout, someone has to sell something. It may be selling a vision to a potential employee, selling the promise of a significant improvement to a potential user, selling the hope of future riches to a potential investor or selling the firm to another company.

Whatever is being sold, the key to being effective is to remember that selling is primarily about finding someone who needs what is on offer. Therefore, the most important things to understand are what the need is and who the person with the need is.

This chapter provides a structure and process for uncovering customers' underlying needs, creating a strong desire for the unique attributes that the business offering possesses, presenting a solution in such a way as to overcome all obstacles to the signing of a contract and, finally, making sure the money is paid.

Getting started – the sales and marketing plan

In the university course Marketing 101, students are taught the 'five Ps of marketing':

- product;
- price;
- place;
- promotion; and
- package.

In essence, this examines the principles of establishing a viable product. In practice, however, the five Ps deliver an abstract conceptual representation of the solution rather than a real-world return on investment (RoI) case for which a customer will pay.

A real problem with most marketing is that it is fun. It is easy to spend time fiddling with presentations and talking to advisers from public relations and advertising agencies. It is much less fun cold-calling new prospects to set up appointments. Unfortunately, without customer input to guide it, a product presentation will not relate to any of the customer's needs and therefore cannot support the sales effort.

In Sales 101, students rapidly learn that the five Ps of marketing only equate to the first of the 'four Ps of selling':

195

- proposition;
- prospects;
- proposal; and
- payment.

This is because selling concerns itself with all aspects of revenue generation, not just the ability to satisfy a particular client's needs. The four Ps have first to be identified and then codified into a plan that the business will work towards. Developing a superior technical product must be subordinated to developing the entire offering that will fit with the potential clients' needs.

The sales and marketing plan should clearly identify:

- the target audience(s);
- the communications channels to get to the audience(s);
- the expected sales revenues and timelines;
- the overall proposition;
- the sales organisation;
- the required skills profiles for the sales team; and
- the salary/commission structure.

Finally, the plan needs to be communicated in a way that everyone in the spinout team can understand so they can all support the sales process. This means a mission statement, company positioning statement, 'elevator pitch', regular briefings on sales progress to the entire company and an effective set of collateral for the sales team to use.

Proposition

The only way to bring a new product successfully to market is to create a differentiated business proposition that is economically viable for buyer and supplier alike.

It takes time or money, or both, to build a great proposition. However, the process is straightforward: identify potential users for the business solution, identify their needs, test the assumptions and proposition with them, select the best target market and start selling. Exhibit 16.1 illustrates the various steps involved in developing and honing a proposition for a business offering.

If the business offering or proposition is not obvious, or it is a struggle to build it, a good starting point is to discuss the project with an industry heavyweight, commentator or journalist. The university spinout can often access such people through the technology transfer office (TTO). Alumni should also be willing to listen to you and act as an adviser.

If money is available to buy expert input, buy it – it will provide access to invaluable experience, insights and contacts. This can dramatically accelerate the process of finding a target market for applications of the intellectual property.

Identifying and targeting an audience

The first step is to define the business offering as a solution, and to determine who has the need (and the budget) for it. This is usually an 'off-line' exercise and is best done by experienced business people who understand how markets operate, know what problems firms face and can tell the business how its offering may be packaged as a solution that might address them. This will create a generic proposition for the business.

Exhibit 16.1

Getting ready to sell

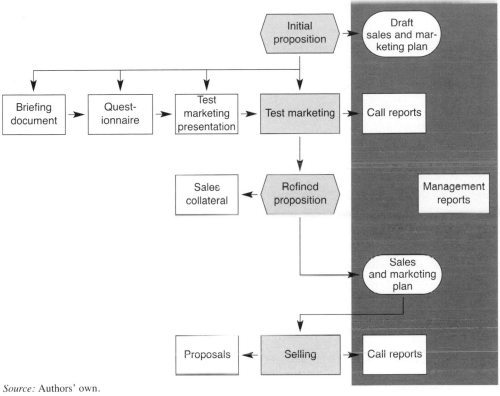

Source: Authors' own.

Next it is necessary to identify which markets might be most suitable. Build on the proposition to develop it into a presentation and an accompanying questionnaire, and then visit a selection of firms to make the pitch.

This becomes the basis for achieving 'proof of market' – essential to get funding from investors. Can investors be shown that there is a genuine demand for the offering, not just that it is technically feasible? The process may need to be iterated through several different markets and sectors until a pressing need in a niche sector can be identified and the business proposition perfected.

To do this successfully, the person making the presentation needs to know exactly who he or she is going to talk to and what responsibilities lie with that post. It also needs to be a 'research pitch', not a sales pitch, if it is to be used to gather valuable intelligence. That means two things: listen and do not talk too much. Remember the old sales adage: 'You have two ears and one mouth – use them in that ratio.'

The pitch

The pitch needs to be simple, not complex. It should discuss your understanding of the issues more than the business offering. If it is truly innovative, it must not give too much away to potential competitors. Ask open questions as much as possible, but be specific where specific

197

information is needed. Creating a questionnaire will help to ask the right questions, but be careful to tune it for specific industry issues where possible:

- What are the priority problems?
- What are the budget priorities?
- Does this solution fit into one of the priority areas?
- What are the criteria for buying from a new supplier?
- Keep asking – are these assumptions right – have we missed something?

If the solution is sufficiently compelling and the person presenting the pitch is genuinely interested in the feedback, the interviewee is more likely to open up and be receptive to the ideas as well as provide valuable information. Do not forget to reflect other people's opinions into the session: 'I was talking to a senior manager at a similar firm the other day who said…' or 'I read about … in the news last week, do you think that's likely?' This also gives them an opportunity to discuss and debate rather than being questioned. Read specialist magazines and research the web to get up-to-date information about the industry and company. The interviewee will be more receptive if the interviewer can come across as knowledgeable.

Finally, write up the results, collate and review the information. It is surprising how much more can be remembered when it is written down. Looking over several reports also gives a better feel for the details that can make a difference.

During the process be sure to identify:

- who will make the decision to buy;
- who will influence it;
- who will sign the contract; and
- who determines the budget.

It may be that an engineer or scientist has the authority to buy low-value items but major purchasing decisions are usually decided by a senior manager – or even by the board – and the finance director controls the budget and signs the order/contract.

It is useful to find out at an early stage what internal processes and paperwork have to be prepared to get an order. As the selling activity progresses, this will give the spinout a vital insight into how likely it is to receive an order or whether it is simply wasting time.

The economics of pricing

Pricing is the most obvious – and the most difficult – part of taking any product or service to market.

The right way to price a product or service is by reference to the value it brings a customer – this can then be 'tweaked' for each individual set of circumstances. To do this, however, it is necessary to offer a differentiated solution to a well-defined problem. It is really necessary to find out what the business solution means to prospective customers, particularly the savings and return on investment (RoI) case that can be built.

For example, it could be that the business offering increases the accuracy of a process and thereby reduces the amount of rework that needs to be done. This should be expressed as a percentage of salary so that it is easy to quantify the value to the customer (such as 5 per cent productivity = US$75,000 per annum if salaries plus overheads are US$100,000 and there are 15 employees). If the firm is looking for a payback within 12 months and an RoI of

25 per cent, the price in the above example could be US$60,000 annually. This is as applicable to a new enzyme or process as to a software program or tool.

Unfortunately, much pricing is done by reference to the production cost or to the market leader. This is unlikely to offer a satisfactory return to the business because it brings three key economic factors into play:

- risk premium;
- substitution; and
- inferred quality.

The risk premium refers to the well-documented impact that high market share and perceived market dominance can have on the price of alternatives. This risk also attaches to new technologies and under-funded firms. In the 1980s, IBM hardware carried a price premium of 17 per cent (in other words, competitors had to price their products more than 17 per cent cheaper than IBM to secure a sale). In the 1990s, Microsoft Office sported a greater than 90 per cent risk premium over Lotus and other office productivity software.

Substitution refers to the fact that there is always more than one way to approach a problem and that, at some point, the cost of the total solution means that alternative approaches become viable. Moreover, it is important to consider the overall cost of the solution – not just the price of the component the new business is providing but the cost of procurement, change, implementation, training, parallel-running, resources from the client and so on.

This is why the 'in-house' solution is always the most difficult to win against – the cost of staff under-utilisation or redundancy can always be added to the price of a bought-in solution to make it uncompetitive. Against them is usually a multi-year track record of over-promising and under-delivering. The certainty of delivery of the new business offering when weighed against the risk of waiting for a competing solution to be designed and developed is a powerful factor, as is the immediacy of delivery when weighed against the time lost and the cost of missing an opportunity while waiting.

Under these circumstances, it is critical to get the users on the side of the new business. For example, information technology (IT) and procurement are support functions and will seldom risk open warfare by refusing point blank to implement the solution preferred by the user communities – the chief information officer or IT manager usually has much less clout in the boardroom than the finance director or other directors. Another useful tack is to ensure that the new business complies as much as possible with whatever standards apply to the sector, whether it is an International Organization for Standardization (ISO) quality standard or a technology standard. This defuses many of the internal arguments.

Inferred quality is the most often-overlooked factor – the credibility of any product correlates to its price. Hence the expression 'it's too good to be true'. Pricing too low exacerbates the risk premium because it makes buyers fear for the long-term survival of the business; they will therefore ignore it if they are looking for a mission-critical purchase.

The effect of 'follow-the-leader' pricing for new spinouts is to be the lowest-priced substitution option – an undifferentiated offering that is hard to sell because of the risk premium and one that lacks credibility because of its low price. Few investors or buyers are interested in such an offering.

The pricing model

Having worked out how much to charge, the other issue is how to charge. The staging of

199

payments should reflect the need to have cash-flow and the customers' need to generate a return on their investment – noone wants to pay out a large sum in the hope of future bene-fits, they would rather pay for results. Technology customers want to see a price based on some combination of:

- the number of processors being used;
- the number of people who will use it;
- upgrades and fixes;
- the hours they can contact you for support (nine to five, five days a week to 24 hours a day, 365 days a year);
- the response time to problems based on their priority/critical nature (service level agree-ment); and
- payment options for technology, including support, training, enhancements, quantity discounts.

You can charge a one-off price for the technology followed by an annual maintenance charge for upgrades and support, or a licence fee that includes maintenance, billed annually or monthly. Payment options for a life sciences offering might include:

- an up-front commitment fee;
- staged licence payments (say every three months);
- bonus payments for milestones such as clinical trials, drug submissions and approvals; and
- a percentage royalty fee on revenues in line with volumes sold or royalties received, per-haps varying over time and by territory profitability, with a life-time collar and/or cap.

The agreement could also include the rights to variations on the drug or other drug developments. A 'service offering', such as testing, offers a third way of illustrating the pric-ing approach.

- An up-front charge to design the process and set up the interfaces between the two companies.
- A monthly fee based on the number of users accessing the service or the number of items being tested.
- A minimum fee for a fixed number of items, with a sliding scale of charges based on vol-umes that exceed the monthly total.
- A fixed fee per item with an annual rebate based on total volumes or on total revenues. The latter gives an incentive to purchase for additional services that the business may wish to offer.
- A bonus structure that charges a premium for exceeding the service level (in other words, quality and time) thresholds that have been agreed. However, note that this is usually accompanied by penalties for failure to attain the required service level.

All of the above factors are negotiable and could vary with each deal – it depends on who the business is dealing with. Exclusivity/non-exclusivity is another powerful factor in pricing an offering, and applies to technology distribution deals as much as to drug licensing.

The management team of a new business should always set prices where it wants them to be in two years' time, then give discounts to early adopters, launch customers and so on. It is much easier to discount initially than raise prices later. The business will also benefit from charging maintenance on a high base price.

Prospects

A business cannot sell without prospects – in general, the more the better. Test marketing the business proposition will have helped to identify the kind of people who have the need and the budget to buy the offering. The business then needs to contact them. A constant flow of prospects will keep revenues and cash-flow steady and the management team will not get bogged down in chasing opportunities that are more hope than reality.

Early stage spinout companies do not have enough money to indulge in lots of brand-building activities such as advertising. Instead, they need to be in direct contact with people who might be interested in what they are offering. This is done by writing to them, e-mailing them or phoning them, or the easier option of meeting them at events and conferences or through third-party introductions or contacts. Get a list of potential companies to contact. Several are available commercially, and in general you get what you pay for.

Another approach is to join a society or organisation that contains the target customers for the business, and then attend every meeting they run in order to network. This is a very effective mechanism and much easier than calling. A good technique is to ask them what they do, prompt them with a few comments like 'that sounds as if you must...', and then wait for the inevitable 'So what do you do?' This is an opportunity to spend five minutes explaining the business pitch to a captive audience – use it well.

Whatever approach is taken, be prepared with a short pitch that says who you are, what the business offers and what benefits it can deliver. Remember – the point is to get an appointment, not to waste an hour on each person encountered.

Once a meeting has been secured, send a thank you letter in an e-mail to confirm the meeting. Include a summary of the business proposition. Do not give too much away – save your thunder for the meeting. The day before the meeting, call to confirm the appointment. It is professional and it saves making a journey to find that the person is unwell or an emergency has dragged them away.

Meeting with the prospect

The most important things to do are:

- Find out whether there is a budget. If there is, it is usually possible to find a way to make the business solution fit their need. Without a budget and authority to spend it, their need will not make the supplier a penny.
- Find out who has the authority to sign a purchase order, and whose approval they need in order to proceed. Do not assume that managers operate dictatorially – the good ones delegate to others with specialist knowledge. There will often be a series of meetings at which different people will pick over the business offering.
- Work towards advancing the meeting to gain some form of commitment or agreement, otherwise time is being wasted. Negotiate these meetings carefully, to achieve a firm commitment from the signatory that:
  - if everyone agrees, the contract will be awarded; and
  - he or she will provide a detailed list of everyone whose approval is needed and an e-mail from the signatory to them to support the follow-up call.
- Identify any competition – a lot of firms will keep a supplier working on their problem just to force down the price of the preferred supplier.

Proposal

If all goes well, the companies targeted will be interested in the business proposition, and will ask for a detailed price proposal and contract terms.

The time to develop these is when the startup begins prospecting for business: do not wait until asked. The proposal and contract are linked –the details of what the business is going to deliver can be specified in the proposal, so that the contract simply needs to specify that the business will deliver what was specified in the proposal.

There are several templates for proposals and contracts that can be used. The proposal should set out:

- the customer requirements;
- the proposed solution;
- the generic benefits of the solution;
- how the solution can be applied to meet the customer's requirements;
- the major technical features of the product, focusing on the industry and technical standards that it supports;
- how the solution will be deployed, including the allocation of responsibilities between the supplier and the customer. This should include a sample project plan highlighting the major milestones;
- the service level agreement (support hours, response time, fixes, upgrades, and so on);
- the price for each element in the solution and any discounts that are to be applied;
- payment terms – what percentage will become due at each milestone during the contract, plus how soon payment should be made after the invoice is sent; and
- the contract, which will specify liabilities, indemnification, IPR (intellectual property rights) ownership, confidentiality, and so on.

If the proposal is as standard as possible the structure and language can be honed and made as compelling and accurate as possible. The only variance should be the description of the customer requirements and the benefits to be delivered by the supplier. Include service levels and the price. This makes it easier to update it as you get feedback from customers or as you add new features.

Payment

Closing the deal

Eventually the time comes to ask for the order. If a supplier does not ask for an order, it is unlikely to receive it. The challenge is to find a way to ask for the order that both the supplier and the buyer are comfortable with. Examples include:

- Can you please authorise this contract so that we can proceed?
- If I agree the discount will you order today?
- Can we move to implementation?
- When should we deliver?

A smart way to work out how to approach this issue is to keep a look out for 'buying signals' such as the prospect:

- selling the new offering to their colleagues;
- asking when you can deliver and if they can have a particular support person;

- talking as though they already had your offering installed;
- telling you about all the other issues your solution will address;
- identifying who is to be trained or asking where the machine is to be sited; and
- describing future enhancements or potential uses for your offering.

When this happens, ask for the order. At the end of each call, always ask for confirmation on how the sale is progressing and the next action and get the next appointment into the diary. Calls that just collect more information are not worth making. Whatever else, aim to advance the sales process by getting the buyer to commit to some specific action, such as giving access to a decision-maker higher up the chain.

Handling objections and final negotiations

If you get objections, do not panic: they are often 'buying signals', the prospect is trying to find additional reasons to buy and clearing away any confusion or concerns they may have. To handle objections, isolate the issue, confirm it, clarify that understanding and respond to it and then confirm that it has been dealt with satisfactorily and ask for agreement to proceed. Minimise cost differences over five years as a monthly cost and compare them to the total cost of ownership, including all of the client's costs of implementation.

If the business offering is completely rejected, always ask for the reason why. It is possible that the prospect has misunderstood part of the proposal, and this gives an opportunity to address it. In any event the management team will learn something that can be used in the future.

The final hurdle to gaining the order is often a negotiation, frequently on price. Before entering a negotiation, the person representing the supplier should prepare a list of what the business wants:

- better payment terms – more paid on order in exchange for discounts;
- press release and case study;
- opportunity to bid for more work; or
- ownership of the IPR for all developments, and so on.

Think about the other things the prospect might ask for as well as discounts. Get all their issues out before agreeing to anything. Keep reminding the prospect of what the business offering will deliver. Always trade what the buyer wants for what the supplier wants and achieve a win/win. Never just give anything away for nothing, otherwise they will keep asking for more.

Challenges to closing the deal

A major challenge in managing the sales process for complex products and solutions is keeping control over the cost of sales. If it is going to take a long time and a large investment of resources, think carefully about whether the business can afford to lose it – the time spent on it could be used to win other contracts.

In some cases, if there is a large number of people involved in approving the purchase decision, a good technique is to run a deployment workshop where all the issues can be raised with all the interested parties at the same time. This has several other advantages:

- it gives the supplier access to all the key people at the same time;
- it presumes that the decision will be 'yes' (a presumptive close);

- it turns the focus of the meeting (and their mindsets) into a 'how to do it' rather than a 'why might this fail?'
- it encourages participants to actively find solutions to potential problems rather than relying on the supplier to find the answer – this is vital since many problems will be internal to their organisation and nothing to do with the business offering; and
- the decision of the meeting will be binding on all participants, and a positive outcome gives the signatory the authority to proceed with signing a contract.

Getting paid

The most common reason for businesses to fail is because they run out of cash to pay their staff and creditors. It is seldom lack of sales and profits. A startup business must be careful when spending money – it is always easier to spend than to generate.

The cheapest, easiest and quickest way to get cash into a new business is from customers. Think of all the things that can be charged for, break them out of the overall solution price and charge separately for them. This generates cash during the sales cycle, and has the effect of reducing the price of the core offering, making it more competitive. Also, break the solution price into staged payments, which eases cash while more closely aligning payments with results. For example, it is possible to charge for:

- audit of existing process/technology;
- return on investment study;
- preparation of a statement of requirements;
- design and configuration workshop;
- trial of the system, process, product or enzyme;
- successful testing/start of live usage;
- training of support staff and users;
- manuals and course materials;
- grant of patents; and
- stages in drug approval and delivery.

To a large extent, getting paid depends on the way the proposal and contract have been written. For longer projects, factor in stage payments for completion of critical project milestones so that cash-flow will not suffer during the project. Always ask for a payment on signing the contract.

- Ensure that invoices are raised and sent as milestones are achieved – waiting until the end of the month means a payment cycle may be missed and the supplier waits another month to get paid.
- Find out how the customer's payment cycle works and plan around it. This can mean setting target dates for activity completion in the third week of the month, to leave enough time to get the work signed-off by the customer and invoiced in time for the cheque run.
- A small company can often ask for special treatment and get paid early. Offer discounts in exchange for early payment.

A final point to note: pay sales commissions when the payments are received, rather than when the contract is signed or when the invoice is sent. This makes the salesman focus on ensuring the customers are satisfied with what they are getting, and acts to dissuade them from promising more than can be delivered.

Lessons learned; tips for entrepreneurs

- Selling starts at the earliest possible stage. It should not begin when the technical details of the product are 100 per cent perfect – by then it is far too late to start thinking about addressing the customer's needs.

- The whole purpose of a business is to sell what it offers to someone who needs it. Therefore make it as easy as possible for them to buy. Understand their business and phrase the offer in their language.

- Business people buy solutions to their issues and problems. They understand 'return on investment', and 'total cost of ownership', arguments. They will rarely, if ever, buy technology for technology's sake.

- Proactively create opportunities to meet potential buyers. Target them through the press they read, from the conferences and exhibitions they attend or through calling them to make appointments to demonstrate the business solution offered and to capture better information about their needs.

- Ensure enough time is allocated to selling. Creating momentum towards closing a sale may involve numerous engagements and meetings. Bear in mind that selling may take as much time in the first three years as it took to develop the offering in the first place.

- Put yourself in the buyers shoes and answer the 'so what?' question to the sales presentation. When success is achieved, keep pushing your luck with prospects and suspects to build a pipeline and close it.

- If what the business is doing does not work and yield results, get external help to examine what the business is doing in the market. Also try something different – change the proposition, try a different route to market, change the target market, move the price up by at least five if not 10 times the original price, try using test marketing rather than actually selling and, if necessary, change the people. Do not give up until everything has been tried.

Chapter 17

Building and managing productive relationships with investors

Iain Wilcock
Quester Capital Management, London

Introduction

Investors come in all shapes and sizes and have different expectations and objectives. Before selecting an investor, it is important to understand the investor's motivation. The objectives of the management team and investor need to be aligned. This chapter provides a spinout's management team with an understanding of investor's motivations, and shows how an effective communication plan can be developed and employed. It also discusses the tools used by investors to monitor investments and to influence change.

Experienced financial investors look for investment opportunities that resemble successful corporate models and where their experience may add value. One of the key judgements for a spinout CEO is the selection of appropriate investors. A mistake at this stage will seriously damage the prospects of the spinout and may prove fatal.

It is usually the case that capable investors aim to manage actively their investments and thereby increase the probability of survival, and rapid growth to create more value. How an active investor exerts influence will depend on the specific circumstances and the management styles of both the investor and the management team. It is, therefore, important to discuss with any prospective investor their expectations in respect of post-investment relations.

Good management teams encourage input from their investors and will actively seek out investor views on specific issues both in formal situations such as board meetings and informally through ad hoc individual conversations. The converse situation, where managers avoid or ignore investor suggestions (which are usually well intentioned but not always right) will quickly lead to a breakdown of relations with the investor. Hence, effective communication in an early stage company must be an active process.

Characteristics of successful investor relationships

The investor

Professional investors need to spread the individual technology risk by investing in a balanced portfolio, typically comprising 20–30 companies. Individual investee companies will be contrasted and compared with other companies in the portfolio. The quality of the investor relationship can have a material effect on the attitude of the investor towards particular portfolio companies and their commitment to support the company.

Successful investor relations depend on the establishment and maintenance of trust. This can be difficult to establish in the early stages of a relationship – particularly if your investors are from the 'trust needs to be earned' school of thought. However, experienced investors understand the high degree of uncertainty and ambiguity that is associated with early stage technology companies.

Open and supportive investors are desirable. Investors' approach to the pre-completion negotiations will provide some insights into their 'house style'. Experienced early stage investors will have a pragmatic and flexible approach to post investment modifications that may need to be made to the business plan, in the light of accumulated experience. Logical development of a plan should strengthen investor relations not undermine them.

Professional investors appreciate the pressures that the uncertainty with early stage technologies can place on the management of a spinout. They can provide constructive advice on how to manage this type of fluid and fast-moving situation. Investors expect management teams to keep them informed of developments and to minimise the information asymmetry. Investors do not expect to have to chase managers for information.

A spinout's management team should be aware that professional investors need to report, normally quarterly, on their portfolio to the investors in their funds. It is important that spinouts ensure that their investors have sufficient information to satisfy their reporting requirements and appear informed about their portfolio of investments. Professional investors dislike unexpected surprises because it makes them appear poorly informed about their investments. One of the objectives of investor relationships is to allow your investors to manage other interested parties' expectations. Investors cannot do this effectively without an open and informative flow of information from their investee companies.

Another management objective of investor relations is to find ways to involve investors in the development of the business and enable investors actively to add value. To embrace this type of investment risk as an investor requires an open, creative and supportive approach. Broad experience of the management issues associated with spinouts refines the investor's judgement and develops networks of general contacts that can be useful to such companies.

The spinout management team

One of the barriers to building a successful relationship with an investor is the asymmetry of information that exists between the management team and the investors. It is always worth bearing in mind that an active investor will be responsible for a number of companies and that you are competing for the limited resources of that investor. Inexperienced management and investors frequently fail to work effectively together because this asymmetry undermines the relationship between these groups.

Good spinout managers should actively use the due diligence process prior to investment, and develop management information systems after completion, to minimise this asymmetry. Investors need appropriate information from the company on which to make decisions and actively contribute to the development of the company. Spinout managers should welcome tough questioning from investors that will help investors develop an informed view of the investment proposition. This initial exchange of views should not degenerate into an interrogation. When tackling the information asymmetry to build relationships with investors, the managers of a spinout need to focus on the 'four Cs', namely credibility, clarity, creativity and control.

Credibility, clarity, creativity and control

Spinout management teams should keep in mind that an investor has presumably 'bought into the business plan' and is aware of the key risks associated with it at the point the investment is made. Spinouts will have established some credibility with the investor. Effective communication should:

- be designed to continue to build credibility with the investor;
- provide a balanced and realistic presentation of the opportunities; and
- provide an assessment of key risks and areas of uncertainty.

Too much or too little detail is undesirable – ideally an investor should be kept informed of material matters that could affect the viability of the commercial proposition. A spinout's management team needs to exercise a degree of judgement in this area – good judgement will further enhance the credibility of the management and vice versa.

When it comes to developing technology-based spinout companies, things rarely go according to the original plan. However, provided there is an effective flow of information between management and the investors, changes in the plan based on new knowledge should not undermine the relationship. Problems can occur when the investor is not aware of the key issues in the business and 'discovers' them by chance.

Clarity and control are often key ingredients that investors look for in managers when changes in the original plan are required. In extreme cases, this could result in investors deciding the future course for the business and taking effective control of the business. Good spinout managers are able to:

- identify the reasons for the change, for example, a delay in the technical programme, slower expected sales of a product, external market dynamics;
- secure support for their recommended new course of action; and
- ensure that the investors agree with the analysis of a situation and the proposed adjustment to the original plan.

Early stage investing involves making decisions, often on scant information. Good spinout managers are able to:

- make intuitive decisions that enable the business plan to evolve as more information becomes available;
- ensure there is a flexible development plan that allows alternatives to be explored; and
- avoid betting the entire business on a single option.

Usually it is only when one of the four Cs has not been addressed that investors take unilateral action. Active investors do intervene and make management changes (assuming they have the legal or financial power to do so), but usually only reluctantly.

Arguably, if it is necessary to make key changes in the management team without the consent of the executive team, the investor has made a mistake in backing the company in the first place. Active intervention of this type is always disruptive and costly.

The need for a communication plan

Keeping active investors informed of material developments in a rapidly developing early stage company requires management to make a conscious effort. Typically, active investors will be involved in a number of companies and will not expect to have to chase companies for updates. Developing a communication plan ensures that managers recognise the need to keep investors informed of both scheduled progress against plan and unexpected news (either good or bad).

Early investment of management time usually will save time later because investors will be informed and should be in a better position to respond to changes to the business plan. Active and appropriate communication will also enhance the credibility of the management team with the investor. Conversely, the absence of appropriate communication usually means investors will need longer to consider developments at the investee company. There is an increased risk in these situations that detached investors make inappropriate decisions because they have not considered all the material information in a timely fashion.

Consideration of investors' requirements

Typically, early stage spinout companies are resource-constrained and operate in new and uncertain markets. Developing responsive and lightweight communication systems will demonstrate to investors that the management team has control over the business and has identified the key issues that investors are interested.

After a financing round has been completed, it can be helpful to set out a rough Gant chart or project management chart that covers the next couple of years. On the chart the key milestones of the agreed business plan should be charted – these milestones may be:

- scientific (such as results of an important series of experiments);
- technical (such as commissioning of a prototype);
- commercial (such as execution of a key collaboration or first sale of a product);
- operational (such as opening of a new site);
- management (such as recruitment of key senior staff); or
- financial (such as securing further backing for the business)

Having identified the major events that are expected to occur, the appropriate method of tracking and reporting on each should be considered. Generally, investors like to track 'value creating' events. The basic objective of communicating with investors is to keep them appraised of progress against the agreed plan and to ensure that they are aware of any modifications that are necessary. The execution of a plan nearly always involves modification and decisions – to maintain credibility, clarity, creativity and control, the management team needs to ensure that the company's investors are involved in this process.

When to engage with your investors

The following subjects can be seen as opportunities for investor communication:

- key strategic decisions;
- seeking discretionary support; and
- reporting on updates on financial and operational performance.

For example, a business plan should have several key strategic decisions (either implicit or explicit) that are expected to be made during the period covered by the plan and based on information that is expected to become available. Active investors will wish to be involved in these important decisions and will need to have the key information presented to them. Ensuring that the communication plan covers this area in sufficient detail should be discussed with each investor.

At the other end of the scale is keeping investors informed of the financial performance against the approved budget. Investors need to prepare their own internal reports to monitor their portfolio companies. Therefore, understanding the management information investors require and their reporting deadlines should enable the communication plan to cover this area.

One of the surest ways for a management team to demonstrate it has lost control of its business, is to fail to produce appropriate management accounts and/or produce them late.

How to engage with your investors

The best vehicle for achieving this objective will depend on the type of investor and experience of the investor representative board member. Management should select the appropriate method to deliver particular types of information:

- general day-to-day issues can be dealt with by e-mail contact and phone calls;
- financial information is usually set out in a report; and
- strategic decisions are usually best handled by a presentation to the key investors followed by a discussion in a formal meeting.

Managers should ensure that they make full use of the different channels – over-reliance on a single method, such as informal conversations or written reports, should be avoided.

Developing a balanced management style

Entrepreneurs and founders can have unusual management styles and find it difficult to adjust as a company grows and the management team expands. Identifying and adopting appropriate styles is vital to the maintenance of group cohesion. Experienced investors can help this development. The failure to establish a balance of preferred styles within a business is often a source of conflict and can lead to costly mistakes.

Investors are looking to build a successful combination of styles into a team. Styles are not right or wrong, ideal or not ideal. Style refers to the way key members of the management team behave. One of the major contributions that experienced investors make is their first-hand experience of working within and developing successful early stage management teams. Striking a productive balance within a new team is one of the major indicators of the effectiveness of a CEO in the investors' perception.

Creative tensions and constructive solutions

Experienced investors will spend time considering the dynamics of a new management team and seek to modify their own styles to meet the needs of the situation and to exert their influence in the most effective way. A well-balanced management team does not necessarily mean that tensions do not exist within the group, but it does mean that differences of viewpoint can be expressed and accommodated within a constructive and supportive framework of relationships.

Tensions will exist in any creative group of people, and is to be expected in an entrepreneurial new management team. One of the benefits of having investors that are experienced in these situations is that they can assist in directing creative tensions into finding constructive solutions that reconcile the initial differences of viewpoint. Sometimes it is not possible to find a middle path, in which case it is important to ensure that the 'collective decision' is accepted by all.

Monitoring investments and influencing change

Monitoring investments is one thing – bringing about change in investee companies is another. It is useful to separate these two distinct activities and to consider what each involves. For example, one of the most difficult judgements an active investor has to make is when to suggest that management change may be necessary to accelerate value creation. Changes often have to be made sooner than expected and can be a cause of major tension between the investors and executive management team. Finding a way through these issues requires maturity and experience – something an experienced investor will have acquired through previous investments.

All professional investors need to monitor their investments – this should be a mechanical, but structured activity. Reporting/monitoring activities often focus on tracking quantitative actual performance against a plan. The obvious monitoring activity is tracking the monthly financial performance against the approved budget.

Early stage investors also often like to monitor qualitative indicators of progress, such as staff recruitment, technical milestones or business development activities. It is useful to agree a small number of performance indicators that should be tracked and agree with the investors an appropriate method of presenting the data. Over time it is also sensible to review these indicators and revise them – competitors can move the goal posts. Having agreed the performance indicators, it is vital that the managers own them. Satisfying investor monitoring needs is a basic requirement of board meetings.

Tools to influence change

Active investors need to be able to influence change – this is an ongoing process during the life of any investment. The key tools that are used to influence change are:

- the business plan;
- staffing changes; and
- other strategic decisions.

It is important to ensure that investors are openly involved in these areas, otherwise there is a risk that off-line discussions between investors will start and an alternative investor plan will start to develop often involving changing the management. As the spinout develops, so do its management needs and an important role of active investors is to prompt discussions concerning the development of the management team. Establishing a remuneration sub-committee of the board that involves the investors is a useful way to structure this type of input.

Investor representatives and non-executive directors

An active early stage investor can always be expected to negotiate board representation rights. An effective investor representative should be on top of the issues facing a company. The representative's role should be one of increasing awareness and assisting the management's efforts to build the business. Investor representatives may have some additional controls, such as investor consent provisions, but these controls should be used sparingly.

Sometimes it is necessary to be forceful and directive when dealing with new management team who may be relatively inexperienced compared with the investor. However, if an investor representative is going to influence the management team successfully, first he must gain their confidence.

When joining a board, an investor non-executive director (NED) should focus on issues such as:

- style of the management team (for example, defensive or expansive);
- team building/maintaining commitment;
- keeping the peace where possible;
- ensuring the managers manage;
- potential reaction to changes;
- watch for early warning signs;
- crisis management; and
- planning for an exit.

The investor representative will also expect to be involved in the normal board functions as follows:

- setting of agendas and agreeing key procedures;
- financial review;
- strategy;
- setting of budgets;
- review of executive performance;
- taking key board level decisions;
- corporate governance; and
- discipline.

Danger areas for less experienced investor representatives are a lack of independence. It is necessary to avoid others around the board being unsure about who you represent – are you a NED or an investor? The converse of this risk is when an investor 'goes native' – in this case there is a risk that the individual will not be able to convince venture capital colleagues to support the business because of this apparent lack of objectivity.

Active support or interference?

The line between active investor support and interference can be a fine one. Investors should always remember that they are not the managers of the spinout. There is a danger that an active investor dominates the spinout company's thinking and the executive management team fails to take responsibility for the business. This is to be avoided – managers should be allowed to manage and investors should not usurp their powers. Generally, investors do not make good managers.

Different investor approaches

Active investors have distinctive styles and it is worth considering what impact a particular style may have on the business. At one extreme, an investor may appoint a senior industry figure who is content to allow the management team to deal with the day-to-day operation of the business. He or she only expects to provide input to strategic discussion (normally at board meetings) and provides broad feedback to the investors. Typically, this is a non-interventionist approach. The investor will tend to provide direct feedback at the point the business needs to raise further funds or at the stage that the company needs to seek investor majority consent.

At the other end of the scale is the serial entrepreneur and investor who can be more inclined to act like a shadow CEO and/or finance director. This type of investor will often be in weekly or daily contact with the management team and will be involved in every aspect of the day-to-day operation of the business. In certain cases, the business will be located in the key investor's offices. Provided the investor does not hinder the development of an independent management team, soon after company formation this type of intensive support can be valuable.

Does size and experience count for anything?

It is true that spinout companies may benefit at different stages in their development from different types of investors' interaction. Experienced investors will be sensitive to the need for their input in a company to evolve. Often the trigger to change the way an investor handles a particular investment is linked to the raising of finance. As new investors are attracted to a company, existing investors will discuss with the new investors how the board of the company should be structured to enable the new investor to make a contribution. Frequently this will result in one or more of the existing investors stepping down from the board.

There is always a personal risk associated with active investors. Larger financial organisations tend to have more staff turnover and movement amongst offices than smaller organisations. This means that in larger investor groups, it is less likely that during the entire life of an investment the same individual will be responsible for a particular investment. This can create a degree of uncertainty about the level of support that a particular investor will provide. In some cases, a supportive investor can become a disenchanted one because of a staff change or a change in the investment strategy of the investor.

Smaller specialist investors tend to have stable teams and it is usually expected that the individual who recommends the investment will be responsible for it for the entire investment cycle. These investors tend to place the decision-maker on the board of the company. This means that at board meetings the investors' expressed views are less likely to change after reporting back to head office. This directness can be important when dealing with fast-moving situations that require subjective judgement that are always more difficult to make from a distance.

Managing interactions between different investors

It is also worth considering how different investors may interact. Management should be aware of these potential tensions. For example:

- Professional active investors can often be direct competitors. This can create a difficult board dynamic where these investors have invested at different times and on different terms.

- Investors may not agree on a course of action and therefore there is a stalemate over a key strategic decision. In some cases this can lead the business to fail.

The management team of a new business can help to avoid problems like this.

- Look for evidence that potential investors have worked successfully together in other syndicates in order to improve the chances that the syndicate works well.
- Ensure that active investors are able to make their contribution, but that they are not allowed to interfere unduly with the management of the business.
- Apply strong executive management and independent non-executive management to counteract these dangers and ensure that the board is focused on moving the company forward, not deflected by specific investor agendas.
- Look for evidence of this 'added value' when selecting investors. This is a good discipline. It usually indicates that the investor has a constructive way of working within an early stage management team.
- Look for relevant experience that can significantly enhance the prospects of the business. Experienced investors should improve the chances of and increase the speed of accessing further capital as well as attracting the most talented management.

It is worth, however, stressing that investors do not have a monopoly on wisdom. Clearly, experienced and active investors do make mistakes and some of their investments will fail despite their best efforts – or even because of their worst efforts (for example impatience, loss of nerve or changes of internal policy).

Tips for entrepreneurs

- Understand the perspectives, needs, objectives and motivations of your investors.
- Use the due diligence process and negotiations to clarify the objectives of the investors and ensure that they are consistent with those of the spinout management team.
- Early on in the relationship, work to establish the basic information requirements of individual investors.
- Developing a simple communication plan around the investors' needs is a good way to start to develop an open relationship.
- Agree a small number of performance indicators that should be tracked and agree with the investors an appropriate method of presenting the data.
- Having agreed the performance indicators, it is vital that the managers have ownership over them if they are to create and deliver value.
- Management should be aware of potential tensions and a difficult board dynamic where different investors have invested at different times and on different terms.

Chapter 18

Post funding challenges and opportunities: the value of venture capital

Ravi Belani[1]
Draper Fisher Jurvetson, Menlo Park, California

Introduction

Much of what is presented in this chapter is inspired by experiences from the Draper Fisher Jurvetson fund and its portfolio companies. The chapter outlines the resources, capabilities and knowledge that a good venture capital firm may provide. It also presents some key defining pitfalls and challenges that most academic spinouts face post financing. University spin-outs come in many forms in terms of stage, industry focus and goals. The issues discussed here give universities and academic inventors a general overview and will need to be filtered according to each unique business opportunity. Some ideas discussed may be provocative or controversial, but like all interesting topics, they can be treated as one view among many.

Building a business

The real work for a university spinout begins after it has gone through the various stages to secure funding.

In many ways, securing financing hallmarks the transition between the academic and the business world. While the process of financing is a relatively contained and defined process, building a business is not. It is during this phase of a spinout's life that the culture of academia – which rewards rigorous thought, development and reflection – may bump heads with what is required to succeed in business – execution, making tradeoffs and sweat. Academia provides a nuturing environment for cultivating innovative ideas that may result in patents for seeding a business, but business building requires distinctly different skill-sets (see Exhibit 18.1).

There are many good venture capital firms that have already been down the path to financing, and more that will be going down it in the future. These firms should be able to provide resources, networking and advice. Most importantly, the venture capitalist (VC) chosen by a spinout should be someone that the entrepreneur can trust and for whom it will want to make money, and someone who can serve as a mentor.

Draper Fisher Jurvetson believes that great entrepreneurs build great companies. It tries to help entrepreneurs from the earliest stages of a company to build lasting businesses by providing a network of resources, people and support. It backs companies because it wants to see an entrepreneur's vision realised. The firm is vigilant about being supportive, but not controlling. Micromanaging an entrepreneur's vision can often cripple it, especially for the most innovative companies that are disrupting convention.

Exhibit 18.1

The patent is not everything

A patent that may have inspired the start of a company is just that: a start.

- Adrian Tuck, executive vice president of Ember, has a useful points system for putting things in perspective. An entrepreneur gets:

  - one point for having an idea, and one point for the patent;
  - 10 points for articulating an idea and developing a rational business model;
  - 100 points for getting funded; and
  - 1,000 points for landing a customer.

- Landing a customer is the goal – a patent, venture-backing and a great team are only valuable insofar as the business has, or can get, a customer who pays.
- Do not use patents to hold the company hostage if tension arises as a company grows. Make sure there is a 'no fault divorce' provision – a type of prenuptial agreement that provides a mechanism for resolving disputes regarding licensing a technology if members of a company decide to go their separate ways.
- It is usually better to take stock instead of a royalty for the patent. Stock puts the founder on the same team as the other shareholders, and can usually make more money in the long run.

Source: Adrian Tuck, executive vice president, Ember Inc, Massachussetts.

Getting assistance with key challenges and opportunities

There are multiple challenges and opportunities post funding. Three that are particularly common and important are highlighted below:

- building out the team;
- acquiring the first customer; and
- raising further finance.

Each challenge is discussed in the same way that a VC would walk an entrepreneur through the options and choices they have.

Building out the team

Receiving funding marks a critical point of change for most academic spinouts. Prior to funding, money is often scarce, but time is ample. Once a spinout is funded, money is available, but time becomes expensive to spend. It is critical to understand this shift, and where this first comes to a head is in building out the team. In fact, building the right team is arguably the most important area on which to focus.

Of course, a team may have been assembled prior to funding, but as the spinout develops it will undoubtedly evolve. Right away, a few key questions need answers.

Who is in and who is out?

Good universities can provide inexpensive resources to companies before they are funded. Once funded, however, it is critical for the company to set up an identity and location outside of the university. As a general rule, if anything needs to be done that is critical to the development of the business, it has to be done by people who work for the company. It should not be done by people who work at the university.

Having said that, technology transfer outside the university is a contact sport – it occurs through people.[2] The key technical gurus on the team almost always need to leave academia in order for the spinout to be viable. Professors or university faculty staff involved in the company should think carefully about how interested they are in participating in the company moving forward. If professors are critical to carrying the key technical know-how into the spinout, they will need to be willing to take a leave of absence from the school, and assume the acadmic career risk that might accompany such a leave.

In the authors' experiences, it is very difficult to straddle both academia and the operations of a spinout company. After the key technical insight has been transferred to other members of the team or embedded inside a developed product, a professor may return to academia. Professors who wish to continue to work in the university generally serve best by playing a consulting, advisory or personal mentorship role to the company or other founders.

However, the university provides a wonderful resource for talent that should not go untapped. The academic network should be leveraged well for hiring other members of the team. It is probably best to bring university talent to the company, as opposed to bringing company work to the university. The culture of the university often runs counter to that of a spinout and the business will be well served to bring the talent in-house – doing work in a location that is physically different from the university can have a significant impact on meeting product development needs.

What is the founder's role?

Assuming the founder would like to commit to the company, he or she next needs to determine what role to play.

The founder's role probably will be defined more by his or her interests than capabilities. Founders of companies have taken on every executive role – CEO, chief technical officer (CTO), and head of marketing, sales or engineering. Although success and failure have been seen in each permutation, an academic founder who can assume the CEO position successfully is a rarity.

The founder should think through what ultimately motivates him or her. The next step is to build a team to complement what he or she does and does not want to do. The founder should seriously consider the implications the new role will have on his or her own life. While challenges in a university can often be overcome with intellect and experimentation, a spinout environment will afford little room for mistakes. After the role of the founder has been determined, several questions should be asked.

• Can the company afford to have the founder in that role?

If one person possesses the core understanding of the technology on the founding team, it may be challenging for the team to have that person not play a technical role in the beginning. CEOs, for example, do not spend the bulk of their time focusing on technology development. If the founder serves as CEO, the team may suffer a huge opportunity cost for not having him or her work on the development of the technology. After the founder has transferred that technical know-how, a transition to the business side may be easier.

217

- Does the founder know what the role requires? If not, is he or she willing to learn? Does he or she have the desire to do what the role requires?

The skill-sets of each role are very different. A CEO's job, for example, often seems glamorous due to its role in externally promoting the company and internally building morale. First and foremost, CEOs need to be managers and sales people. Is the founder ready to create and be measured by an operating plan and budget, to pitch and close the first few customers, to manage a board of directors, to motivate the team when money is running out, and to make hard cost-cutting decisions when times get rough?

Similarly, a vice president of engineering needs to know how to build a commercial-grade product through a structured development process. This process often has less to do with technical insight and more to do with managing what can go wrong in the pursuit of shipping a product – such as poor testing, feature creep (where additional features are continually added) and not prioritising requirements.

The founder's ideal role more likely will be determined by desire and experience than by intelligence. If the founder finds that he of she is not executing this role well, it likely will not be because he or she is not smart enough, but because he or she does not have a skill-set born out of experience, or is not happy doing what the role requires.

- If the founder realises he or she is not happy in a given role, will he or she be able to get out of it?

It often takes real personal reflection and maturity for founders to admit that they would be more effective in another role. If the founder does make that decision, someone must fill the role fairly quickly, or critical time will be lost. Make sure that there is a plan for assessing the founder's fit and performance in his or her role, and that he or she has the option to move out of it if it does not seem to be working.

- If the founder is not the CEO, who is?

A leader, not just a functional head, should be hired as a CEO. The CEO should be as good at business as the best technical founder is at technology. There is often a temptation to hire a CEO to fill a functional role that the team or investors feel is lacking – for example, a buddy who serves as a sales head. That is not a CEO. The CEO should complement the team in this functional capacity, but should also pass a higher hurdle of being a real leader as the company grows. Specifically, the CEO should be great at understanding the strengths of people and where to place them to lead a team that can execute. He or she may also be a vehicle to establishing trust between the VCs and the founding team in the early stages of a company.

Is the rest of the team well-rounded?
Complement the skill-set between the founders and the CEO (if different from the founders) with a well-rounded team of sales, operations, finance and marketing professionals. Sometimes, the functional roles that academic entrepreneurs often find less intellectually challenging – operations, marketing and sales for example – are the most important for execution. They should not be discounted. Hire the best people possible, and hire very carefully. The founder should never be afraid to hire people better or smarter than himself or herself.

The following case study provides an example of how a VC can work closely with their portfolio company to build out the management team.

Case study

Imago Scientific Instruments

In 1998, Tom Kelly, PhD, Professor of Material Science and Engineering at the University of Wisconsin-Madison, re-mortgaged his house to found Imago Scientific Instruments, a company based on a novel 3D atomic scale microscope he had developed at the university.

Tom Kelly knew he needed business expertise to help him build the company, and initially brought on a business consultant to help guide him on certain issues. His brother, Ed Kelly, was an MBA-educated, 20-year seasoned business executive from the publishing industry, and in August 2000, Ed Kelly came on board as the business head. Tom Kelly maintained the title as CEO, while Ed Kelly served as president.

New investors

In September 2002, Draper Fisher Jurvetson led a US$7 million financing into Imago. Managing director Warren Packard spearheaded the investment, bringing in two of the other three outside venture funds into the company. Packard was no stranger to university spinouts: prior to joining Draper Fisher Jurvetson, he had co-founded Angara Database Systems, a main-memory relational database company spun out of Stanford University.

The new investors helped build out the Imago team. As part of the financing, Imago was able to bring on Sanjay Tripathi as a full time chief operating officer (COO). Packard also worked with the Imago executive team to revamp and update an antiquated employee stock option plan they had in place to incentivise new and existing hires to come on board.

Ed Kelly had guided the company well, raising US$5 million in angel funding during his leadership. But Ed Kelly lacked domain expertise in the markets Imago was attacking. Ed Kelly worked with Packard to find his replacement, who would serve as CEO of the company while Tom Kelly assumed the chief technical officer (CTO) role. Packard led the sourcing of a CEO search firm, and along with other board members, interviewed multiple CEO candidates until they found Tim Stultz, PhD, a former vice president of Veeco Instruments Metrology Group.

New CEO

In his previous role, Stultz was instrumental in bringing to market the world's first fully automated Atomic Force Microscope, an analytical tool of similar sophistication and areas of application as Imago's. He brought an instant perspective to many of the core issues Imago was wrestling with, including:

- developing an intellectual property (IP) strategy;
- forging partnerships; and
- developing sales.

> Stultz had worked with many of the same companies that Imago was pursuing. He could assess how real their business development relationships were, and also recommend firms that the company had not worked with that they should have. Imago would later secure an additional US$5 million in financing at an upswing in valuation in February 2004.

Acquiring the first customer

The second key challenge post funding is acquiring the first customer. In most cases, university spinouts start out with solutions in search of problems: highly disruptive innovations looking for a market that rewards them. At the same time, technologists can often become so enamoured with the further development of a technology that they lose sight of a market beckoning for a solution that their technology is already well-suited to address. Finding the niche – the initial market where a technology can gain traction – is often the most difficult task an academic spinout addresses. The problem also needs to be re-addressed as markets shift.

Every spinout differs in nature and development when it comes to finding that niche and acquiring its first customer. Listed below are the milestone events that can be abstracted from the authors' collective experiences with university spinouts. It is assumed that the spinout's innovation is at a proof-of-concept stage when funded. These questions underlie the product development and customer traction milestones that successful spinouts hit in the first 12–18 months of operation. These are not set in stone: a particular business may be further along in development or the nature of the business may prioritise certain milestones over others.

What is unique and who wants to buy it?

The innovation being spun out from the university may be a novel proof-of-concept at the funding stage, for example, an elegant algorithm, a new process or a material with compelling properties. It is now important to determine where the uniqueness of that innovation may be most relevant for someone to pay for it.

The company should seek smart people outside the core founding team who can position the technology relevant to the landscape of innovations and markets they see.

- A VC, for example, often sits between technologies and markets and can facilitate matching the two.
- Smart people at the nexus of business and technology are most relevant here, such as:
  - technology decision-makers within leading corporations;
  - professors serving as consultants or board members of leading corporations;
  - technology market analysts; and
  - other market-savvy technologists with creative bents.

Try to have multiple conversations quickly, but be wary of prolonging or over-structuring this process. The business's positioning will most likely change, and the best insights will often come from unexpected places. It is most important to iterate: develop a perspective on where the business would like to head, but remain flexible as new insights are gathered.

How quickly can a prototype be built?

The next goal is to build out a prototype to engage prospective customers. The prototype does not need to be, and should not be, flawless. The incremental time spent on perfecting the prototype at the expense of not being in front of a prospective customer sooner likely will not be worth it. In fact, presenting an imperfect product to a prospective customer will force the customer to prioritise how important the flaws are, or to think creatively about ways to fix them.

Development time of the prototype should in general be on the scale of months, not years. A good prototype is one that gives the team credibility in the eyes of a customer prospect, and makes the product just real enough for customers to be willing to pay for further development of it or to think about where it would be most useful to them.

Track who buys into the vision of the prototype and why, but, more importantly, track who does not buy into the vision and why. There is a tendency to view those who agree with the vision of the prototype as successes and those who do not as failures. However, many new markets can be found by discovering why the prototype did not resonate. Is there another point of pain that the prospective customer faces that the technology can address? A greater point of pain means more dollars – if the real point of pain can be found, see if the business vision can be adjusted accordingly.

Who will step up first to pay for the product?

The next critical goal is to find the initial customer who will pay for the product and over-deliver in servicing them. The most relevant customer is someone who will move the fastest in closing a deal, pay the business to cover its costs and evangelise the successful product. The initial customer does not need to be in the ultimate target market, or even a big brand name. What is far more critical is a proof point where the business can demonstrate early on the uniqueness of the technology that has been articulated. The business can then parlay this success into other markets.

Treat this first customer as a partner. The business and its customer are going to work together in building out the first product, and the customer is going to give the business credibility to the market. Having said that, it is critical that the first customer pays the business, and ideally enough to cover both material and labour costs, as well as the overhead associated with the product. The business may not achieve a profit on the first customer, but should expect to cover its costs. Adequate payment will ensure that each party has a continuing interest in the product, and also can provide a good litmus test to decide who the initial customer should be.

The following case study provides an example of how a VC can work closely with their portfolio company in the stage prior to securing the first customer.

Case study
Ember Corporation

In February 2001, MIT graduate students Rob Poor, PhD, and Andy Wheeler moved their nascent company Ember into the Cambridge Innovation Center, an office suite designed for startups, located across the street from the Massachusetts Institute of Technology (MIT) campus in Kendall Square. They were attempting to build a business around an embedded wireless networking technology that they had developed at MIT's Media Lab.

Housed on their floor at the Cambridge Innovation Center was Draper Fisher Jurvetson New England, the Boston-based affiliate fund of Draper Fisher Jurvetson. Managing director, Todd Hixon, became friends with Poor and Wheeler at the coffee machine in the community kitchen, and soon Poor and Wheeler shared their plans and ideas with Hixon.

Excited by Poor and Wheeler's vision, Hixon teamed with Bob Metcalfe at Polaris to put together a term sheet that led to a US$3 million seed round, with an initial anchor investment in July 2001. In the process of fund raising, Poor and Wheeler were introduced to Adrian Tuck, whom they brought in as an interim CEO, while Poor and Wheeler assumed responsibilities as CTO and vice president of engineering, respectively.

Hixon would work with the team daily in their first seven months post funding. A former senior vice president of the Boston Consulting Group, Hixon helped craft and continually revise the initial go-to-market strategy. He interviewed almost every new hire the team brought on board, and mentored the team on the key milestones they needed to achieve prior to achieving their subsequent funding.

Some 13 months later, in October 2002, Ember would secure US$20 million of additional funding with a significant increase in valuation, impressive referenceable customers, a strong pipeline and many industry accolades. How did they do it? Below are some comments from Adrian Tuck.

Keep the whole company focused on a few key goals
- In the beginning, it is the really simple things that need to be executed: find a happy customer, ride that customer and get five more.
- Ember kept one wall in the company with a very detailed project plan with every task that they needed to achieve over the following six months listed out, as you would in a Gantt chart. Everybody could see their tasks and how they had an impact on those of everybody else.

Set expectations with the board on what 'success' means for the next funding event and exceed them
- Ember's board reports were simple: they focused on the five key areas to the business with traffic light signals for how they were tracking.
- Business plans continually evolved, and were never more than 10 slides.

Do not get stuck in analysis paralysis: find someone who wants to buy what the business has and move fast
- Initial market analysis had Ember looking at markets as diverse as home networking, health care, agriculture, automotive and construction. Ember landed their first customer eight months post funding by cold calling a list of contacts and finding a water filtration plant with a need that fit.
- Do not underestimate the power of a story in closing the first customer. People love a story on how the technology will change the world, and how they will contribute to that evolution by being the first adopter.

Over-deliver to the first customer, and parlay that to success with others
- Although water filtration was not necessarily Ember's target market, their first implementation proved the technical capabilities of the product to help them sell into other markets.
- Their first customer paid them to cover their costs, and more importantly, provided fantastic quotes for future sales.

Raising further finance

The third key challenge post funding is raising further finance. The initial venture investment will typically provide capital to fund 12–24 months of operations. The business might need to start the process of acquiring more capital fairly soon. If the business decides to pursue another round of venture funding, as opposed to debt financing, federal grants or revenue from customers and partners, the following questions should be asked.

What is the founder and the board interested in?

Prioritise what is important to the founder and the board. Is the business just seeking new capital, a specific addition to the investment team (a corporate investor, for example) or a certain valuation? The board will have to approve the new financing, but, more importantly, they can set a floor for an acceptable valuation – they may opt to internally finance a company for any valuation that comes below a certain price.

What are the target investors looking for?

Series B (second round funding) investors are different from Series A (first round funding) investors – they will expect more progress along product development, customer traction and revenue visibility than their earlier peers. Also, Series B investors will differ among themselves in terms of industry preferences, risk preferences and investment appetites.

- Begin by having a list of who to target and what their expectations might be. Work with the Series A investors on fine-tuning the pitch to be presented.
- In the process of presenting, ask for feedback and listen carefully, especially to those firms who decline funding. Is the business at a fundable stage for that investor? If not, what would they like to see before they invest?
- Make sure there is enough cash in the bank to bring the company to a point in its development where it is fundable. If, in order to receive funding, the business needs to hit milestones that were not anticipated, the business plan must be readjusted and the cash burn rate (the month-by-month rate at which the remaining cash within the company is used) reduced to give the business time to hit those milestones.
- It is wise to err on the side of starting the process earlier to reality test assumptions on where the company needs to be to receive Series B funding.
- If the business is capital intensive, Series B may be the first time that the business requires cash to build significant facilities or capital expenditures. Those expenditures need to be justified to the Series B investors.

- Be opportunistic in fund raising. If there is interest from others to put more money into the business before it had planned to solicit funds, think about terms that would be attractive to the business. Conversely, if the capital markets are cold despite the progress the business is making, reduce the cash burn rate until the situation turns around and focus on executing in the business.

- Cast a wide net, but prioritise who to speak to. Fund raising can be a time-consuming process. It may be useful to keep an updated list of the business's top 10 investor prospects and only add a new investor prospect to the list when one of the original 10 ends their interest.

The following case study provides an example of how a VC can work closely with their portfolio company to help with fund raising.

Case study

ZettaCore

In 1999, Randy Levine, PhD, founded ZettaCore, a developer of next generation electronic memory based on research from the University of California Riverside and North Carolina State University. ZettaCore garnered US$5.55 million in Series A funding in December 2001; Draper Fisher Jurvetson was the largest investor.

In May 2003, ZettaCore aimed to raise Series B funding, giving themselves a nine-month timetable to raise the funds. Levine's board had helped him to put together an initial list of venture funds to contact, and helped with the initial fine-tuning of the pitch he would make.

A year earlier, ZettaCore board member and Draper Fisher Jurvetson managing director Steve Jurvetson had highlighted ZettaCore to Vinod Khosla, a general partner with Kleiner, Perkins, Caufield and Byers, at a conference. Now that the company was fundraising, Steve took the opportunity to re-introduce the company to Kleiner Perkins, one of the initial target firms.

Core team and milestones

In the course of presenting the company to the Series B prospects, it became clear that the Series B investors wanted to see the company complete its next milestone in an aggressive development programme (a compelling prototype). The company focused its efforts on completing that prototype prior to returning to the group of investors who were most interested in the company.

In the meantime, ZettaCore rounded out its team of directors. After an introduction from Jurvetson, Levine invited and brought on Herb Goronkin, a vice president of Motorola Labs, to the board of directors. Jurvetson also provided an introduction to Les Vadasz, one of the founders of Intel, who joined the board as well.

With an aggressive milestone schedule on track, and an impressive board of directors filled out, ZettaCore re-visited its most promising Series B prospective investors. In

December 2003 – six months after having begun their push for Series B funds – ZettaCore secured over US$17 million in financing, led by Khosla at Kleiner Perkins, at a significant upswing in valuation from their Series A price.

The value of venture capital

Given the post funding challenges presented above, what value can a venture capital firm bring? Academic studies have shown that venture-backed companies (regardless of the firm) bring products to market faster, attract management talent more easily and receive financing more quickly than non-venture capital backed startups.[3] If the growth of the business is constrained by a lack of cash, resources or advice, venture capital can often provide an injection to catalyse its growth.

Venture capital firms provide financial support, mentorship and resources to the entrepreneurs they champion. They help their entrepreneurs focus on a strategy and operating plan, provide a rolodex of contacts to help build out the business, and serve as a sounding board for issues that young spinout companies wrestle with, based on their experience of seeing early stage companies grow. A good firm will often challenge an entrepreneur's assumptions to help them think critically, but will rarely dictate what they have to do.

Beyond advice and mentorship, venture capital firms can often provide an entrepreneur with the following key resources to overcome key challenges and build the business.

Capital

If the business is constrained in developing the product, pursuing customer leads, or exploring new opportunities, the most immediate relief that a venture firm will provide is the capital itself. More importantly, the firm should have additional capital reserved for follow-on investing in later rounds. Indeed, the business should know how large a fund the venture capital firm is investing out of, and how much additional capital the fund might have in reserve for follow-on investing.

A venture capital firm will also have relationships with other institutions to help with the capital needs of the business. These should include other venture funds for future private equity rounds, commercial banks that can provide debt financing, and investment banks that can provide liquidity and public financing when the business is thinking about a public offering. A good VC cannot get the extra money, but they might get the business better terms, better rates or a more successful initial public offering (IPO).

Credibility

Receiving financing from a brand name venture fund can provide a powerful signal of the viability of the business. Leading venture capital firms receive a plethora of business plans for every company they back. Venture capital backing can serve to differentiate the company from the rest of the startup pack, indicating to others that this business has deep-pocketed financiers behind it who see huge potential.

Access to the Global 2000 Major Corporations

Venture capital firms often have strong connections with the Global 2000 corporations of major corporations. These connections can help secure an introduction to a large enterprise that may become a customer, channel partner, system integrator, value-added reseller, original equipment manufacturer (OEM), original design manufacturer (ODM), or other partner in developing the technology.

There are multiple ways that a venture capital firm may have a relationship with a large enterprise.

- Large enterprises are often limited partners in venture capital firms.
- For many of the top venture capital firms, individual partners may serve on the boards of public companies they financed when they were private, or they may have sold a previous company to a Global 2000 player in the past.
- Large corporations with their own venture capital arms often maintain tight relationships with independent venture capital firms, since the independent funds lead financing rounds that the corporate funds participate in.
- Often, venture capital firms serve as hubs for large corporations that want to reach out to emerging companies.

In short, a good venture capital firm will usually have at least an initial contact into a major corporation that can be helpful to a business.

Access to other portfolio companies of the VC

A venture capital firm's portfolio of companies can be a rich source of resources as well. For companies building businesses in novel areas, the most important suppliers and partners to the business may be other emerging companies in the venture fund's portfolio. The fund's portfolio can also serve as a network of best practices for emerging companies and technologies. Once funded, the business team joins an instant community of executives building out businesses, who may serve as sounding boards for various operational, strategy and technology development areas being faced.

Access to providers

Many venture capital firms are natural hubs for industries that support emerging company operations – legal support, financial accounting, information technology infrastructure, human resource benefits, consultants, real estate brokers and so on. Indeed, the venture capital firm may not only be able to provide an introduction, but may even provide a discount to some of these services.

Acquiring talent

Building out a team with the right people is arguably the most important task that a founder will undertake. Good VCs can provide a rolodex of contacts who can serve as key management hires, potential members of the boards of directors and advisers, and other staff. A firm's website often serves as a résumé-generating source – a business may post openings on the venture firm's website or the firm may forward on résumés submitted to its site by those seeking to join the company.

Promotion

A good portion of some VCs' time is spent in educating and promoting new industries. The press often courts VCs to obtain emerging-technology stories. A VC may spend significant time at conferences, serving on panels or delivering keynote speeches about emerging technology areas. A firm cannot only be a hub to direct media inquiries towards a business, but individual VCs are natural spokespeople as well who can promote the company to others (assuming this is desired).

Exploiting an investor's resources, networks and knowledge

All venture funds will trumpet at least a subset of the above resources. However, VCs will not build a business for the founder – he or she and the team are ultimately responsible for that (and deserve the recognition when the company is successful). The VCs investing in a business want to see it succeed – indeed, both the founder and the VC will have a significant stake in the company and their incentives should be aligned.

Getting the most from investors

Entrepreneurs should be proactive about exploiting their investors' resources once funded.

- Do not be shy about asking for introductions in areas you are seeking.
- Bring VCs into your problems, and do it early. VCs do not expect you to be 'all knowing'. Do not be scared that the board will fire you if you need help. In fact, the board will be far more disappointed if you bring them into your problems too late. The board would much rather help you, and indeed will respect you more, for pointing out issues early than for confronting them with surprise issues that have been ballooning in the background without their knowledge. Being viewed as cautious is always better than being viewed as incompetent.
- VCs tend to be social beasts. Even if a business's VCs cannot come up with the critical insight into a problem, they probably know someone who can. Brainstorm with them so they can effect an introduction to someone who can help, if they cannot help directly.
- Develop individual relationships with each board member outside of the board meeting. The board meeting itself is sometimes a legal formality – individual interactions will allow you to see another side of your board member. Ask if you can come over and meet them for breakfast or lunch, especially if there is an issue brewing. Sometimes, you can set up regular individual meetings outside the board setting. Especially target individual meetings with board members that are not always around for the meeting itself.

Getting the most from your board

Serving as a CEO can be a lonely job. The CEO has to make decisions to ensure the viability of the business with an objectivity that often separates the CEO from the rest of the company. The board can serve as a source of mentorship and coaching for the CEO.

At its most basic level, the board of directors keeps the company honest. The discipline of presenting to a board every four to six weeks can be a worthwhile exercise in and of itself. A great board, however, possesses the quality of a great team. It will not only keep a company honest, but also push the company in new directions using the combined experience, knowledge and guidance of the board members.

Surrounding yourself with the right people on your board will make a real difference to achieving your goals. A well-rounded board with complementary skill-sets will best serve spinout companies.

- Choose members who can serve not only as mentors you trust, but also as representatives of different skill-sets and experiences.
- Bring in people with domain expertise, strategy and operations experience to the table.
- Get a VC, but also get someone who has run a similar company before (if the VC has not). It may also be beneficial to have a customer or supplier on the board (unless the business wants to keep its margins secret from them).
- Finally, don't be scared to go outside your comfort zone and bring in people who look at the world differently.

Tips for entrepreneurs

- Venture capital can serve as a shot in the arm to catalyse the growth of your business. Look for a firm that has the resources, advice and money you need to build out your dream, and an individual VC you trust and want to work with.
- Build out a well-rounded board that you trust. Communicate with them both in and outside the boardroom to make sure that you are getting what you want from them, and that they will not feel surprised when problems occur. Set realistic expectations for them to judge you by, and hit or exceed those expectations.
- Once funded, focus on landing the first customer. Determine what is unique with the product, build out a prototype quickly, and over-deliver to the first customer who will pay for the product.
- Use the VCs on the board. Have them help build out the team by introducing and interviewing candidates or executive search firms. Leverage their expertise and network in fine-tuning the pitch and determining the audience for subsequent rounds of funding.
- Finally, none of these are hard and fast rules. In fact, often the best successes use approaches that are entirely new, and break all the rules and norms. Entrepreneurs, by their nature, are agents of change. Go out and change the world.

---

[1] The authors are indebted to the following key contributors for their invaluable insight – Entrepreneurs: Tom Kelly (Imago Scientific Instruments), Randy Levine (ZettaCore), Udi Meirav (Luminus Devices), Norman Shumaker (Molecular Imprints), Adrian Tuck (Ember); Venture Capitalists: Tim Draper/Steve Jurvetson/Warren Packard (Draper Fisher Jurvetson), Todd Hixon (Draper Fisher Jurvetson New England), Rajeev Motwani (Dot Edu Ventures), Michael Sheridan (Mohr Davidow Ventures). The ideas expressed do not necessarily represent those of the contributors.

[2] Special thanks to Michael Sheridan from Mohr Davidow Ventures for providing this analogy.

[3] Hellman and Puri, 1999 & 2001, Stanford Graduate School of Business.

Chapter 19

Adding value – strategic alliances and corporate partnerships

John O'Donohue
Motorola Ventures EMEA, Basingstoke

Chris Winter
New Venture Partners, Adastral Park and New Jersey

Dr Kenny Tang, CFA
Oxbridge Capital, London

Introduction

This chapter, illustrated by three case studies, addresses the motivations of large corporations in partnering with young spinout companies. It also assesses the benefits and risks to spinouts when considering strategic alliances and corporate partnerships with major corporations.

Developing a win-win situation

New high-technology spinouts have a short time in which to become established in competitive marketplaces. An important way to achieve this is by creating timely strategic partnering relationships with established corporate players. These relationships range from key product purchase commitments to distribution agreements, original equipment manufacturers (OEM) deals, joint technology development and equity investment. Major corporations, especially those with corporate investing arms, have strong relationships and experience in key markets, thereby providing ideal corporate partnering opportunities for young spinouts.

Corporate research and development laboratories: adding value?

Corporate research and development (R&D) laboratories are a rich source of intellectual property (IP), and the goals and spending priorities of these corporates mean that the original research is often both well-directed to commercial goals and global markets, and well protected. However, the coupling between corporate R&D and its exploitation through the corporates' customer-facing lines of business is often poor or missing. These problems can be summarised briefly.

- The stage at which a corporate R&D team is prepared to develop the technology is much earlier in the product cycle than when a product team will want to take it on.
- There are always more technologies than the company can invest in internally.

- The technology may end up being better if exploited in a market that is not strategic to the corporate.
- New technologies are normally sold as products, components or materials. The R&D facilities of service companies (such as the major telecommunication network operators) are often poor at product delivery and the lines of business would prefer to source the best of breed internationally to build into their service offerings. For product companies, components and materials seldom differentiate a product sufficiently in the marketplace and it is better to exploit them more widely than keep them in-house.
- A single technology is seldom a customer solution on its own: it often needs a wider suite of intellectual property rights (IPR) and related developments to create a product family and a sustainable business.

Response: spin in or spin out?

Increasingly, large corporations are looking to spin out technologies from their laboratories in order to create value, and to look for other investors to help in the productisation of such technologies. When they do so, they are often interested in sourcing the products back to include with their own offerings. This breaking of the vertical R&D model is leading to concepts such as 'open innovation', where corporate R&D labs are looking for other companies to share their R&D facilities, to source new concepts from startups and to see spinouts as the natural way to exploit disruptive technologies. This creates an ecology of interdependent suppliers of research and products that feed into the main corporation's lines of business.

Large corporations are also looking to source technologies by buying outside companies or investing in them (referred to as 'spin-ins'). Buying ensures access to the technology, but has a patchy record of success. Investing has, arguably, been less successful, especially if the investing arm of the corporate is not well-aligned with the lines of business.

Corporate R&D: in-house or outsource?

For corporate strategic investors facing today's challenges, university spinouts provide an opportunity to seek out and invest in promising companies worldwide. In the last 20 years the vertically integrated business model has declined, and as a result corporates have increasingly outsourced key functions or processes to optimise their business model and remain competitive. However, for technology or product companies, R&D has remained largely an internal activity. Typically, the resource distribution of high-technology firms is correlated to the business cycle.

In a positive economic cycle, the R&D budget is increased (R&D as a percentage of sales) and corporates have more scope to invest in new product or market opportunities. From 1997– 2000, for the Fortune 500 high-technology group, as much as 30 per cent of the budget focused on stretch (ie, the concept of pulling the business forward from its existing market or product boundary) and new (ie, new products and/or new markets) opportunities (compared with 70 per cent for existing product/market) (see Exhibits 19.1 and 19.2). However, after the dotcom bubble burst in 2000, and as the sector went through radical downsizing, the R&D budget diminished. The reduced R&D budget reverted to 90–95 per cent for existing products and markets and 0–5 per cent for stretch or new opportunities.

As a result, many corporates were forced to look at the efficiency and effectiveness of their R&D investment. In addition, many corporates survived by cutting any activity that was

Exhibit 19.1

Core R&D focus versus new/stretch opportunities

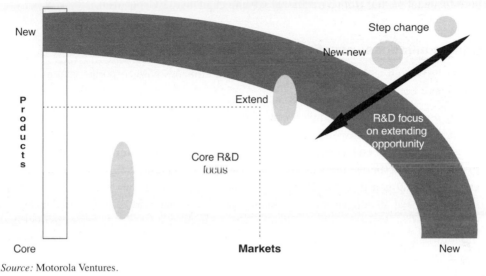

Source: Motorola Ventures.

Exhibit 19.2

R&D budget as a percentage of sales

	For existing products/markets	*For stretch/new opportunities*
Positive economic cycle (%)	70	30
Downturn (%)	90–95	0–5

Source: Authors' own.

not directly related to near-term revenue. As the next positive economic cycle emerges, corporates are looking for growth opportunities, but the R&D pipeline is restricted.

Corporates' competitive responses

Corporates have three broad competitive responses that can be used in an effort to increase their new market and product pipeline.

- *Acquisition*. Obtain new technology or increase the product base through acquisition. This is highly risky and subject to financial market dynamics.
- *License*. License the technology or products from a competitor or complementary supplier. This results in a distribution of the profit in the value chain and constrains the profitability of the corporate.
- *Strategic alliance*. The corporate forms a strategic alliance to acquire the product or technology to develop market growth.

The different types of strategic alliance occur in a broad spectrum. Pure commercial or OEM agreements lie at one end of the spectrum, whilst a deep relationship backed by an equity investment is found at the other end. For an early stage company or university spinout, investment, collaborative alliances and revenues are all required. Therefore, a corporate partner with a venture investment capability (normally termed corporate venture capital, as opposed to pure financial capital from a traditional venture capitalist (VC)) is ideal.

Strategic alliances: benefits to spinouts

The benefits to high-technology spinouts of strategic alliances with corporate venture capital arms of major corporations are as follows.

- *Equity investment*. Financial investment in the company.
- *Technology and business validation*. The investment by a corporate in a high-technology spinout is a credible endorsement by an established player of the potential in the business. In the absence of corporate investments, many startups take investment by well-regarded VCs as validation of their potential. However, the knowledge a VC has about the quantum of the market potential, in comparison to a corporate already in that market, is open to debate.
- *Global reach and distribution*. An alliance with a corporate can provide access to their distribution and global reach, which alleviates the need for a high-technology spinout to divert resources into establishing its own global distribution.

The following two case studies highlight how such strategic alliances and corporate partnerships have successfully opened new customer opportunities.

Case study[1]

Motorola and Apertio: successful testing and validation opened customer and partnership opportunities

Apertio is a telecommunications software startup based in Bristol in the United Kingdom. It is a leading provider of open infrastructure software solutions for mobile operators. Apertio's flagship application, its Home Location Server (HLS), is part of Apertio's open infrastructure platform for second and third generation mobile networks. A traditional Home Location Register (HLR) manages subscriber information like feature preferences, mobility and location information. The Apertio HLS runs on low cost, volume hardware and occupies 1/100th of the footprint of a traditional HLR while offering unprecedented scalability and multi-site reliance. Additionally, by opening up access to the subscriber data, using standard interfaces, the Apertio solutions enable the rapid and cost-effective deployment of advanced services.

Demand for Apertio product offering

The demand for the Apertio product offering is fuelled, on the one hand, by Home Location Register (HLR) end-of-life replacements, which are due within the next three to four years at practically all major mobile operator and carrier networks. On the other hand, demand is fuelled by green-field mobile networks which are launching in Asia and the Americas.

At an early stage, Apertio realised that it needed to form effective partnerships in order to be highly successful in selling to leading mobile operators. Partnerships were needed to overcome the specific hurdles that it faced as a relatively small company.

- access to global customers;
- big-ticket, mission-critical solutions;
- long sales cycles;
- strong incumbent competitors; and
- turnkey network sales (total solution sales where the supplier takes responsibility for the whole network in contrast to the buyer purchasing individual components and putting them together).

Motorola identified as a strategic partner

Apertio identified Motorola as a potential partner because, in addition to mitigating the above, they fulfilled a number of Apertio's key strategic requirements:

- a recognised and respected brand;
- no internal competing products; and
- a large embedded customer base and strong presence in global growth markets.

Paul Magelli, CEO of Apertio said: 'It is essential to work with partners that understand the industry and add value during the early growth phase of a company's development. Motorola's certification of Apertio's products provided our customers with confidence and gave us an edge as a young company.'

At this time, Motorola was re-entering development and sales of core network components with the acquisition of Winphoria (a leading wireless softswitch vendor). The partnership with Apertio was viewed as highly complementary because it completed their core network offering with technically and commercially compelling next generation solutions. In addition to stand-alone sales, network solutions such as HLRs are typically sold as part of an overall green-field network deployment or growth onto an existing network. These turnkey solutions are for complete networks including radio access and switching products, which Motorola offers in its portfolio. It is only through partnerships with vendors such as Motorola, with its broader portfolio of products, that Apertio can address these opportunities.

Apertio solutions differentiate themselves due to their market leading performance, small size, scalability, open interfaces, resilience and total cost of ownership.

As these solutions are mission-critical components of an operator network, Motorola completed three months of in-depth performance, functionality and interoperability testing to validate the Apertio HLS in the Motorola laboratories. Through the testing, both Motorola and Apertio gained increased confidence in the solution. As with all interoperability testing, issues were found, but they were quickly resolved. The resulting solution was a better product for both parties.

Successful testing and validation opened opportunities

The successful conclusion of testing has (a) enabled Apertio to validate independently the technical capability of their system, and (b) accelerated their time to market. As a result, it has also opened up new customer opportunities and partnership opportunities to them.

Furthermore, the successful completion of the testing programme meant that Motorola not only technologically validated their investment but also gained the confidence in the solutions to bid for contracts through their global sales teams. This has opened up opportunities for Apertio across Russia, India, Africa, Western and Eastern Europe, and the United States that would have been difficult to address directly by Apertio.

The regional sales teams are fully trained on the suite of products and therefore able to bid standard solutions without the additional support of Apertio. Regular sales review calls are held with Motorola Product Management to ensure alignment on both sides. On a tactical level, the Apertio and Motorola local sales teams meet frequently, reviewing opportunities in their respective accounts and maximising the chances of success.

Leading investors

In December 2003, Motorola Ventures invested in Apertio as part of a US$6 million Series A financing round that included Deutsche Venture Capital, in addition to the Tokarz Group and Eden Ventures, who provided the first round funding.

John O'Donohue, managing director at Motorola Ventures, said: 'We are very confident that this latest round of financing will help establish Apertio as a leading software company in one of the fastest-growing areas of mobile technology: software-based infrastructure solutions, including the mission-critical HLR. There are huge opportunities now that 2G [second generation] networks are becoming more widespread and 3G [third generation] networks are starting to launch around the world.'

The Motorola testing and validation enabled Apertio to secure US$6 million of additional funding with leading investors, impressive customers and a strong pipeline working in conjunction with Motorola. How did they do it? Here are some tips for others to follow, from Wallace Ascham, director of strategic partners at Apertio:

- Do create partnerships to increase coverage of the limited sales resource of a startup, particularly in a market with long sales lead times and that opens up new markets.
- Do focus around a specific, tangible sales opportunity.
- Do ensure both partners' goals are aligned. Do they have competing products? Is this opportunity strategic or tactical for them? What are their alternatives?
- Do test the solution as early as possible because it builds significant confidence in the partnership.
- Do seek to limit exposure and up-front costs.

- Do get financial commitments – test of commitment ensures alignment and effort to sell once the honeymoon period is over.
- Do plan for a long negotiation in both cost and time – the dating is quick, but the prenuptial agreement takes an age.
- Do write in milestones for achieving specific, tangible events that add value to the startup company and to the partnership.
- Do not be blinded by the opportunity – big companies require significant maintenance and support and 'priming the sales pump' takes considerable effort and time.
- Do be realistic about the cultural and procedural differences between large and small companies.

Case study[2]

BT and Vidus: access to corporates' customers and channels

The focus on technology in a startup often misses the key point: it is channels and customers that determine success. In a corporate laboratory there is a natural access to the lines of business that can perform the role of both a customer and a sales channel. Given the expense of establishing the latter, this is a major advantage to the startup and spinout if it can be exploited. The startup will not only benefit from the sales but also the association with the brand of the corporate parent that can overcome the reluctance of many companies to buy from new startups.

A good example of this model working is the British Telecom spinout, Vidus Ltd (formerly a.p.solve Limited).

Vidus exploits BT's field service management software (called 'taskforce'), developed over many years and underpinned by powerful artificial intelligence algorithms, which internally schedule all of BT's engineers every day and is credited with large annual savings. The technology was then repackaged as a stand-alone business, with the first customer being BT.

John Davies, chief operating officer of BT Wholesale said: 'The implementation of Vidus's taskforce has enabled BT to offer unprecedented levels of customer response that are highly valuable to both residential and business customers. We are achieving 95 per cent utilisation from our highly skilled engineers located countrywide. Taskforce is undoubtedly one of the most advanced work allocation systems in the world.'

The solution has helped BT to generate 36 per cent field productivity improvement, reduce dispatch control costs by 76 per cent, achieve savings through automation that total £175 million (US$321.4 million) a year and introduce new lucrative service offerings based on its new speed of provision and repair. However, once the system was independent of its parent company it was possible to offer the product to other blue-chip companies with similar workforce issues.

Many of these companies had expressed an interest in using the technology when it was inside BT, but no investment capital existed for the purpose. The BT line of business was able to approach major customers offering the platform and related services. Major customers were lined up by the channel to do a trial and buy the system, reassured by the existing record of deployment in BT and the association with the BT channel. As Vidus deploys mission critical software, this BT relationship is key in exploiting the technology. Already in its first year of independent business, Vidus has grown its client list to include Centrica, NTL and Hungarian energy provider, E.On.

Strategic alliances: risks to spinouts

Beyond the normal challenges in forming new relationships, high-technology spinouts face the following risks.

- *Being over-focused on corporate requirements*. The high-technology spinout becomes focused on the requirements of the corporate and may lose viability in the wider marketplace. In essence, they become an 'outsourced' R&D organisation and this may limit the opportunity to exit (sell the business).
- *Being over-dependent on corporate revenues*. The spinout becomes dependent on the corporate for revenue and the corporate grows to represent a disproportionate amount of revenue. The spinout is overly exposed to the fortune and whim of the corporate so that the chances of survival in any change from the corporate are reduced.
- *Exclusivity*. Any exclusive relationship that a spinout has with a corporate should be balanced by the limitation this places on the spinout in forming value relationships with other major industry players.
- *Mismatch of capabilities*. Developing strong partnerships between big established companies and new high-technology ventures can be difficult. There is a mismatch in capability between a big corporate and a spinout. The corporate is familiar with business scale attributes, such as clearly defined processes and documentation; early stage companies are immature in this area.

An optimised model

The normal driver for a spinout is to develop into a stand-alone company or to achieve an exit (trade sale). In achieving this long-term goal, it is desirable that the spinout does not take any short-term actions to compromise this. The model in Exhibit 19.3 represents an approach for a spinout.

The spinout forms strategic alliances backed by a corporate equity investment. The key consideration is that it should first seek partnerships that create mutual strategic value for both the corporate and the spinout. If this is optimised then it should accelerate the financial value creation for the spinout. For example, if a corporate utilises the spinout's core technology, then this validation should enable the spinout to license the technology to other participants in the industry.

Exhibit 19.3

Securing strategic value with the right partnership adds to financial value

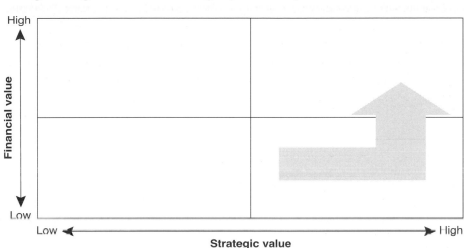

Source: Motorola Ventures.

Case study[3]

Motorola and Magic4: strategic beach-head customer backed by corporate investment

Magic4 is a world leader in seamless mobile messaging technology. Mobile communications are creating an open world of opportunities that allow people and companies to reach their full potential. With leading-edge expertise in Seamless Mobile Messaging applications, Magic4 delivers interoperability that breaks down the barriers between applications and devices, and provides a common set of application interfaces for easier integration and time to market advantage. It developed open standards that were critical to success in the mobile messaging field.

Magic4 was a high-technology spinout with seed venture investment from Philips Enterprises of £2 million (US$3.7 million) in 1999. Co-founder and CEO, Simon Wilkinson, previously held a number of senior international positions at Philips Consumer Communications. In 2000, 3i invested £9 million (US$16.8 million).

Beach-head customer
In 2003, 'Motorola became their beachhead customer' according to Steve Langkamp, chief operating officer of Magic4. For Motorola, Magic4 was also a strategic customer because of two factors: (a) it was consistent with Motorola's desire to reduce costs through outsourcing, and (b) it recognised that interoperability is critical to its future success.

Mala Chandra, vice president and director of Client Architecture and Applications at Motorola's Personal Communications Services (PCS) Division, said: 'We chose Magic4 because they have proven their solutions all across the globe'. Magic4 has tested their software with 64 mobile operators in 40 countries. Used by handset manufacturers worldwide, Magic4's solutions are delivered on multiple platforms and in many devices. Large and mid-sized global mobile operators have formal procurement cycles, including development cycles for their handsets and strategic requirements. These operators pay Magic4 to do the testing (a) in the laboratories, and (b) for features, functionality and future product roadmaps. Magic4's strategic relationship with a leading handset manufacturer such as Motorola, enables them to capture additional handset manufacturers globally to use their software.

Corporate investment

After Motorola signed a long-term strategic agreement to utilise the Magic4 solution in two of its handsets, Motorola backed up this commitment with a US$5 million corporate venture investment in Magic4.

Simon Wilkinson, CEO of Magic4, said: 'We are delighted to have Motorola Ventures join us as part of our team. Our existing strong relationship with Motorola's handset division (PCS) continues to deliver benefits to both companies. We believe the Motorola Ventures team's experience and connections in the wireless arena will add an important customer and industry perspective to our Board.'

Benefits to both parties

Motorola gained strategic value by gaining speed to market: it did not need to develop the MMS client internally. Magic4 used the Motorola success to capture additional handset manufacturers to use their MMS clients, and also captured additional financial value. The success led to an exit in May 2004, when Openwave Systems Inc, a NASDAQ-listed company, announced an acquisition of Magic4.

Lessons for spinouts on how to build and exploit corporate connections

University spinouts seldom have the strategic benefits that come with access to corporate laboratories and incubators. However, Exhibit 19.4 lists a number of alternative ways that they could achieve these benefits.

The first two approaches can gain attention in the early phase. However, they are typically with an R&D department in the corporation. The problem with the corporate R&D department is that it is often poorly connected with the lines of business at the right commercial level for a startup to make an impact. The corporate R&D department is better seen as a way to identify and influence the key decision-makers in the corporation. Too many university startups presume that R&D interest will lead to commercial opportunities. It is better to gain a line of business interest first, with the business line looking to the R&D department for validation.

Exhibit 19.4

Approaches to build and exploit corporate connections

	Type	How
Approach 1	Early visibility of pipeline.	Use the university's existing links with major corporations to establish early visibility of pipeline.
Approach 2	Foresee the market.	Establish corporate R&D support during the research phase.
Approach 3	Create a larger company with corporate profile from joint IPR pool.	Identify corporate laboratories with supporting technology and then build value from joint IPR pool while tapping market reach of the major corporations.

Source: Authors' own.

The third approach, whilst fraught with deal problems, enables a stronger company to be created with corporate visibility from its initial creation. Given the difficulty in developing world-class companies, finding world-class CEOs, creating channels to market and gaining investment, it is surprising that more effort is not put into identifying wider pools of IPR to exploit. Many patents or technologies are insufficient to build a company alone. The future of university spinouts probably lies in joining up with major corporate incubators, and then building value from the joint IPR pool and the global market reach that such partnerships with major corporates can offer.

Summary

There are two key issues to understanding the best use of university spinout technology.

For a corporation, it provides an excellent opportunity to access fully invested and supported products (whether from its own laboratories or a university) that can then be thoroughly exploited through the corporation's key channels and customer relationships. The association with the brand of the corporate overcomes the reluctance of many companies to buy from new startups and spinouts.

For a university, the technology on its own is never enough to build and develop a viable proposition. The spinout needs to think of the technology from the corporate partner's angle: the cost and benefits of deploying the system versus an internal solution, and their role as a channel and as a reference customer.

---

[1] This case study benefited from assistance by Apertio – the authors particularly thank Paul Magelli, CEO; and Wallace Ascham, director of Strategic Partners.

[2] This case study benefited from assistance by Vidus – the authors particularly thank Diana Tucker, director of marketing communications.

[3] This case study benefited from assistance by Magic4 – the authors particularly thank Simon Wilkinson, CEO; Steve Langkamp, COO; and Guylaine Klein, marketing manager.

Chapter 20

Active portfolio management: the Imperial College case study

Susan Searle
Imperial College Innovations, Imperial College, London

Brian Graves
Imperial College Innovations, Imperial College, London

Dr Kenny Tang, CFA
Oxbridge Capital, London[1]

Introduction

This chapter addresses the role of a university's technology transfer office (TTO) when managing its portfolio of spinout companies – what are the challenges faced by the TTO as the number of spinout companies increases or as they mature in terms of company development? The chapter includes two case studies: one on the partnership between Imperial College and a leading investor, Fleming Family & Partners, and one on the training provided by Imperial College for later-stage spinout companies.

The core skills of a university's TTO are needed in the early stages of spinout development – working with academics to investigate promising research ideas to turn into commercial opportunities, and in developing and incubating early stage spinout opportunities. TTOs are not normally expert in the later stages of spinout development, such as the raising of significant funding for spinout companies. Nor are they usually experts in seeking exits (that is, either a trade sale or listing on a stock exchange) or corporate partnership opportunities. Therefore, as the number of spinout companies increases or as spinouts mature in terms of company development, what do they require from a TTO?

Management of spinout companies – what is an active approach?

An active approach to spinout company development means getting the spinout company to a stage at which it can be regarded as investment ready. At this stage it is ready to receive a significant capital increase, and prepared and capable of using this money effectively and efficiently to build and grow the company, increasing its value and potential return of capital to the investors. If investors cannot see how their investment will be grown and returned to them, then it is unlikely that they will be persuaded to part with their cash. An active approach will include the following five steps.

240

1. *Inventions and assessing their potential*. Academics are creative by nature and there is never a shortage of new ideas. However, judging the commercial potential at such an early stage is very difficult and TTOs seek advice from as many sources as possible to decide which ideas to patent and whether it will be best commercialised through either a licence agreement or spinout. Only 3–4 per cent of new ideas are likely to be suitable for venture investment. Once it is decided to pursue the spinout route, the TTO moves to step two below.

2. *Developing the business proposition*. The TTO will now conduct some more in-depth market research to identify the size, scale and entry points to the market opportunity. From this, strategic partners, potential product ideas, and technical and marketing requirements will often emerge. This initial plan is also useful to sell the proposition to potential members of the spinout's management team and identify someone with the appropriate skills and circumstances to embark on the key role of commercial manager/CEO.

3. *Building the business structure*. With the assistance of the TTO, the commercial manager/CEO will produce the business plan that will be used to find the first funding for the company, attract a board of directors and promote the business to other strategic partners and stakeholders. A key skill for the commercial manager/CEO at this stage is the ability to work with the academic inventors and founders to introduce them to the commercial drivers and disciplines of a commercial organisation.

4. *Company formation and incubation*. When the funding, management team, board of directors, and business and technical development plans are secured, the TTO also supports the early legal needs of the spinouts. Support to the spinouts may also include access to market intelligence and a network of business partners, some of whom may be corporate venture capitalists. In addition, the TTO may continue to provide active intellectual property (IP) management for the company until it has the resources to manage this itself.

5. *Active support and monitoring*. The process of active monitoring requires the companies to send the TTO periodic reports on their progress and financial situation. These reports are actively reviewed for any telltale signs of trouble. In addition, for early stage companies, there is a need to maintain a more frequent personal dialogue to keep up-to-date with developments, since the fragility of these entities can place them more at risk and some nurturing can help.

An active approach versus a passive approach

An active approach and a passive approach differ significantly. The purpose of active portfolio management is to take an active role in increasing the value of a portfolio of assets. On the other hand, a passive approach is simply to monitor an investment in the spinout. It would require little more than observing the company's press releases and reading the annual reports.

An active approach requires the shareholders to take an active and continuing interest in the fortunes of the company and do what is required to improve them. For example, it may be as simple as monitoring the company's cash position and offering to help with fund raising where necessary. It may involve sitting on the board of the company and leading the initiatives to oust an ineffective executive. Or it may involve carefully scrutinising company communications and refusing to endorse them until the board answers certain questions.

Such an active approach can be unpopular with spinout companies and accusations of 'mothering', 'nosiness' and interference can fly. However, this is part and parcel of good corporate governance practice and is preferable to being alerted to irreconcilable problems at the last minute.

Resources to implement an active approach

The first step is to put a relationship manager (RM) in place for each spinout. This approach improves the process for monitoring companies, as well as enabling proactive management of ongoing issues. The RM is the person within the TTO who maintains regular contact with and supports the company, in particular with the appointee director (ie, the director appointed by the TTO), identifying critical issues and helping to resolve them where appropriate. The RM provides another channel of communication apart from the appointee director, who may be someone from outside the TTO.

The other is the development of a database to capture more fully information on the portfolio of spinout companies. Such a system captures:

- the key financial and shareholder information;
- various strategic documents, including the business plan, milestones, IP tracking, and so on; and
- various management and monitoring information, including management accounts, board minutes and so on.

The development of a web-based system assists the TTO in the active relationship/portfolio management of its spinout companies. Also, the web-based system enables the RMs, the appointee directors and the university decision-makers and administrators to have up-to-date and strategic information at their fingertips. Such information is provided at various levels of access depending on their need for such information.

Case study

The Imperial College–Fleming Family & Partners partnership: active management of later-stage spinouts*

How did the partnership come about?

Imperial College wanted to realise some of the equity value held in its existing portfolio of spinout companies. It wished to realise only a minority interest because it believed that the upside was still to come in most of the portfolio of spinout companies. Furthermore, its TTO (Imperial College Innovations) was not experienced in the area of portfolio management, nor was it experienced in the area of later-stage financing of its spinout companies.

A second objective was to find a partner who would acquire a stake but also work closely with Imperial Innovations to provide this expertise. Imperial Innovations looked for a partner that would not threaten other existing investors in the spinout companies, but would be seen as providing complementary expertise. This meant discounting working with any of the major venture capitalists because their role would have been too dominant, especially as external parties would have assumed that they would want to lead investment rounds in all the companies.

Imperial College had been working successfully with Gordon House Asset Management, who introduced Fleming Family and Partners (FF&P). Gordon House and FF&P formed a partnership with Imperial College. Subsequently, Gordon House merged with FF&P. FF&P stated clearly upon acquisition of their interest in the partnership that this did not mean they would want to position themselves as lead investor for the companies in the portfolio, nor did they have the right to do so, but that they would make selective follow-on investments to maintain their shareholding.

The objectives of the partnership

The objectives are to work closely together to maximise the potential return from the partnership's portfolio. FF&P has the right to acquire an interest in future portfolios of Imperial Innovations as they are assembled. In this way it should have access to all Imperial College's winners. FF&P, like Imperial College, believes that there are some major potential winners. The expectation is of a number of companies to list on major stock exchanges and a much larger number to trade sell. FF&P's objectives are to make a good financial return whilst recognising that, because this is an early stage portfolio, many failures are expected, along with some substantial big winners.

The expectation is to be regularly exiting from the portfolio of companies as they either trade sell or list. This would provide an annual income stream to Imperial College in multi-millions from which Imperial College will expand and develop research activities (thereby generating more IP and so on).

What was Imperial College looking for in a partner?

Imperial College Innovations has core skills in developing and incubating spinout opportunities. It is not an expert in fund management or exits. Therefore, it was looking for a partner with experience of later-stage funding as well as experience of portfolio management of companies.

Imperial College Innovations sought a partner who could share its vision. A partner who would work with it to enhance value, who would not try to dominate the spinouts in terms of their evolution but would be a supportive investor with Imperial College. Furthermore, given the lack of experience of follow-on funding, that partner's experience of later-stage funding and a broader business network was critical.

What is the vision for the partnership?

The vision is to realise a significant financial reward from Imperial College's portfolio of new and existing companies. It is understood that there would often be short-term issues, but that longer term a big gain would be realised. FF&P did not intend to get in and out during the short venture capital horizon, but to get a much more substantial return over a longer period.

Together, the University and FF&P have developed a strategy for each of the spinout companies in the portfolio. In particular, the top quartile is analysed and the board meets regularly with the chairman, appointee director and CEO to look at what can be done to help each of these companies.

Role of Fleming Family & Partners
FF&P has fulfilled a number of roles:

a) *Relationship/portfolio manager.* The burden of monitoring and active portfolio management of the 30-plus spinout companies has been spread between Imperial Innovations and FF&P. FF&P's own requirements to report to its own investors meant that this practice has now been adopted within Imperial Innovations as part of the development of its own portfolio management skills.

b) *Friendly foil.* FF&P provided an authoritative voice to assist in the critiquing of spinout companies' strategies and business plans. It has provided a reality check on the spinouts through an external perspective. This includes helping spinout companies to tailor their message to the appropriate financial audiences, especially during the process of fund raising.

c) *Access to finance and markets.* FF&P has used its considerable network of contacts and investors to provide the spinout companies with both commercial leads and access to investors. This, together with the advice in (b) above, is incredibly useful in grooming the spinout companies prior to making investor pitches.

d) *Provider of finance.* FF&P has also made direct investments into the spinouts themselves.

Another challenge has been to enhance the value of the spinout companies while bringing in experienced non-executive directors to help in the process. Imperial College and FF&P decided to create the Corporate Directors' Programme (CDP), described in the second case study.

---

* A copy of the press release dated 15 May 2002 is included as an appendix to this chapter.

Case study II

The Imperial College Corporate Directors' Programme

The key objective for Imperial College is to enhance the value of the spinout companies by bringing in external experienced non-executive directors. The CDP programme brings together a group of people who share a common cause, to enhance the value of the portfolio, share experiences and networks, and help each other across the portfolio. It extends the network of expertise. CDP also trains the directors in areas of need.

Most problems faced by startups come down to the lack of funding in the market for early stage companies. With lack of funding it becomes difficult to get the right people involved early on because there is still a relatively small pool of people prepared to take the risk of joining a small startup. True entrepreneurs are in demand and there are too few of them. A strategy of engaging people later on in their career to join the board may prove useful: usually such people are willing to give advice or put in effort because they are excited by the opportunity, and not because they need to be paid.

Creation of the pool of directors

FF&P and Imperial College senior management pooled together their networks of experienced non-executive directors. They then went through a formal two-step interview process. The first step was to ascertain whether they had the skills needed and to explain the programme to be implemented. The second interview panel was drawn from directors of the partnership and was more formal in nature. In parallel, a full diligence process was carried out on each executive, including reference checks.

Credentials required for the pool of directors

Experience as a non-executive director is essential, especially in working with small growing companies. Added value was also sought in a range of areas that would encompass some, but not all, of the following:

- financial knowledge;
- fund raising;
- market knowledge;
- commercial negotiations; and
- strategy and development.

Financial incentives for the directors

The directors are free to negotiate a compensation package with the spinout company. Often in very early stage companies this may be in the form of deferred payments (contingent on the company raising finance) or an equity instrument. In addition, and to encourage the collegiate mechanism of the pool, the directors will equally share a 5 per cent carried interest in the portfolio.

Connecting and matching the right directors to the right spinout opportunity

The directors' pool is chaired by an experienced non-executive director, who maintains a regular line of communication with the directors and Imperial College's RMs. In discussion with the RM, the needs of a particular spinout are elucidated and the most appropriate member of the pool is approached to join the board.

Training programme for the CDP

Training includes a range of topics. There is a formal programme called the Entrepreneurs' Programme, run in conjunction with the Tanaka Business School's Entrepreneurship Centre which covers:

- the roles and responsibilities of directors; and
- developing strategic thought – training for the board.

The training is provided in several one-day workshops. Short master classes cover a range of topics, including:

- raising finance;
- getting the most from the lawyers;
- developing the management team; and
- marketing and product development.

Also, there are short specific sessions, including:

- how to turn a company around in a critical situation; and
- growing the board and the executive team.

Key roles for external directors

Spinout companies typically face two issues: the problem of growth and how to develop the management team as the company moves through different stages. The external directors have the services of an experienced recruitment agent to facilitate the process. The other key issue concerns the management of the cash position and the consequences when the cash runs out. External directors are called upon to advise on how to protect a company from its creditors and turn it around

Appendix

PRESS RELEASE

IMPERIAL COLLEGE BUILDS SPIN-OUT PARTNERSHIP FOR FUTURE GROWTH

For Immediate Use
15 May 2002

Innovative deal signals long-term partnership between the parties

A long-term partnership between Imperial College London and two London-based investment houses will, for the first time, create a route for external investment in the growth of Imperial's portfolio of spin-out companies.

Imperial, Fleming Family & Partners Limited (FF&P) and Gordon House Asset Management Limited (Gordon House) today announce a financial arrangement that will generate cash for the College to expand its existing spin-out development activities and exploitation of intellectual property.

FF&P and Gordon House will buy, on behalf of their clients, a 30 per cent stake in Imperial College's shareholding in a portfolio of 36 unlisted spinout companies, typically between one and four years old. The College will receive a multi-million pound cash sum.

The partners will form a Limited Liability Partnership to hold the portfolio of shares, named Imperial FF&P Gordon House LLP. FF&P and Gordon House will own 21 per cent and 9 per cent of the partnership respectively.

Imperial College Innovations Ltd, the College's technology transfer company, was instrumental in engineering the partnership on behalf of the College with legal advice provided by lawyers Bird & Bird.

As well as releasing cash for the College from its equity portfolio, the deal offers private investors the opportunity to buy into the portfolio of Imperial College spinouts before they list, through the funds managed by FF&P and Gordon House.

Individual spinout companies will additionally benefit from FF&P's and Gordon House's extensive industry expertise in business planning and structuring funding arrangements.

FF&P and Gordon House also have an option to purchase interests in further portfolios assembled by Imperial for a period of seven years. Both FF&P and Gordon House intend to make follow-on investments in Imperial's innovative technology companies within the portfolio, and specific funds within the partnership have been set aside for this purpose.

FF&P and Gordon House will also assist Imperial in managing the portfolio to enhance value for the benefit of the College and their own investors.

Susan Searle, Managing Director of Imperial College Innovations, says: 'This is the first partnership of its type to be created by a university. Its a new way of monetising value created in early stage start-ups whilst giving the investor a spread of risk across a diverse range of spinout companies. The deal illustrates the increasing importance of university technology transfer activity in contributing to economic growth.'

Sir Richard Sykes, Rector of Imperial College, says: 'This is an important deal for the College and a first in the university sector. It demonstrates both the financial expertise of Imperial College Innovations and its ability to build a portfolio of quality spinouts from the College's research. This is also an important success for Public and Corporate Affairs, a new organisation managing the commercialisation of the College's intellectual assets, fundraising, alumni relations, marketing and corporate communications.'

Sir Roger Gibbs, Chairman of FF&P, says: 'Fleming Family & Partners is delighted to have established a long-term relationship with Imperial College, which it is hoped will generate significant value for all parties concerned.'

David Donnelly, Chairman of Gordon House, says: 'Gordon House is very pleased to be a member of this important partnership. The combination of long-term capital and world-class science will foster the commercialisation of innovative technology in the United Kingdom for many years to come.'

Notes to editors
The Management Board will consist of Dr Tidu Maini, Pro Rector, Public and Corporate Affairs at Imperial College, Susan Searle, Managing Director of Imperial College Innovations, Michael Stoddart of FF&P and David Donnelly of Gordon House.

Fleming Family and Partners Limited
Fleming Family & Partners Limited is an independent, privately owned investment house, managing funds and trusts for its clients and making direct investments. It was established in August 2000 and has some £1.3 billion in funds under management. FF&P Asset Management Limited is a wholly owned subsidiary of Fleming Family and Partners Limited.

FF&P's heritage is the investment business of Robert Fleming, which was founded in 1873 and which, as Robert Fleming Holdings, was sold to the Chase Manhattan Bank in August 2000. Its target client base includes large family groups, including the Fleming family, high net worth individuals, charities and institutions. www.ffandp.co.uk

Gordon House Asset Management Limited
Gordon House has provided a variety of specialised services to professional investors since 1989. The private equity division of Gordon House provides advice and arranges finance for university spinout companies in order to commercialise proven IP. Gordon House advises on strategy, drawing up a business plan and recruiting commercial managers. Finance is raised from both private investors and institutions.

Gordon House has recently funded two Imperial spinouts, raising £5 million for Powerlase Limited and £1.75 million for Gene Expression Technologies Limited. The lead investor in Powerlase is a fund managed by Cazenove & Co whilst Fleming Family and Partners is the largest investor in Gene Expression. www.gham.co.uk

Imperial College Innovations Ltd

Imperial College Innovations Ltd is one of the United Kingdom's leading technology transfer companies, having created over 50 spinout companies and concluded over 60 licence agreements in the last four years.

The portfolio of spinout companies created by Imperial College Innovations includes two that are publicly quoted, over 15 that are venture capital/private equity-funded and over 30 that have initial seed funding. In addition, there are more than 36 embryonic companies which represent a pipeline of future spinout companies.

The diverse technology areas covered by the spinout companies include analytical tools, biotechnology, chemicals, drug discovery, instrumentation, renewable energy, materials, software, surgical devices and telecoms.

Imperial College London

Imperial College of Science, Technology and Medicine is the largest applied science, technology and medicine university institution in the United Kingdom. It is consistently rated in the top three UK university institutions for research quality, with one of the largest annual turnovers (£390 million for 2000–01) and research incomes (£202 million for 2000–01). In the December 2001 Research Assessment Exercise, 75 per cent of staff achieved a 5-star rating, the highest proportion in any UK university. Visit: www.ic.ac.uk

------ End of Press Release -----

Post Press Release: Gordon House have merged with FF&P.

---

[1] This chapter benefited from interviews and comments from Simon Jamieson, Director of Fleming Family & Partners Limited; Richard Garraway of Imperial College Innovations; and Anthony Everett of Everett-Mitchell Consulting.